gel Blundell is a journalist who has worked in Australia, the United States and Great Britain. He spent 30 years in Fleet Street before becoming an author and contributor to national newspapers. He has written more than 40 books, including several bestsellers on crime.

THE WORLD'S MOST EVIL GANGS

NIGEL BLUNDELL

JOHN BLAKE

Published by John Blake Publishing Ltd
3 Bramber Court, 2 Bramber Road
London W14 9PB, England

www.johnblakepublishing.co.uk

www.facebook.com/Johnblakepub facebook
twitter.com/johnblakepub twitter

First published in paperback in 2013

ISBN 978 1 78219 467 5

British Library Cataloguing-in-Publication Data:
A catalogue record for this book is available from the British Library
Designed by www.envydesign.co.uk

Printed and bound in Great Britain
by CPI Group (UK) Ltd, Croydon, CR0 4YY

1 3 5 7 9 10 8 6 4 2

© Text copyright Nigel Blundell 2013

Papers used by John Blake Publishing are natural, recyclable
products made from wood grown in sustainable forests.
The manufacturing processes conform to the
environmental regulations of the country of origin.

Every attempt has been made to contact the relevant copyright
holders, but some were unobtainable. We would be grateful
if the appropriate people could contact us.

To Juliet Morris
for her dedicated research into some of the
world's most frightful dens of iniquity

CONTENTS

INTRODUCTION

Crime DOES pay. There's no denying it. And in pursuit of riches and power, those outside the law have always tended to band together – spawning today's murky, brutal world of organised crime.

The origins of the archetypical, modern gangster can be traced to 1920s America, when Prohibition turned street-corner hoodlums into rich and powerful businessmen. But today, highly organised and ferociously protective gangs are prevalent throughout the world – their labyrinthine networks affecting every aspect of our lives.

How did these secret societies first evolve? How did they become so all-powerful? By what fearsome means do they control their empires? And how do they evade the massive forces of law and order arrayed against them? Another question worth asking reflects our own viewpoints as law-abiding citizens: Why, despite their despicable deeds, do they hold us in such enduring thrall?

It's an enigma that warrants exploration because it's all too easy to glamorise gangs and gangsters, and what this book aims to do is the very opposite – to show them for the grubby, grasping, often barbaric villains that they really are. We are rightly horrified by their activities, yet stories about gangland culture never fail to fascinate. Perhaps it is because it's the 'bad guys' who always star in the best narratives. 'The Devil,' it is said, 'has all the best tunes.' From the works of William Shakespeare to Mario Puzo, the villains of the piece take centre stage.

Which might be why so many of them get away with it. We, the law abiding public, are forced to accept the existence of a criminal subculture as a fact of life. Unwittingly or otherwise, we become consumers of the crooks' tainted services. And ultimately, when civilised society turns a blind eye, these criminal cancers fester, creep out of the gutter and end up influencing mainstream society.

That is how the rural, peasant-run Italian Mafia grew to global pre-eminence. Its power allowed American Mob mogul Meyer Lansky to boast: 'We're bigger than US Steel!' That was in the 1950s. Today it wouldn't even be a boast. Crime organisations that have evolved out of the old Mafia now run economies bigger than those of entire nations. One-time drug peddlers control armies. Bent bankers bring down governments.

In short, gangs and gangsters have 'grown up'. Even the nuances of the terms have changed. A 'gang', after all, was what kids traditionally joined to play games. 'Gangsters' used to be those cool dudes in cheap movies. But both terms nowadays encompass the underworld's bigger players.

As will be seen, the first chapters of this book are devoted to the Mafia and its offshoots, simply because that multitentacled organisation represents the largest grouping of gangsters of all time. They have taken over entire industries, controlled organised labour, manipulated showbusiness superstars, influenced presidents (one of whom they may have helped assassinate) and even hired themselves out for international invasions. Their wisest leader was the inspiration for the character of Il Capo di Tutti Capi (The Boss of all Bosses) in Puzo's The Godfather. But under Carlo Gambino's low-profile management of the Mob, by the mid-Seventies when the frail 73-year-old died peacefully in his bed, the Mafia had apparently vanished into the woodwork.

So where does that now leave the most pervasive criminal organisation the world has ever known? Their ill-gotten billions didn't just evaporate; they were long ago laundered into legitimate businesses. And the pot still grows. The difference is that instead of seeing blood on the streets of the western world's cities, the public now suffers a secret 'taxation' by the Mafia bloodsuckers.

Sadly, of course, there are many crime centres of the world where blood still stains the city streets, and they are fully explored in this book. In the former Soviet Union an extraordinarily wealthy breed of super-crooks have carved up an entire country. From the Far East, the Chinese Triads and Snakeheads have spread their particular brand of extortion and people-trafficking into every continent. In India, gangs have developed 'specialised' markets, from contract killing and smuggling to kidnapping and child-snatching. And in Brazil's shanty towns, where murder has reached epidemic proportions, gangbusters face an Olympian task in the run-up to the 2016 Games.

Across the developed world, terrifyingly tattooed biker

gangs rule the roads (and the backstreets) from Brisbane to Berlin. As for the Eurozone, it might be in financial meltdown but it's still boom time for crime across Europe's illegal markets, boosted by an influx of street-gang migrants from the ex-communist eastern states. In Britain, where once the capital suffered the curse of the Kray and Richardson gangs, new, even more merciless families have seized control. And in Italy, from where the Sicilian Mafia once spread across the globe, a new ruthless mob has quietly assumed power – the 'Ndrangheta, described in a recent government report as 'the country's richest firm'.

Sometimes a shift of power in the global hierarchy of the underworld reduces the influence of one category of mega-gangster, but usually only in favour of a successor. That is what has happened in Colombia where the crushing of the old warring drugs cartels was welcomed by law enforcement agencies around the world. Sadly, however, even more violent villains were waiting in the wings. The ultimate control of the international drugs industry has switched from Colombia to Mexico, where the government has been shamed by its inability to control the crime lords who terrorise the country with seeming impunity. Mexico has become a battleground, with a military offensive against the cartels costing a six-year death toll of more than 70,000 police officers, traffickers and civilians. Decapitated corpses are regularly found at roadsides. Commuters drive under the bodies of men and women hanged from highway overpasses. Fourteen human heads were delivered in cooler boxes to a city hall. A cartel put a 'warning' video on the web showing the execution of two of its own members, beheaded by chainsaw while still alive.

Yet, as author of this book cataloguing so many accounts of

brutality, one story seemed to stand out. It was a brief news agency report that made a couple of paragraphs in the press just as this book was to go to print. Wiretaps, it was reported, had led Italian police to uncover a new method of drug smuggling by international gangs. Cocaine produced in South America was sealed in packets which dogs were then forced to swallow. In some cases, Mexican vets carried out surgery to cram larger quantities around the animals' organs. The dogs were then flown to Europe as prospective 'pets'. Police discovered that a consignment of 48 animals had recently been imported through Milan's Linate airport. Once safely through customs, the drugs had been retrieved – by butchering all the dogs.

That's how today's gangsters treat animals. They don't treat humans any better. But somehow we expect that.

The story of the butchered dogs is a tiny but very telling example of the criminal mindset. Greed is the driving force that justifies to gangsters unconscionable excesses of callousness, cruelty and corruption. Given this globally gruesome state of affairs, it might be expected that the comparative fate of 48 butchered dogs would fail to shock us. But we should be glad that it still does, because it at least sets us apart from the darkest depths of the underworld, into which we delve in this book exploring the world's most evil gangs.

CHAPTER 1

FROM THE GUTTER TO A TRILLION-DOLLAR BUSINESS

If you're an American, you don't have to deal with the Mafia. All you need do is refrain from drinking, smoking, doing drugs, looking at porn, gambling, investing in the stock market, travelling, buying clothes, living in apartments and eating. In other words, the Syndicate has its greasy fingers in everything.

'We're bigger than US Steel,' said Mafia financial whiz Meyer Lansky, mogul of the Mob and brains of the underworld, who died in 1983, aged 80. He made that comment in the Fifties. Today his boast would be a terrible understatement. Organised crime costs America well over a trillion dollars a year. It is estimated that two cents of every dollar spent in the US goes into Mafia pockets.

The notoriously gun-toting days of the Mafia's rise, the Roaring Twenties and Thirties upon which legend thrives, were certainly exciting. But were they really profitable? The big inroads into all aspects of American life came only after World War Two. It was then that the Mafia moved in on the giant American trade unions and, through terror tactics, dominated them. Even back in the Chicago of 1928, Al Capone had gained control of 91 trade unions and companies. Today this power base has mushroomed. It has given the Mob the ability to use the unions as a weapon against the employers for the benefit, not of the workers, but for their own enrichment. 'Things cost a lot more because of the Mob,' said ex-prosecutor and former New York mayor Rudy Giuliani. 'In fact, nationwide there are hidden taxes on all kinds of goods and services – all imposed by the Mafia.' And because of the Mafia's control of many American unions, he added: 'You want the job done? You pay the Mob's price.'

It is estimated that one quarter of the cost of many construction contracts goes directly to the Syndicates. The Mafia's evil tentacles snake out everywhere. They're into banks, airlines, construction, real estate development, the oil industry, the fashion business, car repairs, waste disposal, the music business, the list is endless. They even reach into Wall Street stockbroking firms, where the Syndicate's fantastic wealth can be sifted back into the system for even greater profit.

Mafia investors infiltrate law-abiding firms and use them as fronts, while the really bad boys operate the main, illegal, money-spinning businesses from behind the scenes. And they don't always see the need to strong-arm their way into a legitimate company. With vast resources from their criminal activities, they can afford to lay out cash where others would have to scramble for credit.

Nationwide, the Mafia's illicit operations and the use of tax shelters cheat the US Treasury out of untold billions. It is thought that some 50,000 people are involved in Mafia-linked trade. So, from the day an American is born to the day he dies, anything he touches will have been touched in some way by the Mafia before him. It's a brilliantly organised operation that has the whole of the world's richest nation in its grip. In the old days, a mobster picked up by the cops would protest: 'I'm a businessman.' True in a way, then. Very true now. For organised crime is in the hands of men who've had their training at prestigious business schools.

The FBI estimates that the Mafia own, control or exert influence over some 20,000 legitimate major businesses, ranging from pizza restaurants to banking. No one can escape – not even the FBI itself. The Bureau was fleeced by the Mob when administrators at New York's FBI headquarters were found to have paid way over the odds to have furniture moved from one of its offices to another. The contract had been rigged by the Mafia!

So how did it ever get to this stage? Why was civilised society turning a blind eye while a criminal 'cancer' festered as it gradually grew out of the slums?

The Mafia has been America's most costly import. Italian immigrants brought both the Mafia and its Neapolitan equivalent, the Camorra, across the Atlantic with them in the late 1800s – and it was in the city slums of the US that the two groups merged.

According to the official FBI history of the American Mafia, a villain named Giuseppe Esposito was the first known Sicilian Mafia member to emigrate to the US. He and six other Sicilians fled to New York after murdering the chancellor and a vice chancellor of a Sicilian province and 11 wealthy landowners. He was arrested in New Orleans in 1881 and extradited to Italy.

New Orleans was also the site of the first major Mafia incident in the US. On 15 October 1890 New Orleans Police Superintendent David Hennessey was murdered in a planned execution. Hundreds of Sicilians were arrested and 19 were eventually indicted for the murder but their eventual acquittal generated rumours of widespread bribery and intimidated witnesses. Outraged citizens of New Orleans organised a lynch mob and killed 11 of the 19 defendants. Two were hanged, nine were shot, and the remaining eight escaped.

Ironically, this gave an early boost to the fledgling secret societies in exile. The government paid $30,000 compensation to the widows and families of the hanged men but the money was expropriated by the criminal brotherhood. With further massive influxes of southern Italians around the turn of the century, the Mafia took its hold on immigrant ghettoes of the major cities.

It was there that the huddled masses of poverty-stricken Italian immigrants first felt the need to assert their power, particularly in New York, where they were terrorised by the city's most preponderant group, the Irish, who dominated politics, police and the legal system. From their early days as street vigilantes, the Mafiosi grew to become a protection agency – offering security at a price. Then their activities spread to illegal gambling, loan sharking and prostitution.

The American Mafia evolved as various gangs assumed – and lost – dominance over the years. The Black Hand gangs operated in New York around the turn of the century. The city's earliest Mafia 'family' were the Morellos, led by Peter 'Clutching Hand' Morello for 30 years until his murder by mobster rivals. The Five Points Gang were the dominant racketeers in New York through the 1910s and 20s, their most feared operator being Ignazio 'The Wolf' Saietta. Related to the Morellos, 'The Wolf' ran a notorious 'Murder Stable', where he systematically tortured and butchered his victims. (Almost uniquely, he was allowed to retire from the Mafia and went into small-time business, dying of natural causes in 1944.) From the 1920s, the focus switched to Chicago, where Al Capone's Syndicate controlled America's new crime capital through bribery and corruption of police, lawmakers and city officials.

The introduction of Prohibition in 1920 was probably the biggest single factor in the success story of the Mafia. The market in bootleg liquor to help America drown its sorrows through the Depression was seemingly limitless. Every one of the several, fragmented, ill-organised Mafia families spread across the nation worked together to fulfil that demand and generate enormous profits.

It was this decade that produced gangsters like 'Scarface' Capone, 'Bugs' Moran, 'Legs' Diamond, 'Machine Gun' McGurn, 'Deanie' O'Bannion and 'Dutch' Schultz – names that have gone down in American folklore, portrayed in films, in books and on television as somehow glamorous characters, sometimes even turned into heroes. However, the truth about these gangsters of the Twenties is far from glamorous. They lived vile lives and most died violently, an exception being the most notorious gangster of the age, Al Capone, who died peacefully but mad from syphilis.

While Chicago seemed to produce the most dramatic examples of Mob mayhem through the Roaring Twenties, two of the hoodlums mentioned above brought an unwelcome taste of the Windy City's style of gang warfare to the streets of New York. They were Jack 'Legs' Diamond and 'Dutch' Schultz.

Both were brutal killers yet lived flamboyant lifestyles, both changed their names to glamorise their image – and, almost inevitably, both died by the gun, cold-bloodedly executed by their own kind.

'Legs' Diamond was born John Noland in 1896 in Philadelphia but moved to New York in his teens and, after an apprenticeship of petty crime, was enlisted in the early Twenties as a hitman by racketeer Jacob 'Little Augie' Orgen.

Diamond earned enough to enjoy a lavish lifestyle, supporting a string of mistresses and earning the nickname 'Legs' from a brief spell as a professional dancer. He bought shares in a number of nightclubs and eventually purchased a top nightspot of his own. When in 1927 his boss Orgen was assassinated and Diamond himself wounded, he 'retired' from gang warfare and set himself up in the illicit booze business.

His partner in this enterprise was an established bootlegger who went by the name of 'Dutch' Schultz but who was born Arthur Fliegenheimer in New York in 1902 and had followed a similar criminal career to Diamond. Indeed, 'Legs' and 'Dutch' were so similar in character that they spent most of their partnership trying to cheat one another.

One night, Diamond killed a drunk in his club and had to flee town. Schultz took over his business, so Diamond retaliated by hijacking Schultz's liquor trucks. Diamond felt safe from further retaliation having teamed up with another gangland figure, New York gaming club and brothel owner Arnold Rothstein. But just as he had lost a friend in the assassinated Orgen, so he did again in 1928 when Rothstein was murdered in a poker club after welching on a $320,000 debt.

Now it was Schultz's turn to get his own back on his ex-partner. He dispatched a hit squad to kill Diamond, whom they found in bed with his mistress. They sprayed the room with gunfire but, although five bullets entered his body, Diamond survived. Two further attempts on his life failed. Finally, in December 1931, unknown hitmen, possibly Schultz's goons, finally got their man. They followed Diamond home from a girlfriend's apartment, waited until he had retired to bed, then smashed the front door off its hinges and shot him dead.

Schultz now believed he had a free reign to openly run his liquor, gambling and protection rackets, which together brought in an estimated $20 million a year. But his gun-slinging style of business was inimical to the new, rising breed of Mafia leaders, like Myer Lansky, who were trying to inhibit the excesses of the old-style New York gunslingers.

There was further embarrassment when Schultz went on a bender to celebrate the result of a sensational tax evasion case, in which he was acquitted after succeeding in having the trial moved to a small upstate courthouse. During a drinking binge, he accused one of his gang, Jules Martin, of 'skimming' money collected from his New York restaurant protection rackets. A witness to their dispute later related what happened next:

'Dutch Schultz was ugly; he had been drinking and suddenly he had his gun out. Schultz wore his pistol under his vest, tucked inside his pants, right against his belly. One jerk at his vest and he had it in his hand. All in the same quick motion he swung it up, stuck it in Jules Martin's mouth and pulled the trigger. It was as simple and undramatic as that, just one quick motion of the hand. Dutch Schultz did that murder just as casually as if he were picking his teeth.'

Prohibition had ended and the rip-roaring days of casual public shootings, such as those regularly orchestrated by

Schultz, were embarrassing to the new Mafia leaders. On 23 October 1935, 'Dutch' Schultz was dining with three friends at a Newark, New Jersey, restaurant when two men with machine-guns entered and shot them all. The last of New York's old-style gun-slinging gangsters was out of action for good.

It took just as many years to rid Chicago of the scourge of its street-war gang leaders, epitomised by Al Capone, who was responsible for the most brutish villainy of the age. Head of some of the cruellest cutthroats in American history, he inspired gang wars in which more than 300 men died by the knife, the shotgun, the tommy gun and the pineapple, the gangster adaptation of the World War One hand grenade.

Alphonse Capone was born in Naples on 17 January 1899, the son of an impoverished barber who emigrated, with his wife and other eight children, to New York and settled in Brooklyn. A street-fighting thug who gained his nickname 'Scarface' while working as a bouncer for a Brooklyn brothel, he looked up to an established Brooklyn hoodlum named Johnny Torrio, who was 17 years his senior. When Prohibition was imposed in 1919, making all manufacture, purchase, or sale of alcoholic beverages illegal, Torrio moved to Chicago to go into the bootlegging business and, short of tough minders, sent for the 'Fat Boy from Brooklyn'.

As it happened, Capone urgently needed to get out of New York, where he was wanted for questioning over the death of a policeman. He arrived in Chicago to find that Torrio was not his own boss but under the thumb of an old-time Mafioso, 'Big Jim' Colosimo, who ran labour and extortion rackets as well as about 100 brothels in the city. The one business he did not seem to be involved in was bootlegging.

At this time, Torrio fell out with Colosimo, not only over his lack of interest in the illicit booze trade but because he divorced his first wife, who happened to be Torrio's aunt, and married a singer, Dale Winter. Colosimo and his new wife held court nightly at his restaurant on South Wabash Avenue, surrounded by minders as well as politicians and entertainers. On 11 May 1920, Torrio arranged to meet his boss there to sign for a delivery of whiskey. As Colosimo waited in the empty restaurant, Al Capone stepped out of a phone booth and, acting on Torrio's orders, shot Colosimo dead, then took his wallet to make the killing look like a robbery. Both Capone and Torrio mourned at Colosimo's funeral – then took over his crime empire, added bootleg liquor to the criminal portfolio and set about amassing a fortune.

The bloodshed had only just begun, however. And Capone's creed – he once said: 'You can go a long way with a smile. You can go a lot farther with a smile and a gun' – meant it would continue for another decade.

In the early Twenties, Chicago's underworld was shared between the Mafia gang run by Torrio and Capone and the mainly Irish gang of Charles Dion 'Deanie' O'Bannion. A baby-faced ex-choirboy once destined for the priesthood, O'Bannion's childhood friends included future gangsters Hymie Weiss and George 'Bugs' Moran, all members of a strong-arm crew called the Market Street Gang. They started in a small way during what became known as the 'Chicago Newspaper Wars', in which the city's competing newspapers hired thugs to beat up paperboys who sold the competition's journal.

O'Bannion next tried his hand at robbery but after being arrested for a safecracking job he went to work in the more convivial environment of the city's dive bars, where his speciality was drugging patrons' drinks and then robbing them when they passed out. As part of this scam, joke-cracking O'Bannion also did stints as a singing waiter in a nightclub that was frequented by criminals. They found the entertainer so engaging that they helped him set up in big-time business for himself. He ran his operation from a flower shop, the grandest in Chicago, catering for the city's high society weddings and funerals. But his core moneymaking trade was in illicit brewing and distilling.

O'Bannion had style and principles. Unlike his Italian rivals in neighbouring parts of Chicago, the Irishman would not allow brothels in his area and refused to sell any but the best-quality booze. He sneered at the crudity of the Mafia gangsters but in 1924 he cracked his most costly joke at their expense. He sold Johnny Torrio a half-share in a brewery for half a million dollars – without revealing to Torrio he'd been tipped off that it was about to be raided. O'Bannion ensured he had an alibi when the police swooped but Torrio, who had been careful to avoid any police record, was booked. Revenge was swift and bloody.

Three hoodlums working for Torrio and Capone dropped into O'Bannion's shop to buy a wreath. The 'joke' being played on the Irishman was that the wreath was for himself. One of the thugs held the Irishman down while the others shot him dead. O'Bannion's funeral was attended by Chicago's richest and most influential citizens, as well as murderers, thieves and bootleggers. No one stinted on the wreaths, said to have cost over $50,000.

O'Bannion's gang, including the notorious George 'Bugs' Moran and Hymie Weiss, now went on the attack, ambushing Torrio as he returned home from a shopping trip. The hitmen gunned him down, shooting him in the jaw, lungs, groin, legs, and abdomen. Moran tried to deliver the coup de grâce into Torrio's skull but ran out of ammunition and he miraculously survived. After recovering in hospital, Torrio was picked up by the police and jailed for nine months over the illicit brewery. On his release, he fled Chicago in 1925 with a reputed $50 million and with Moran and Weiss still on his trail, and settled in his family's hometown, Naples. He returned to New York in 1928 and worked an enforcer for Mob mastermind Meyer Lansky (of whom much more in the next chapter) until being jailed again for tax evasion. He died of a heart attack in 1967.

Capone was now master of the richest territory in the underworld, running a thriving empire in prostitution, bootlegging, gambling and extortion, but he had started a gangland war that he could not finish. Before the Twenties were out, more than 1,000 bodies were to end up on the streets of Chicago in a string of bloody reprisal raids. And one of the earliest was against 'Scarface' himself.

Capone's headquarters was the Hawthorn Hotel in the wholly corrupt Chicago suburb of Cicero. From there he ran his $5 million-a-year business in the most flamboyant manner, playing host to the city's louche glitterati, from politicians to showgirls. In September 1926 'Bugs' Moran and Hymie Weiss, having failed to settle their score with Johnny Torrio, led a motorcade past the Hawthorn Hotel and sprayed it with hundreds of submachine-gun bullets. Capone was unhurt but his pride was ruffled and he had Weiss gunned down in the street shortly afterwards.

Moran proved more elusive so, while maintaining a price on his head, Capone turned to other business matters that needed settling. The Genna family, a gang of six Sicilian brothers, led by 'Bloody' Angelo, were established suppliers of 'medical quality' alcohol. Both Capone and Moran wanted to muscle in on their business and one by one their gang members were gunned down until the remaining brothers fled the city.

Capone then turned on one of his own men, Francesco 'Frankie' Yale, one of the hitmen hired to assassinate 'Deanie' O'Bannion. Suspecting Yale had short-changed him on a liquor deal, he was lured to a fake appointment in New York in 1928 and machine-gunned to death from a passing car. Back in Chicago that same year, an attack by unknown assailants also gunned down 'Diamond' Joe Esposito, another hoodlum who had become a bent politician controlling police, politicians and union leaders.

The next obstacle to Capone's monopoly of power in the West Side of Chicago was another bootleg liquor supplier, Roger Touhy. As a means of driving him out of business, Capone in 1931 kidnapped his partner, Matt Kolb, and when Touhy paid the $50,000 ransom demanded for his release, shot him anyway. When Touhy still held out against Capone, the gangster got corrupt police to frame him for a separate kidnapping and he was jailed on perjured evidence. Days after his release, he was shot dead in a Chicago street.

But to Al 'Scarface' Capone, the sweetest act of revenge was always going to be the elimination of his most hated opponent, George Clarence 'Bugs' Moran, the O'Bannion aide who had tried to kill Capone's old partner Johnny Torrio in 1924. For the task, Capone employed his deadliest hitmen to enact what would become the most infamous gang shoot-out of all time – the Saint Valentine's Day Massacre of 1929.

On a snow-covered Chicago morning, men in police uniforms burst into a garage used by Moran's North Side Gang. Seven of his men, who had gathered to await a liquor delivery, were lined up against a wall. The fake cops then motioned to the Mafia executioners just outside. Machine guns spat death.

Neither Capone, who was vacationing in Miami at the time, nor Moran, were in the garage that morning, the latter only narrowly missing his assassination. But six Mob associates and a car mechanic were killed. It was a massacre at the height of the Chicago Mob wars that shocked a nation already accustomed to headlines announcing random street killings. It also shook Moran himself, who fled town, leaving the 'Windy City' to Capone.

The actual hit is thought to have been organised, and possibly carried out, by one of his most trusted lieutenants, Vincenzo DeMora, who liked to be known as 'Machine Gun' Jack McGurn and sidekick Anthony 'Joe Batters' Accardo. McGurn, who had joined Capone as a hired gunman after his father was killed by the Genna family, had a fearsome reputation. By 1929 at least 25 bodies had been found with his 'calling card', a nickel coin pressed into the palm of the victim's hand. His fees for contract killings allowed him to buy shares in a number of Chicago clubs. In 1927 when a comedian, Joe E. Lewis, refused to work at one of them, he was beaten up by McGurn and had his vocal cords cut. McGurn himself was machine-gunned to death by three masked executioners in a bowling alley in 1936, seven years and a day after the St Valentine's Day Massacre.

McGurn's sidekick, Anthony 'Joe Batters' Accardo, went on to succeed Capone as head of the Chicago Mafia. In old age, he gave way to Sam Giancana (of whom, much more in a further chapter).

McGurn's killers were never traced but the prime suspect was 'Bugs' Moran. He largely disappeared from public view after his men were massacred and it was not until 1946 that he resurfaced in Ohio, where he was jailed for bank robbery. Shortly after his release in 1956, he was again caught after robbing a bank. He died in Leavenworth prison in 1957.

After forcing Moran to flee for his life following the 1929 massacre, Capone had taken over control of the entire criminal network of the city of Chicago. But his empire would soon crumble. In 1931 what the police failed to achieve in a decade the taxman managed in a few weeks. On 4 October after a speedy trial, Al Capone was found guilty of tax evasion. He was fined $50,000 and ordered to pay $30,000 costs – chickenfeed to him. But he was also sentenced to a jail term of 11 years. It broke him.

When he was released in 1939, Capone was already sliding into insanity from syphilis. He hid himself away on his Florida estate, shunned by neighbours and even his fellow Mafia veterans until his death, alone and deranged, in 1947. The new breed of Mob leaders wanted nothing to do with the loud-mouthed, brutish scar-faced relic of a blood-spattered era.

CHAPTER 2

MONSTERS WHO BECAME MOGULS OF THE MOB

A young Polish immigrant was walking through the streets of New York when he saw a girl being assaulted by two men. The 16-year-old rushed to her rescue, fists flying. In the ensuing fight, police were called and all three men were arrested and kept in prison for 48 days. Their brief incarceration changed their lives. The girl's two attackers were young thugs 'Lucky' Luciano and 'Bugsy' Siegel. The plucky teenager was Meyer Lansky. Despite his attack on them, the thugs took Lansky under their wing … and all three went on to become Mob magnates.

Well, it's a nice story. (And even as an author of crime books, I also once believed it.) But like so many myths about the Mafia, it paints a glamorised picture of what is, in stark truth, a grimy, grubby, barbaric criminal subculture. There are no 'Robin Hoods' in the ongoing history of the Mafia, only hoodlums and their manipulative masters, the Mob bosses.

Take 'Lucky' Luciano, who liked to think of himself as a heroic wartime agent for the US government. In fact, his real name was Salvatore Lucania, Sicilian-born pimp and drug pusher who was a bully and cheat almost from birth. 'Bugsy' Siegel – so nicknamed because he was 'as crazy as a bedbug' – presented himself as a handsome playboy, who mixed with Hollywood's rich and famous. But Benjamin Siegel was really a nasty thug and cheap chiseller who, when entrusted with millions of dollars to run his own business, stole from his friends. Seemingly self-effacing Meyer Lansky was, to all appearances, a polite, mild-mannered businessman. But the bent accountant, born Maier Suchowjansky, was as guilty as any of the murderous mobsters who worked for him – a cynical mover of money earned from the vilest criminal undertakings that cost untold lives.

The story is true, however, that Luciano and Lansky met early in life. Born in Sicily in 1897, Luciano arrived in the United States in 1906 and got into trouble within hours of disembarking from his migrant ship – for stealing fruit from a handcart. The following year the ten-year-old was charged with his first crime, shoplifting. He also launched his first racket, charging Jewish kids a penny or two for his 'protection' to and from school. If they refused to pay, he would beat them up. In 1915 his life of petty crime led him to a custodial sentence for the first time for drug peddling but his year in reform school left him a hardened criminal. Luciano became a leader of Manhattan's Five Points Gang and police named him as a suspect in several local murders although he was never indicted. Fellow members of the gang at various times were Johnny Torrio and Al Capone.

Meyer Lansky, born in 1902 to a Russian family, arrived in

the US in 1911 and was one of the Jewish kids that Luciano targeted, offering him protection at a price. Lansky refused to pay, and after Luciano failed to beat him up they became friends. Like his Italian pal, Lansky formed his own small gang while still in his teens, mainly involved in gambling and car theft. Luciano was at first Lansky's mentor and later his associate. They controlled a number of New York gangs, mainly Italian and Irish, involved in robbing homes, shops and warehouses. But there was an area of crime in which Luciano specialised and which Lansky abhorred: prostitution. The Jew would have no part in the vice trade because, while a teenager, he had fallen desperately in love with a young prostitute, then found her one night in an alley with her throat cut, probably by her pimp.

Between 1918 and 1932, Lansky was arrested seven times on charges ranging from disorderly conduct to murder but he had to be released on each one because of lack of witnesses. Luciano was more successful in keeping out of police custody. He and Lansky had both become affiliated to the gang of Jacob 'Little Augie' Orgen, who made a fortune from union and organised labour rackets. On Orgen's behalf, Luciano became New York's most feared hitman, whose favoured weapon was an ice pick. His reward was a string of Manhattan brothels that, by the Twenties, were estimated to be earning him more than $1 million a year.

While Luciano was the epitome of a brutal gangster, Lansky took the softly-softly approach. Seeing how fellow Jews were intimidated by their Irish and Italian neighbours, he began offering their businesses 'protection' – at a price. But he needed 'muscle' to make his racket work, and the first person Meyer recruited was fellow Brooklyn boy Benjamin Siegel, also of

Russian Jewish descent, though born in New York in 1906. Siegel had already devised his own protection racket, forcing Manhattan pushcart merchants to pay him a dollar or he would incinerate their merchandise. From his teenage years, the tough thug was building a criminal record that included armed robbery, rape and murder.

Siegel, Meyer and Luciano formed a firm friendship, reinforced when Siegel saved Lansky from beatings and when Lansky helped Luciano organise his rackets to the best financial advantage without interference from the tax authorities. It could hardly be said they were 'life-long' friends, however, for two of them would end up sending a hitman to 'rub out' the third. But the years following the World War One were boom times for the trio.

Their key to untold riches came on 17 January 1920. When the Prohibition law banning alcohol was introduced, the trio went into the bootleg booze business big-time, teaming up with tommy gun wielding thugs to ensure a constant supply of illicit alcohol to New York. Principal among their associates in the northern states was Alfonso Capone, who was fiercely loyal to Lansky and Luciano.

In 1927 the evil duo were joined by a third ruthless killer and future crime czar, Vito Genovese. Born in Naples in 1897, Genovese had been a friend and neighbour of Luciano since the former's arrival in New York. A petty thief with only one arrest, for carrying a revolver, he too had graduated to organised crime while working under contract to Jacob Orgen. Despite the combined reputations of Lansky, Luciano and Genovese, the gang of three were still not the most powerful mobsters in New York. That accolade was being fought for between two old-style Mafia leaders, Salvatore Maranzano and Giuseppe Masseria, bitter rivals whose territorial battles had left as many as 60 of their 'soldiers' shot dead in a single year.

Individually, both Maranzano and Masseria tried to woo Luciano, Lansky and Genovese into their organisations, probably fearful of the trio's growing power. They refused. By way of persuasion, Maranzano lured Luciano to an empty garage, where a dozen masked men lay in wait. Maranzano had him strung up by his thumbs from the rafters and punched and kicked until he lost consciousness. Luciano was repeatedly revived so that the torture could continue anew. Finally, Maranzano slashed him across the face with a knife. The wound required 55 stitches.

Unsurprisingly, Luciano told his tormentor that he had changed his mind and was now happy to join his Mob. Maranzano relented and offered him a role as his associate – but only if he would first dispose of his Mafia rival, Masseria. With little choice in the matter, Luciano agreed. In April 1931 he approached Masseria, pretending that he was now keen to join forces with him, and invited the Mafioso for a meal. They sealed the deal and toasted one another across the table at his favourite restaurant, Nuova Villa Tammaro, on Coney Island. When Luciano retired to the bathroom, four gunmen burst in. Masseria must have known his fate the moment he saw them. They were Vito Genovese, Bugsy Siegel and two other Lansky men, Albert Anastasia and Joe Adonis. Masseria was cut down in a hail of bullets as he tried to flee the restaurant.

Salvatore Maranzano was delighted with the result and paid due tribute to Lansky and Luciano for their handiwork. The 63-year-old Mafia boss could now claim to be the first true Godfather. After Masseria's death, this elegantly dressed

Sicilian, who had once trained to become a priest, called a meeting of the New York families in a hall where the walls were hung with crucifixes and other religious emblems. He drew up a constitution in which he proclaimed himself the effective 'Capo di Tutti Capi' of what he termed 'La Cosa Nostra'.

These and other terms that are such an intrinsic part of the Mafia vocabulary were becoming familiar to the American public for the first time. Luciano and Genovese used this Mafia patois and their Jewish cohorts Lansky and Siegel were also fluent in it. But despite the traditional Cosa Nostra oaths of fidelity they all expressed, loyalty was not their strong point. The new Capo di Tutti Capi, Salvatore Maranzano, was the man who stood between the Luciano gang and the pinnacle of power in the US underworld. And in September 1931 Luciano settled his old score with him.

One morning four 'tax inspectors' called at Maranzano's real estate agency on Park Avenue. His bodyguards kept their guns hidden as the four identified themselves as Internal Revenue Service investigators and demanded to see the books and the boss. Ushered in to his private office, they revealed themselves as 'Bugsy' Siegel, Albert Anastasia, Red Levine and Thomas 'Three Fingers' Lucchese. All four drew knives. Just five months after pronouncing himself Godfather, Maranzano was killed – stabbed several times and then shot for good measure. Over the next few days about 40 more of Maranzano's team and their associates were systematically eliminated.

The new Mob magnates were now firmly in power. Luciano became the Boss of Bosses. His predecessor, Maranzano, had very conveniently formed the La Cosa Nostra code of conduct, set up 'family' divisions and structure, and established procedures for resolving disputes. Luciano now instituted the

'National Crime Syndicate', consisting of the major Mob bosses from around the country and the so-called 'Five Families' of New York. The Syndicate was meant to serve as a deliberative body to solve disputes, carve up and distribute territories and regulate lucrative illegal activities. The solely Italian-American Mafia had their own body, known as 'the Commission', which ruled all La Cosa Nostra activities.

In this way, by the early Thirties, the old-style trigger-happy Mafia leaders, derisively termed 'Moustache Petes', had largely been replaced. The Syndicate of crime families brought in accountants and corporate executives. They still needed those ultimate persuaders, the hired killers, but, in order to show the authorities that the Mob had cleaned up its act, the assassins operated at arm's-length from the men in suits. Thus, under Luciano's aegis, while one wing of the operation was labelled the National Crime Syndicate, the other became known in the press as 'Murder Incorporated'.

The most feared hitman of this mercenary death squad was Albert Anastasia, one of the killers of both Masseria and Maranzano. Known as New York's 'Lord High Executioner', he was founder member of Murder Inc., appointed by Luciano as a reward for his loyalty, along with second-in-command, union racketeer Louis 'Lepke' Buchalter. Together, they meted out death on contract for a quarter of a century.

Their 'soldiers', sometimes known as the 'Brownsville Boys', were predominantly Jewish and Italian killers who operated out of the back room of an innocent-looking candy store called Midnight Rose's, in Brooklyn's Brownsville neighbourhood. The shop was owned by Louis Capone, no relation to Chicago's Alphonse Capone but still a thoroughly nasty killer. From this base, Murder Inc. is estimated to have carried out between 900 and 1,000 gangland murders in the New York City area. Throughout this period, their boss, Albert Anastasia, remained largely untouchable, his business card claiming that he was a sales representative for a company called the Convertible Mattress Corporation.

Anastasia, born Umberto Anastasio in southern Italy in 1902, had arrived in New York illegaly just after World War One, jumping ship and taking a job on the Brooklyn waterfront. In 1921 he was sentenced to death for the muder of a fellow docker – but, when retried on a technicality, he had to be freed because all the witnesses had mysteriously disappeared. In 1928, by which time Anastasia had become a union leader in the corrupt Longshoremen's International Association, he was charged with a murder in Brooklyn – and again freed when the witnesses either disappeared or refused to testify. In 1932 he was indicted on charges of murdering another man with an ice pick – but the case was dropped due to lack of witnesses. The following year he was charged with yet another killing – but again there were no witnesses willing to testify.

Anastasia's more high-profile 'contracts' included the murder of top trucking union official Morris Diamond in 1939. That same year he organised the murder of Pietro Panto, an activisit trying to expose corruption in the 25,000-member Longshoremen's union. When Panto refused to take a bribe to desist from his campaign against the intimidation and violence that kept the union's members in line, he was kidnapped, brutally battered, then strangled. His body was later recovered on a farm known to be a Murder Inc. dumping ground in New Jersey.

Murder Inc. finally over-reached itself in 1941. A gun-for-hire gangster named Abe Reles was arrested on murder charges and admitted that he had been supplying Anastasia and Buchalter with hitmen for the past ten years. To save himself from the death penalty, Reles offered tesimony that put seven members of Murder Inc. in prison. He also offered information that could implicate Anastasia in the slayings of Diamond and Panto.

Fearful of prosecution, Anastasia offered a $100,000 reward to anyone who would 'rub out' Reles. In November 1941, the 'squealer' was being guarded by police at a Coney Island hotel during an ongoing trial. Despite his police guard, Reles was found dead on an adjacent restaurant roof. An official inquiry ruled that he had accidentally died while climbing down the building using knotted sheets.

Most New Yorkers, however, firmly believed that Anastasia had had Reles murdered – a view reinforced the following year when another informer was found dead. Like Reles, a Murder Inc. associate named Anthony Romeo had been arrested and was willing to implicate Anastasia in several murders. However, in June 1942 his body was discovered in Delaware. He had been beaten before being shot several times.

The silencing of informers was very much in Murder Inc.'s interests but the removal of unco-operative criminal cohorts or commercial rivals was also a money-making activity. It was, as the character Don Corleone says in Mario Puzo's novel *The Godfather*, 'not personal – it's strictly business'. Those gory bits of 'business' might often be ordered by – but seldom if ever witnessed by – the Mob leader who always maintained a low profile, Meyer Lansky.

Lansky, the so-called 'Mob's accountant', had become the main money manipulator for the Mafia barons from the early Thirties. His expertise was much needed. When Prohibition was repealed in 1933, a principal source of income dried up and new forms of investment had to be found. Loan sharking, the numbers games, protection rackets and vice kept the money rolling in but new areas of exploitation were needed. The growing drugs market was one of the most potentially lucrative, and the Mafia built up European and Far Eastern connections to supply it. Another was legal gambling, with the golden boom in casino towns like Las Vegas, Reno and Atlantic City. The third main route away from the Mafia's tawdry roots was into the labour movement. Trade unions were cynically milked for the funds that could be misappropriated and, more importantly, for the 'muscle' they could lend to any extortion situation where a strike could prove costly.

Despite being Jewish in a predominantly Italian society, Lansky, the wily diplomat, helped maintain peace within the crime Syndicate. He helped fuse the rival Mafia families scattered around the nation into a 'federal' unit. Autonomous in their own area, they nevertheless came together to seek agreement on major policy issues – and it was Lansky's advice that they often accepted. He persuaded them of the logic of maintaining a low profile, that the days of street warfare were over. Any such 'contracts' could be left to Murder Inc. As he became increasingly trusted as an 'independent' Mafia advisor, more concerned with money-making than internal power struggles, his associates allowed him to invest their ill-gotten gains in respectable industries and in the gambling havens of Las Vegas, Cuba and the Bahamas.

Lansky looked after his known interests too, of course. Following Al Capone's 1931 conviction for tax evasion, Lansky saw that he too was vulnerable and, to protect himself, transferred his illegal earnings to a Swiss bank account, the anonymity of which was assured by the 1934 Swiss Banking Act. He eventually even bought an offshore Swiss bank, which he used to launder money through a network of shell and holding companies. Lansky made billions for the Mafia and an estimated personal fortune of $300 million.

An associate, Joseph Doc Stacher, once said of Lansky and his partner Luciano: 'They were an unbeatable team. If they had become President and Vice-President of the United States, they would have run the place far better than the idiot politicians.' Unluckily for 'Lucky' Luciano, the partnership was broken up in 1936 by government prosecutors. In June of that year, Luciano was convicted on 62 counts of prostitution and other vice offences and received a sentence of between 30 and 50 years in state prison.

Vito Genovese briefly became acting boss of Luciano's gang but, after being indicted for a 1934 murder, he was forced to leave the country – Frank Costello now replaced him as acting boss of the Luciano crime family. Genovese fled to Naples in 1937, his expatriation cushioned by an estimated $2 million that he had salted away in secret Swiss bank accounts. A vociferous supporter of Mussolini, having contributed generously to fascist funds, he further helped out the Italian dictator's family by becoming the main drug source for his son-in-law, Count Ciano. It is also said that, to impress Mussolini, he arranged the murder of a newspaper editor who was a fierce opponent.

Genovese switched sides hurriedly when the tide of war changed and offered his services to the occupying American forces. He pinpointed black-market operations in post-war Italy and helped close them down – but then quietly resurrected them with his own men in charge. His Italian Connection came to an end when he was extradited back to the

US in 1945 to face an old murder charge. It failed to stick after the principal witness was shot dead and Genovese returned to New York – with an ambition to take over the Luciano family and become the Mafia's Capo di Tutti Capi.

As we shall see in the next chapter, things did not go entirely Vito Genovese's way. Neither was organised crime a passport to a peaceful old age for fellow family members Albert Anastasia and 'Bugsy' Siegel. On the other hand, Meyer Lansky continued to live a charmed life. And 'Lucky' Luciano lived up to his name too.

Luciano must have thought his luck had finally run out when he was jailed for up to 50 years for vice offences. But six years later, in November 1942, he got a visit from his old friend Lansky. The arch fixer told him that he had done a deal with US naval intelligence officers who were concerned that information about Allied convoys was being leaked by pro-Mussolini Italian immigrants working on the New York waterfront. The fears seemed to have been confirmed by the burning of the French liner *Normandie* at its moorings in New York. So many fires had broken out at the same time within the ship that the US Navy, which was due to use *Normandie* to carry troops and supplies to Europe, was certain Italian saboteurs were to blame.

Naval chiefs were willing to offer Luciano a move to a better prison if, from his cell, he would cooperate with a special intelligence unit to flush out Italian spies and saboteurs. The jailbird, through Lansky, improved the deal to win the promise of early parole and possibly complete freedom after the war. At least one other Mafia man was immediately freed from jail at Luciano's request. He was Johnny 'Cockeye' Dunn, who was responsible for the no-questions-asked removal of two suspected German spies. Apart from keeping peace on the waterfront, the team was also credited with locating an enemy submarine off Long Island. Four German spies were captured as they came ashore and, under interrogation, revealed a North American network of Nazi agents.

Even more valuable to the Allied cause were Luciano's contacts with his homeland. Before the invasion of Sicily by British, Canadian and US forces in 1944, Luciano sent emissaries to local Mafia leaders urging that all help be given to the Americans. Four Italian-speaking US naval intelligence officers joined up with the Sicilian Mafia and successfully raided German and Italian bases for secret defence blueprints. Later, in Rome, the Mafia foiled an assassination attempt against Britain's General Sir Harold Alexander and, as a footnote to history, seized Mussolini's entire personal archives.

The American authorities kept their part of the bargain and in 1945, within a few months of the war in Europe ending, Luciano was freed from jail. New York's Governor Thomas Dewey, a former special prosecutor of organised crime who got Luciano jailed in the first place, granted commutation of sentence and had him deported to Italy. His comrade in crime, Lansky, was there to bid him farewell, with a contribution of half a million dollars to help him start his new life. From an ocean's distance away, Luciano continued to hold sway over his American Syndicate until – like Lansky and Genovese, his two principal partners in a lifetime of corruption, torture and murder – he died of natural causes.

CHAPTER 3

'WISE GUYS': OUT OF THE MOUTHS OF MOBSTERS

'Mafia-speak' has slyly insinuated itself into American culture. 'I'm gonna make him an offer he can't refuse' is the instantly recognisable saying of Don Corleone, as portrayed by Marlon Brando, in *The Godfather*. But there are many other titles, words and phrases that are less well-known outside the Italian underworld. Since the street talk of the Mafia is a language unto itself, here are some of the favourite expressions, plus an explanation of the organisation's hierarchy, followed by some of its leaders' pithier language.

When a young hopeful is accepted into the Mafia, he becomes a 'Wise Guy' or he has become 'straightened out'. Later, after he is appointed a fully-fledged or 'made' member of his particular Mafia 'family', he could become a 'Capo' (captain) heading a crew of 'Soldiers', the lowliest rank. Hundreds of criminals who have not been invited by families to join their inner ranks of 'made' members are nevertheless linked with the Mafia as 'Associates'. Some are in influential or powerful positions with companies and government agencies.

The Mafiosi themselves refer to their crime family as 'La Cosa Nostra', which means 'our thing' or 'this business of ours'. Collectively, they like to refer to themselves as 'Men of Honour'.

There are about 25 Famiglia or crime families in America, the five largest and most powerful based in New York. These have branches in other parts of the country or, in some cases, affiliated families tied to them by blood.

The head of each family is the 'Godfather' or 'Don'. An honorary title that the top Godfathers bestow upon one of their number is 'Capo di Tutti Capi', Godfather of Godfathers, or Boss of all the Bosses. Some, who feel powerful enough to ward off any challenge, seize the title. They usually die.

Next comes the 'under-boss', who is usually the tough-guy, the disciplinarian. The 'Consigliere' or counsellor is third in line. He is effectively a family's chief-of-staff. Beneath them are the 'Capos', some of whom, specialising in arranging murders, are known as 'Enforcers'. Some Enforcers are also under-bosses.

Soldiers have specialities too. A hitman will be known as a 'Torpedo' or 'Buttonman' (as in 'pressing the button' on someone). The chief hitman (or sometimes bodyguard) will be known as a 'Caporegima'.

Police make no distinction, calling them all Hoodlums, 'Hoods' for short, or 'Goons'.

Godfathers of most of the Mafia families make up a kind of criminal board of directors, which is known as 'The Commission'. The existence of this body was denied for decades and was only noticed by accident in 1957. Members of the Commission have since been tried in court, charged with the very offence of being members of it.

There is also a group of Mafia bosses known as 'The Club', and this one involves those who participate in trade union racketeering in the construction industry.

Other descriptions of wider groupings of gangsters can be confusing. The word 'Mob' is often used synonymously with 'Mafia'. But the Mob is a looser description of a group of gangsters. During the formative years of US organised crime between the world wars, 'the Mob' was usually taken to mean Jewish-dominated racketeers, while 'the Mafia' admitted only Sicilians. When 'Lucky' Luciano forged his way to ultimate power in New York, however, his Syndicate included such nefarious non-Sicilians as Frank Costello, 'Dutch' Shultz, Joe Adonis, Louis Lepke, and Meyer Lansky. Luciano even toyed with the idea of dropping the Syndicate's Mafia affiliation. He was dissuaded by Lansky, who felt that the spectre of the Mafia would help them keep people in line, even though at one point the Jewish members outnumbered the Sicilians.

The activities the gangs got up to in those early days had their own vernacular too. 'Bootlegging' referred to illicit booze, a boot being best hiding place for a bottle. 'Hijack' was literally the phrase 'Hi Jack', the supposed greeting in a bootleg booze hold-up. And a 'Speakeasy' was an illegal bar, not to be spoken of loudly. All very logical.

Not so explicable is 'Vigorish', a very important word in the Mafia language. The hoods call it 'vig' and it stands for the exorbitant interest the thugs collect every week on a loan. Which leads us to 'loan-sharking'. This is a commonly used word that describes the business of illegal lending, at murderous rates, in which every branch of the Mafia is engaged.

Murder has many names in the Mob – to waste, blow away, hit, terminate, retire, rub out, take care of, remove, or (Jimmy The Weasel's favourite) to 'clip'. Ordering a hit, a Mafioso will still utter the old Sicilian phrase: *'Livarsi na petra di la scapa'* – Take the stone out of my shoe.

Carlos 'Little Man' Marcello, head of the Mafia's New Orleans branch, shouted this curse at the Kennedy brothers, John and Robert. They were both gunned down. But a Godfather will often say nothing to snuff out a life – a nod or a motion of the hand is enough.

When a rubout is 'sanctioned', or approved at the top, the killing is quite often sub-contracted to a third party, perhaps even someone from a different crime family. A friendly Mafia clan in another town will provide the killers, making it more difficult for police to trace them. This practice, which dates back to the Twenties, is known as 'importing'. Alternatively, a 'contract' is put out on someone. This can take two courses – a trusted man can be handed the contract specifically, or it can be posted generally, like a bounty, for anyone to fill.

They don't talk about 'concrete overcoats' any more for encasing a victim's corpse in a cement block; they just call it 'dressing'. Nor are words like 'drill' and 'plug' used for killing. They just 'take care of business'.

'What's doin'?' is a typical greeting in the densely populated districts of New York, where crime is big. The stock Mafia answer is 'What can I tell y'? Nuthin'.' Because the actual meaning of that retort is: 'I can't tell you anything that makes sense because it could cost me my life.'

'D-and-D' is what you stay if you're smart, whoever you are. It means 'deaf and dumb' or plain silent. Squealers, known in the trade as 'canaries' because they 'sing' or 'chirp' to the authorities, usually have a general contract out on them. This keeps them terrified because they never know where the hit might be coming from. The assassin could be their closest buddy. And quite often he is; many of the major victims were at least lured to their execution, if not actually hit, by a trusted friend.

'Omertà' is the code of silence to which every member is sworn. Penalty for breaking it is death. 'Capish?' Do you understand? Bacio del Morte is the 'kiss of death', the traditional light brush on the cheek of the victim-to-be. It's a ritual, now dying out. Some still use it for effect; most don't believe any more in signalling their intentions.

To be 'connected' means to have a link in some way with the Mafia. Even those who don't have that link pretend they do, especially people with Italian names. It brings instant respect. Nobody is allowed to mention the name of the person to whom he is connected. Penalty: death. Those on the outside who use a Mafia name are also killed. Anyone who actually gives a name is almost certainly unconnected!

The Mafiosi used to call themselves 'The Untouchables' because they considered themselves able to operate their various activities totally out of reach of the law. This is reflected in some of the nicknames today's mobsters have.

Aladena Fratianno became 'Jimmy The Weasel' but not because the Los Angeles mobster turned informer on his partners-in-crime. He earned that name long before because of his ability to avoid being brought to justice. This knack of ducking the law turned Antonio Corallo into 'Tony Ducks'.

Matty 'The Horse' Ianiello, of the Genovese family, got his name through his enormous bulk: 29 stone of it. Colombo boss Carmine Persico was known to police and many in the

Mafia as 'The Snake', although he had tried to foster another nickname, 'Junior'.

Sometimes nicknames are wordplays. Joseph Bonanno would be 'Joe Bananas'. Enforcer Aniello Dellacroce's parents had given him an Italian name that meant 'Little Lamb of the Cross'. Aniello turned into 'Mr. O'Neil'. Joe Stracci, scourge of the Garment District, became 'Joe Stretch'. Anthony Provenzano was 'Tony Pro'. Phillip Testa, who headed the Philadelphia family for a year until he was blown to bits, was called 'Chicken Man', not because he was a coward, but because he once ran a chicken farm.

The nicknames often make perfect sense. Benjamin Siegel became 'Bugsy' because he acted like a crazy man, as in Bugs Bunny. Hulking Frank Bompensiero in Los Angeles was affectionately known, until his murder, as 'The Bomp'.

From the inventiveness of their nicknames and the success of their villainy, it might seem the Mafia is made up of pretty wise 'Wise Guys'. This is not at all the case. 'We must remind ourselves that we're not talking about brain surgeons here,' warned New York organised crime specialist Tom Luce. And yet sometimes the Mafiosi will come up with a good line or two.

Al Capone himself had a simple philosophy: 'You can get much further with a kind word and a gun than you can with a kind word alone.' Here are some of his other recorded quotes: 'You can go a long way with a smile. You can go a lot farther with a smile and a gun.' 'Once in the racket you're always in it.' 'Vote early and vote often.' 'I am like any other man. All I do is supply a demand.' 'I don't even know what street Canada is on.' 'Capitalism is the legitimate racket of the ruling class.' 'I have built my organisation upon fear.' 'My rackets are run on strictly American lines and they're going to stay that way.' 'Now I know why tigers eat their young.' 'Prohibition has made nothing but trouble.' 'When I sell liquor, it's called bootlegging; when my patrons serve it on Lake Shore Drive, it's called hospitality.' 'I am going to St. Petersburg, Florida, tomorrow. Let the worthy citizens of Chicago get their liquor the best they can. I'm sick of the job – it's a thankless one and full of grief. I've been spending the best years of my life as a public benefactor.' And finally: 'This American system of ours, call it Americanism, call it capitalism, call it what you will, gives each and every one of us a great opportunity if we only seize it with both hands and make the most of it.'

The masterful 'Lucky' Luciano averred: 'There's no such thing as good money or bad money. There's just money.' 'If you have a lot of what people want and can't get, then you can supply the demand and shovel in the dough.' 'The world is changing and there are new opportunities for those who are ready to join forces with those who are stronger and more experienced.' 'Ever since we was kids, we always knew that people can be bought. It was only a question of who did the buying and for how much.' 'Behind every great fortune, there is a crime.'

The 'Mob Accountant' Meyer Lansky boasted: 'We're bigger than US Steel.' His other advice: 'Don't lie. Tell one lie, then you gotta tell another lie to compound on the first.' 'Don't worry, don't worry. Look at the Astors and the Vanderbilts, all those big society people. They were the worst thieves and now look at them. It's just a matter of time.' And some advice he ignored himself: 'Always overpay your taxes. That way you'll get a refund.'

Hitman 'Crazy' Joe Gallo once prodded an accomplice and

said: 'You like federal judges? I'll buy you one for Christmas!' Carlo Gambino famously said: 'Judges, lawyers and politicians have a license to steal. We don't need one.' His son Thomas Gambino reflected: 'Me I never had the chance to say, "Well I'm going to do something I want to do." I always did it for my family, for my children, for my father, for my mother.'

Carlo Gambino's successor Paul Castellano, sometimes known as the 'Howard Hughes of the Mob', was more reflective: 'This life of ours, this is a wonderful life. If you can get through life like this and get away with it, hey, that's great. But it's very unpredictable. There's so many ways you can screw it up.'

Castellano also explained a Mafioso's sense of duty: 'There are certain promises you make that are more sacred than anything that happens in a court of law, I don't care how many Bibles you put your hand on. Some of the promises, it's true, you make too young, before you really have an understanding of what they mean. But once you've made those first promises, other promises are called for. And the thing is you can't deny the new ones without betraying the old ones. The promises get bigger; there are more people to be hurt and disappointed if you don't live up to them. Then, at some point, you're called upon to make a promise to a dying man.'

But Castellano also exposed his sense of cynicism: 'We're not children here. The law is – how should I put it? A convenience. Or a convenience for some people, and an inconvenience for other people. Like, take the law that says you can't go into someone else's house. I have a house, so, hey, I like that law. The guy without a house – what's he think of it? Stay out in the rain, schnook. That's what the law means to him.' And on political influence: 'If the President of the

United States, if he's smart, if he needs help, he'd come. I could do a favour for the President.'

Thomas DiBella, who was briefly the Colombo family boss in the 1970s, expressed the Mafia philosophy: 'You are no better or worse than anyone else in La Cosa Nostra. You are your own man. You and your father are now equals. Your father, sons, and brothers have no priority. We are all as one, united in blood. Once you become part of this, there is no greater bond.'

Joe Bonanno, who became boss of one of America's most enduring crime families, waxed almost lyrical when he said: 'Mafia is a process, not a thing. Mafia is a form of clan-cooperation to which its individual members pledge lifelong loyalty. Friendship, connections, family ties, trust, loyalty, obedience – this was the glue that held us together.'

Gambino under-boss Aniello Dellacroce was less eloquent: 'You don't understand Cosa Nostra. Cosa Nostra means the boss is your boss. Boss is the boss is the boss. What I'm trying to say is a boss is a boss. What does a boss mean in this fuckin' thing? You might as well make anybody off the street.' 'Things change now because there's too much conflict. People do whatever they feel like. They don't train their people no more. There's no more respect.'

Anthony Casso, a homicidal maniac who ran the Lucchese crime family, nevertheless felt the need to show his sensitive side. 'I truly feel sorry for the younger generation that wants to belong to that life. It's sad for them. There is absolutely no honour and respect today. Little do the newcomers know that there are many made members in the Mafia that wish not to be there and would like nothing better than to walk away from it. So they do the next best thing: stay low-key if possible. The young newcomers will never see the kind of big money that was once made. That's long gone. They don't realise what it means to be free and to have peace of mind until it's taken from them.' Casso also declared his domestic loyalty. 'Most all men in my life, everyone I know, had girlfriends. It goes with the territory. Women are drawn to us, the power, the money, and we're drawn to them. But only in passing. Some guys treated their mistresses better than their wife but that's outrage. No class. Only a *cafone* [ill-mannered peasant] does that. I never loved any woman but Lillian. She and my family always came first.'

But Frank Costello, who was known as the 'Prime Minister of the Underworld', did not think so highly of his family: 'Other kids are brought up nice and sent to Harvard and Yale. Me? I was brought up like a mushroom.'

Family business meant something completely different to Antonio 'Tony Ducks' Corallo, a union racketeer at the head of the Lucchese family, who said: 'Let's take a son-in-law, somebody, put them into the (union) office; they got a job. Let's take somebody's daughter, whatever, she's the secretary. Let's staff it with our people. And when we say go break this guy's balls, they're there, seven o'clock in the morning, to break the guy's balls.'

Jimmy Hoffa, the most infamous union leader of them all, obviously agreed. 'Everybody has a price,' he said – shortly before he was murdered by Mafia hitmen. Talking of which, Los Angeles gang boss Mickey Cohen passed off his murderous ways with the excuse: 'I never killed a guy who didn't deserve it.' But Chicago hitman Joseph 'Joe Batters' Accardo once freed a victim with the words: 'Let him go. He cheated me fair and square.' This was somewhat out of character for the killer hired by Al Capone to attend one of his dinners and publicly beat to death two of the guests with a baseball bat.

Some of the most revelatory quotations from a Mafia leader are those of John Gotti, labelled the 'Teflon Don' because of the number of charges that failed to stick. When he was finally convicted, however, it was partly because of an FBI bug that recorded him describing his criminal activities. On one tape he described his organisational ambitions thus: 'This is gonna be a Cosa Nostra 'til I die. Be it an hour from now, or be it tonight, or a hundred years from now when I'm in jail. It's gonna be a Cosa Nostra.'

Other memorable quotes from the opinionated Gambino family godfather include: 'If they don't put us away for one year or two, that's all we need. But if I can get a year run without being interrupted … put this thing together where they could never break it, never destroy it. Even if we die, be a good thing.'

'When I think of the American Indian I think of their courage, strength, pride, their respect and loyalty toward their brothers. I honour the reverence they share for tradition and life. These traits are hungered for in a society that is unfortunately plagued by those whose only values are self-centered and directed at others' expense.'

'I never lie to any man because I don't fear anyone. The only time you lie is when you are afraid.' 'If you think your boss is stupid, remember: you wouldn't have a job if he was any smarter.' 'I know where my mistakes are, where I made my mistakes. They're too late to remedy, you know what I mean?'

'Don't carry a gun. It's nice to have them close by, but don't carry them. You might get arrested.' 'You will put the garbage in the cans and make certain that the cans are covered. We got to keep our own backyard clean.' 'Be nice to bankers. Always be nice to pension fund managers. Always be nice to the media. In that order.' 'I would be a billionaire if I was looking to be a selfish boss. That's not me.' 'I'm in the Gotti family; my wife's the Boss.' 'All I wanted was to be what I became to be.'

A prophecy that would have been more likely if Gotti hadn't talked so much: 'He who is deaf, blind and silent lives a thousand years in peace.' And a final wrong call before he was sent to jail in 1992: 'Three-to-one odds I beat this.'

CHAPTER 4

THE SYNDICATE SUMMIT THAT SHOOK AMERICA

The American Mafia's 'coming of age' – its transformation from a high-profile killing machine into an invisible corporate entity – had begun with the first man to claim the title Capo di Tutti Capi, Salvatore Maranzano. But he was ahead of his time. Within months of his 1931 peace conference to end blood feuds between the major families, he and 40 of his men were dead. Gang warfare on such a scale had alerted Americans to the magnitude of the crime problem in their midst. It had also alerted the Mafiosi themselves to the dangers of advertising their power in blood.

So the man who ordered Maranzano's killing, Meyer Lansky, took up his assassinated rival's theme of cooperation, saying: 'Crime has moved out of the ghettoes and become nationwide.' Lansky and his contemporaries, 'Bugsy' Siegel, 'Lucky' Luciano and Vito Genovese, made themselves millions by adopting a new, more 'businesslike' approach to organised crime. As Luciano explained: 'The world is changing and there are new opportunities for those who are ready to join forces with those who are stronger and more experienced.'

So what happened to these Mafia 'modernisers'? The previous chapters took us through the blood-stained years to World War Two and highlighted the influence of the original infamous foursome – Luciano, Lansky, Siegel and Genovese – who formed a strong family bond that enabled them to survive that violent era. Extraordinarily, after a lifetime of corruption, torture and violent death, three of the four died of natural causes. The fourth was murdered on the orders of his supposed long-term 'friends'.

The nickname 'Lucky' certainly applied to the Sicilian-born Salvatore Lucania. As one of the most – if not *the* most – powerful men in organised crime, his influence over the US underworld still holds. The first person to challenge the 'old Mafia' by breaking through ethnic barriers and forming a network of gangs, he created a national Syndicate that controlled organised crime long past his imprisonment, banishment and death.

Having genuinely helped the American war effort, albeit to his own benefit, the authorities kept their part of the bargain and in 1945, within a few months of the war in Europe ending, Luciano was freed from jail. New York's Governor Thomas Dewey, a former special prosecutor of organised crime who got Luciano jailed in the first place, granted commutation of sentence and had him deported to Italy. His comrade in crime, Lansky, was there to bid him farewell, with a contribution of half a million dollars to help him start his new life.

From an ocean's distance away, Luciano continued to hold

sway over his American Syndicate. He lived in Rome for a while but grew restless and in 1946 he sneaked into Cuba, travelling in a most circuitous route – by freighter to Venezuela, then by plane to Brazil, on to Mexico, doubling back to Venezuela, and finally landing by light plane near Havana, where he took up residence on a private estate. He had chosen Cuba because Lansky was already established as a major investor in gambling and resorts under the island's corrupt regime. He also wanted to be closer to the United States so that he could resume control over Cosa Nostra operations and eventually return to the American mainland. Meanwhile, couriers were set up to keep him supplied with money.

In December 1946 Luciano and Lansky issued an invitation to leaders of US organised crime to meet him in Havana. The supposed reason was to hear visiting singer Frank Sinatra perform but the real reason was to discuss the expansion of Mob operations in Cuba and Las Vegas and into international drug supply. The week-long conference was held at the Hotel Nacional, where Luciano came face to face for the first time in a decade with his old ally, Vito Genovese. A year earlier, Genovese had been extradited from Italy to New York to face trial on an old murder charge but in June 1946 the charges were dismissed and he was free to return to Mob business. Now his former subordinate tried to persuade Luciano to let him run all his East Coast operetions while Luciano remained in exile. His answer was unequivocal:

'There is no Boss of Bosses. I turned it down in front of everybody. If I ever change my mind, I will take the title. But it won't be up to you. Right now you work for me and I ain't in the mood to retire. Don't you ever let me hear this again or I'll lose my temper.'

The Havana conference rebounded on Luciano. He had made his presence there so public, by dining at nightclubs and fêting Frank Sinatra, that the Cuban authorities could no longer turn a blind eye to his presence in the capital. Before his empire-building in exile could begin, American pressure on Cuba's President Fulgencio Batista forced Luciano's dispatch back to Italy – ignominiously on a Turkish freighter bound for Genoa. On his return he was arrested by Italian police and locked in jail until a judge freed him on stiff parole conditions.

Over the next few years, Luciano was arrested and rearrested several times but always managed to win his freedom. He was, however, placed under curfew at his Naples home, required to report to the police weekly and barred from leaving the city without permission. From 1948 he shared his home with Igea Lissoni, an Italian nightclub dancer 20 years his junior, whom he later described as the love of his life. Although he had affairs with numerous other women, the couple stayed together until Igea's death from breast cancer in 1959.

Despite the restrictions placed upon him, Luciano managed to orchestrate a massive expansion of his Cosa Nostra operation, mainly by introducing fresh drug routes to the United States. In October 1957 he gathered 30 American and Sicilian Mafia leaders for a summit in a Palermo hotel to plan a massive smuggling and distribution system for the flooding of the American market with vast quantities of heroin and cocaine. The cruel aim was to lower the price of these hitherto 'elite' drugs in order to create a market in blue-collar urban communities.

At this stage, Frank Costello, aided by the 'muscle' power of Albert Anastasia's murderous Mob enforcers was still Luciano's acting chief in New York. But Vito Genovese had not foresaken his ambition to take over as Boss of Bosses. He was backed by Carlo Gambino, a turncoat member of Anastasia's crime family.

In May 1957 Genovese ordered the assassination of Costello outside his apartment block but the hitman he hired to do the job, Vincent Gigante, botched it and, although slightly wounded, the target survived. Shortly afterwards, however, the thoroughly rattled Costello conceded control of what became – and is still today known as – the Genovese crime family.

Infuriatingly for him, Luciano was far removed from the action and could only watch from exile Genovese's attempts to carve up his old empire. And a significant blow to his prestige was the murder of his ally Anastasia on the orders of Genovese and Gambino.

Albert Anastasia had enjoyed an eventful and succesful, though hideously bloody career since falling in with Luciano and Lansky. Having run Murder Incorporated during the pre-war era, Anastasia appeared to take a 'sabbatical' from crime during World War Two and in 1942 joined the US Army, attaining the rank of sergeant and subsequently being rewarded with American citizenship. In 1948 he bought a dress manufacturer in Pennsylvania and appeared to be a respectable member of the community. In 1951 the Senate summoned him to answer questions about organised crime but he refused to answer. By then Anastasia was back at his old game: murder.

Anastasia had long been under-boss of the Mangano crime family, run by brothers Vincent and Philip. But he was distrusted by them because of his closeness to Luciano and Costello. In early 1951 both Vincent and Philip went missing. Vincent was never seen again but his brother's bullet-riddled body was found dumped in Brooklyn. It was assumed that Anastasia had ordered them both to be killed.

With Costello's support, the Commission confirmed Anastasia's accession as boss of the renamed Anastasia family. But his growing power became too much of a threat to his principal New York rivals, including Genovese, two of whose henchmen followed him to his barber's shop in a smart Manhattan hotel on the morning of 25 October 1957. With a warm towel draped over his face, he did not see the two gunmen position themselves behind the barber's chair. After the first volley of bullets, Anastasia appeared to try and fight back against his killers – but he was lunging at the gunmen's reflections in the mirror in front of him. The image of a victim covered in bloodied white towels shocked America.

With Anastasia safely out of the way, Vito Genovese now believed himself to be the top boss in the Cosa Nostra. In November 1957 he coordinated what became known as the 'Apalachin Conference', a Syndicate 'summit' of more than 100 Mafia leaders from as far afield as Canada and Italy, at which he expected to be named Capo di Tutti Capi. A local state trooper keeping watch on the conference location, the home of Joseph 'Joe the Barber' Barbara in Apalachin, New York, checked the licence plates of the visitors' limousines and reported the suspicious behaviour to his superiors. A road block was set up and many of the Mafia hierarchy were hauled off. Fifty-eight high-ranking mobsters were arrested and the Cosa Nostra subjected to numerous grand jury summonses. Genovese was blamed for the fisasco and it was an embarrassment and loss of prestige from which he never recovered.

His enemies could now hit back. Genovese's former ally Carlo Gambino deserted him and, with Costello, flew to Sicily for a meeting with Luciano. An elaborate stitch-up was arranged. A narcotics deal was set up in New York – and the plotters ensured that Genovese was heavily implicated in it. They then tipped off the police.

Having eliminated Anastasia along with other rivals, Genovese had savoured the fruits of power for only a year before being jailed in 1959 for drug smuggling. From prison, he continued to control the activities of his crime family, even arranging for his top aide, Tony Bender, to be assassinated because he believed him to have played a part in the drugs plot. Genovese had served ten years of a 15-year sentence when he was found dead from a heart attack on 14 November 1969.

He must have been pleased to have survived his arch enemy 'Lucky' Luciano, who had already gone the same way. On 6 January 1962 he had been waiting at Naples airport for the arrival of an American movie producer planning to film the 64-year-old mobster's life story. But Luciano's luck had at last run out. He dropped dead of a heart attack in the airport lounge. Italian narcotics agents who, unbeknown to Luciano, had been following him with an arrest warrant for drug offences witnessed his demise. The Mafia boss's body was shipped back to the United States and buried in St. John's Cemetery in New York's Queens district. More than 2,000 mourners attended the funeral, Luciano's friend Carlo Gambino giving the eulogy.

One of those publicly mourning his old friend was Meyer Lansky – but he was perhaps not as sorry as his feigned grief might have suggested. As the years of exile dragged on, Luciano's formerly rock-solid relationship with Lansky had begun to falter because the Italian did not feel he was receiving his fair share of profits from the Mob. But there was little that Luciano could do about it – because by the early 1960s the names of Meyer Lansky and 'the Mob' were virtually synonymous.

The diminutive, soft-spoken 5ft 5in tall Russian Jew had been a driving force in forming the national crime Syndicate and became one of its major overseers and bankers, laundering funds through foreign accounts. He developed gambling operations in Florida and New Orleans and also in Cuba, where he arranged payoffs to President Batista. He also funded the early development of Las Vegas as a gambling mecca and sent out his own top aide and good friend 'Bugsy' Siegel to take charge of it.

When Fidel Castro came to power in Cuba in 1959, Lansky switched his gambling operations to the Bahamas, nurturing cooperation from the government of the then British colony to build casinos. He also invested in casinos throughout the Caribbean and in London. He controlled hotels, resorts, golf courses and even a meat packing plant. But his operations were not all 'clean' businesses. He was also into narcotics smuggling, pornography, prostitution, labour racketeering and extortion.

The FBI estimated that by 1970 Lansky had salted away $300million in Swiss bank accounts. But that year he learned of plans to arrest him on suspicion of income-tax evasion and fled to Israel, seeking to remain safely there under the so-called Law of Return. This law, passed in 1950 by the Israeli parliament, the Knesset, grants any Jew the right to seek sanctuary in the country – but excludes those with a criminal past. After two years in Israel, Lansky was arrested and deported back to the US, where he was finally brought to trial on several indictments. However, because the principal witness, a loan shark named Vincent 'Fat Vinnie' Teresa, utterly lacked credibility, Lansky was acquitted of income tax evasion but convicted of grand jury contempt, a verdict overturned on appeal.

Indictments on other charges were abandoned in 1974 because of Lansky's ill health. He lived quietly in Florida and little was heard of him until 1979 when the House of Representatives Assassinations Committee, ending its two-year investigation of the Warren Commission report, linked Lansky with minor Mob figure Jack Ruby, the nightclub owner who killed presidential assassin Lee Harvey Oswald (of which more in a subsequent chapter). Meyer Lansky died at the age of 80 of lung cancer in Miami Beach on 15 May 1983, leaving a widow and three children. He was buried in Miami in an Orthodox Jewish ceremony. By then, his fortune may well have exceeded $500 million but of course no one, least of all the US government, could tell with any certainty how much and where it really was.

So, of those four friends and partners from the rip-roaring Twenties, three of them – Luciano, Genovese and Lansky – who between them had ordered thousands of murders, all died of natural causes. The exception was the fourth member of that merging of Italian and Jewish gangsters, 'Bugsy' Siegel.

Benjamin Siegel hated his nickname, which he had earned early in life. He once said: 'My friends call me Ben, strangers call me Mr. Siegel, and guys I don't like call me Bugsy, but not to my face.' Among the friends he was referring to, the closest and most long-standing was his trusted partner in crime, Meyer Lansky. And it was Lansky who ordered him murdered.

In the Thirties, Siegel had survived a number of attempts on his life. His car was once raked with machine-gun fire and on another occasion a bomb went off in the function room in which he was hosting a meeting with senior mobsters. He survived both attempts and extracted revenge on his would-be assassins. In hospital being treated for minor injuries from the bomb plot, he slipped out of his bed overnight to kill the bomber before creeping back in unnoticed – and with the perfect alibi.

'Bugsy' felt himself safe from his many enemies when, in 1936, his friend Lansky sent him on a mission far away from the mean streets of New York. Prohibition had come to an end and the Mafia and their associates needed to replace their lost income. They decided to expand westwards, into California and Nevada, and on Lansky's advice the Syndicate appointed Siegel as their emissary. This suited Siegel, who in 1935 had been indicted in New York for shooting a rival gang member, one of 'Dutch' Schultz's men, and had therefore been advised by Lansky that he should leave town for a while. So his friend set him up with a $500,000 investment pot and sent him to Los Angeles to team up with local mobster Jack Dragna.

For the sharp-suited, high-living, celebrity-chasing 'Bugsy', California was a dream world. After two decades as Lansky's second-in-command, he was king of his own sun-blessed domain. Siegel settled in Beverly Hills, renting a mansion and joining all the right clubs. In Hollywood, he was on first-name terms with stars like Jean Harlow, Gary Cooper and Clark Gable, but his greatest friend was actor George Raft, famous for his film gangster roles. He and Raft went on a gambling spree on the French Riviera – until Siegel got a cable from Lansky ordering him to 'stop acting like a movie star' and get back to work.

During this exotic period, 'Bugsy' seduced a string of starlets but his closest female companion was a millionairess divorcée, Countess Dorothy Di Frasso, who took the handsome newcomer under her wing. They travelled to Italy, where they met Mussolini, and launched an expedition to seek Spanish treasure on an island off Costa Rica – but after blasting the island with dynamite they returned empty-handed.

Siegel still had business interests back in New York and Lansky regularly remitted money to him. He was a heavy spender and a wild gambler, however, and he also had a very expensive new girlfriend, a spendthrift beauty named Virginia Hill, labelled by *Time* magazine as 'Queen of the Gangster Molls'. Lansky had constantly to remind Siegel that his mission to the West Coast was, after all, to develop new revenue streams for the Syndicate, and he was ordered to start pulling his weight in the partnership with Dragna.

Jack Ignazio Dragna was an old-style Sicilian Mafioso who bootlegged in California through the Prohibition years and became boss of the Los Angeles crime family after the unexplained death of the incumbent, Joseph Ardizzone, in 1931. He was to remain the 'Capone of LA', as the media labelled him, until his own death from a heart attack in 1956. Between them, Siegel and Dragna operated a string of illegal gambling houses and offshore casino ships, as well as drug smuggling operations and even a wire service. The money rolled in throughout World War Two, and in 1945 Lansky helped organise for Siegel a $3 million loan to build a casino hotel in Las Vegas – forerunner of the many monolithic emporia that were to make the desert town into a mobsters' Mecca.

Siegel matched $3 million of his own money with the crime Syndicate's stake and started building The Flamingo, a name chosen by his girlfriend, Virginia Hill. During construction, large sums were salted away into Swiss banks, some of them said to be in the name of Miss Hill. The gaping hole in the accounts did not go unnoticed.

At their Cuba summit in December 1946, when Siegel's East

Coast associates Lansky, Luciano and Genovese met with other leading gangsters to discuss Mob matters, the problem of the errant 'Bugsy' was raised. Lansky, who had once considered Siegel a blood brother, put the case for his friend and won him a reprieve. It was decided that Siegel be asked to repay with interest all of the Syndicate investment as soon as the hotel was open. If he failed to do so, then 'Bugsy' would be 'retired'.

Siegel's luck was out. He opened the Flamingo Hotel on 26 December 1946, with Virginia Hill at his side. The event was a disaster. Bad weather grounded planes in Los Angeles and few of the invited famous faces turned up. The grand opening fell flat, publicity was scant, interest dimmed and the punters stayed away. For two weeks Siegel struggled on. The casino alone lost more than $100,000 before he ordered it to be closed.

The demands for repayment of the Mob's loan became more and more insistent. But Siegel's money was largely tied up in the hotel, and the sums siphoned off to Switzerland did not add up to what the Syndicate demanded. He stung everyone he knew for cash; George Raft lending him $100,000 that he never saw again. Siegel was given one last chance, with a re-opening night the following March, but that too was a damp squib. Worse, the few punters who turned up had a lucky streak and won more than the casino took in profits.

Siegel still thought he could bluff his way out of the crisis, under the protection of Lansky, but his old friend now washed his hands of him. Luciano accepted the task of arranging Siegel's execution. On the night of 20 June 1947, Siegel was sitting on the sofa in the living room of Virginia Hill's rented house in North Linden Drive, Los Angeles, when an unknown killer or killers fired eight or nine bullets at him through a window. The result was not a pretty sight, which would not have pleased the man who had the reputation for being the 'Casanova of the Mafia'. His body was riddled. And one bullet had blown out his left eye – the coup de grâce that was the Mafia's 'calling card'. 'Bugsy' would have preferred a more dignified death. So too would his former Hollywood crowd. Those rich and famous friends steered well clear now that his fame had turned to notoriety. There were only five mourners at his funeral; Meyer Lansky was not one of them.

CHAPTER 5

HOW THE GANGSTER SQUAD NAILED THE RÌMAN

When Bugsy Siegel was bumped off in June 1947 for skimming Mafia money, an associate of the flashy fiend was waiting in the wings ready to take advantage. As one might expect, in this world of supposed family 'honour' but in reality back-stabbing duplicity, Siegel's successor was a former faithful friend who owed his success and wealth to the mobster he helped murder.

Meyer Harris Cohen, later known as 'Mickey', was born into an Orthodox Jewish family, immigrants from the Ukraine who settled in a poverty-stricken part of New York in 1913. He was first arrested for selling prohibition booze at the age of nine. In his young teens, though only 5ft 5in tall, he became an illegal prize fighter before training as a professional boxer. His career foundered when the world featherweight champion Tommy Paul knocked him out two minutes into the first round.

While America was in the grip of the Great Depression, Cohen rode the railways, criss-crossing the country with hobos and making a living where he could. On arrival in Chicago, his mobster career began in earnest and he helped run a gambling operation for Al Capone's younger brother, Mattie. When he bought his first pistol, he said: 'I felt like king of the world. When I whipped out that big .38 it made me as big as a guy six-foot-ten.'

Cohen carried out armed robberies for Mob bosses from the Mid-West to California. He got away with more than 100 before being arrested for the first time as an adult in Los Angeles in July 1933. His mugshot, carrying the number 30732, showed a defiant and lippy 19-year-old glaring at the camera with a crescent-shaped scar two inches long under his left eye.

Just over a year later Cohen was held for murdering a man who tried to rob a casino he had been ordered to guard. But a lawyer on the Capone payroll had him released before a court date was even fixed. Over the next few years he worked as an enforcer for the Mob before his reputation was rewarded with a move to the West Coast.

An FBI report at the time recorded: 'Cohen's prestige in underworld circles had been rapidly mounting even while he was in Cleveland, Ohio. He carried out muscle jobs with dispatch and showed no qualms or compunctions against killing. His debut in California was in the capacity of a pimp. However, he had ambitions to be a major hoodlum and by 1938 an informant advised he was running a bookmaking establishment in fashionable Westwood. By 1938 Cohen was also baiting bigshots from the East by making guns and transportation available when they arrived for visits or enforced 'vacations'.

In Los Angeles, Mickey Cohen was again taken under the wing of fellow New Yorker Bugsy Siegel, for whom he had worked as a hired thug on-and-off for years, and it was under his influence that the newcomer came into his own as a leading gangster alongside the big-time playboy. Years later, Cohen recalled:

'Siegel would throw me ten grand, 25 grand, the biggest was 40 grand. There were no books kept or explanations. All he would say is, "Here, this is for you." Ben Siegel gave me to understand that I was not going to be a fly-by-night hoodlum but that I had ability, stature and personality to do things in a much more respectable manner and that I should start to pay my taxes so I didn't get in any trouble with the revenue.'

It was advice that Cohen would have been wise to have taken. For it was tax-dodging that would be his undoing, just as it had been with Al Capone. But during the late Thirties and Forties Mickey Cohen seemed untouchable.

In 1945 he killed a bookmaker named Maxie Shaman but police efforts to pin the crime on him failed miserably. When 'undercover' cops staked out his home, the mobster had his housemaid take beer and cake out to them. When his gardener discovered the cable to a bugging device, he simply turned up the radio whenever he was discussing his protection rackets. 'I gave them fine music,' he boasted. 'Nothing but the best Bach and Beethoven.'

Cohen revelled in his new-found wealth and notoriety, as author Paul Lieberman revealed in a 2011 book, *Gangster Squad*, covering the crook's crime spree – one of the more fascinating details being how Cohen became addicted not only to fame but, strangely, to water. Suffering from an obsessive compulsive disorder that made him terrified of dirt, he took scalding showers lasting 90 minutes and washed his hands five times during every meal. He was convinced waiters gave him change using the dirtiest bills they could find, thinking that he'd leave them as a tip rather than put them in his pocket!

A more predictable trait of the mobster was disloyalty, as confirmed by another author, his biographer Tere Tereba. In *Mickey Cohen: The Life and Crimes of L.A.'s Notorious Mobster*, she describes how he turned on his mentor, Bugsy Siegel. With Cohen as an 'enforcer', Siegel was developing casino businesses in Las Vegas but secretly siphoning off cash, so in June 1947 Bugsy, who was staying at the LA home of girlfriend Virginia Hill, was 'retired' by the Mob by having a hitman shoot him through the window. Tereba wrote: 'Mickey Cohen was complicit in the plot, beyond a doubt.'

Cohen instantly assumed Siegel's mantle as gangster-playboy. He spent his nights in the clubs surrounded by girls who had flocked to LA trying to break into movies. In time he also got to meet established stars, including Lana Turner, Judy Garland, Frank Sinatra and Sammy Davis Junior, and they began to rely on him for favours. Lana Turner entrusted him with her secrets, including her affair with Cohen's fellow gangster Johnny Stompanato, but Mickey repaid her by selling their love letters to the press.

According to authoress Tereba, Frank Sinatra got help from Cohen to keep his 'torrid affair with gorgeous new star Ava Gardner hidden from the public and allegations of a sexual assault in Las Vegas remained secret'. She added: 'Whenever Judy Garland had problems with her husbands she went to Mickey Cohen.'

The mobster was moving up in the world. He still ran his criminal enterprises, principally drugs and protection rackets, from various 'front' businesses, including a haberdashery shop and an ice-cream parlour, but his public image was that of a debonair businessman and friend of the stars. He tried to lose his rough Brooklyn accent, hiring an elocution tutor to improve his vocabulary, learning a new word or phrase each day. *Life* magazine ran picture-spreads on his home in upmarket Brentwood, including bad-taste features such as his bull terrier's doggy duplicate of his master's bed, complete with 'MC' monogrammed red-velvet bedspread.

But Cohen had enemies in the Mob and survived many attempts on his life, including the bombing of the house where he lived with his wife Lavonne. Bombs and machine-gun bullets failed to kill him. Instead, his notoriety made him a Hollywood celebrity. People asked for his autograph and he was snapped with girlfriends such as Barbara Darnell and Liz Reznay. In 1950 he posed for a remarkable picture surrounded by newspaper cuttings of his criminal exploits.

His flamboyant persona helped portrayals of him in the 1991 movie *Bugsy*, in which he was played by Harvey Keitel as a sidekick to Warren Beatty in the title role. And in 2013 double Oscar-winner Sean Penn played the lead role as Cohen in the film *Gangster Squad*. Which brings us to the reason why this coarse, brutal ex-prize fighter is so significant in the history of organised crime. For the members of the elite police unit formed to smash Cohen and his cohorts were as rough and tough and sometimes as shady and unscrupulous as the criminals they were trying to nail.

The so-called 'Gangster Squad' was made up of eight Los Angeles police officers who employed methods that were dubious even in those politically incorrect days. Their unconventional approach to crime-fighting meant that they carried machine guns in violin cases, took hoodlums into the desert for violent 'chats' and dangled thugs over bridges until they 'squealed'.

The squad was formed in late 1946 when Los Angeles Police Department chiefs realised that corruption in the ranks was so rife that the LAPD was powerless to combat organised crime in the city. In those post-war years, 1,800 bookmakers, 600 brothels and 200 gambling parlours flourished, with raids thwarted by bent cops. One senior officer would warn racketeers of impending swoops by calling them and whistling down the phone.

A former US Marine named Willie Burns was the tough guy chosen to lead the unit that would target this endemic corruption. He recruited like-minded 'heavies' who continued to be officially posted on duty rosters at their old stations but instead 'disappeared' on 'special duties'.

First recruit was a quiet undercover cop called Con Keeler, a World War Two veteran who walked with a leg iron because of a serious injury. A former radio mechanic, he was the team's technical expert, designing bugging devices and planting them along with some of his trademark 'souvenirs'. He once bugged a motel room, leaving a playing card on the pillow of a crooked guest. Since it was the ace of spades, the death symbol, the calling card had the desired effect and the villain fled town.

If Con Keeler was the brains, then 'Jumbo' Kennard was the brawn. A Texan giant, his first Gangster Squad call was to a barber who had tried to bribe a police officer to ignore his sideline, an illegal betting operation. Kennard trapped the barber in a corner while his colleagues trashed his salon – then lathered his head with soap and shaved the quaking shop owner with cut-throat razors. Against other targets, Kennard used to employ his favourite scare tactic: dangling suspects from road bridges until they agreed to talk.

The third main member of the eight-man squad was a clean-cut, church-going detective named Jack O'Mara, who would lift suspects off the streets at gunpoint and drive them into the countryside, where he would interrogate them with a pistol to their ear.

To disguise their mission, the men of the Gangster Squad were based not in an office but in two dilapidated Ford cars. Armed to the teeth, they cruised the city. They carried violin cases with hidden tommy guns. They had spare cash to pay informers. They would smash up illicit businesses by acting as if they were members of rival criminal gangs, but they would never make arrests. Since they were 'invisible', their modus operandi was to set up a victim and then call in uniformed cops to make the arrest.

By these means, the squad forced many lesser criminals to flee Los Angeles. They then turned their attention to the bigger fish – targeting the Bugsy Siegel gang and, after he was shot dead in 1947, his successor, Mickey Cohen.

The squad's principal task was to pin on Cohen the 1945 murder of a bookmaker named Maxie Shaman. In the hope of overhearing a rash admission, the squad dressed as workmen and drove a van onto vacant land near the gangster's home. When Mickey and wife Lavonne went out for dinner, the cops began drilling noisily to divert the attention of his guards. Meanwhile, Con Keeler sprayed ammonia on himself to keep the guard dog at bay and crept into the house to place a microphone and transmitter in a wardrobe. Dissatisfied with the reception, he went back later and put another bug inside a television set.

The bug yielded no useful evidence, however, so the squad reverted to more intimidating tactics. They put false licence plates on a car – indicating that it came from Illinois, home of the Chicago mobsters – and cruised slowly past Cohen's haberdashery shop, raking his most treasured possession, his armoured Cadillac, with bullets. Mickey believed that he had been the target of an assassination bid by out-of-state rivals but merely stepped up his security and became more cautious.

While waiting for evidence to emerge against Cohen, the Gangster Squad turned to one of his rivals, Sicilian-born Jack Dragna, a former member of the Chicago Cosa Nostra and in the post-war years the boss of Los Angeles city's largest Mafia family. His empire was based on gambling and prostitution and he worked in uneasy alliance with the new arrivals in town, Bugsy Siegel and Mickey Cohen. When Siegel was killed, Dragna vied with Cohen to take over Bugsy's rackets. Dragna ordered several attempts on his rival's life but Cohen managed to survive them all. When some of Dragna's 'soldiers' were arrested for the bombing of Cohen's home, Dragna briefly fled the state to avoid questioning but returned to brazen out the crisis and re-establish his leadership.

This blatant inter-gang warfare embarrassed the city authorities and the Gangster Squad was sent in to find any evidence that might stick against the Italian villain. They decided to entrap him on the grounds of his own 'immorality'. The plan was to catch him engaged in any kind of behaviour which contravened California's strict morality laws. To this end, Con Keeler broke into the apartment belonging to Dragna's mistress, a 23-year-old secretary, and hid a bug in the headboard of her bed. They then switched off the power to the block, forcing the couple to have an early night.

This saucy subterfuge had the desired effect. The couple engaged in an offence against California's then puritan morality laws – performing oral sex, or 'French love' as it was termed. Dragna was brought to court and jailed for 30 days for a 'lewd act' of 'moral turpitude'. LA district attorneys argued that this was sufficient grounds for having him sent back to Italy but he successfully fought deportation until his death of a heart attack in 1956.

Six years earlier, in 1950, the California Commission on Organized Crime had singled out Dragna as the head of a Syndicate that controlled major racketeering in the LA area. He was questioned in US Senate hearings but denied all accusations. His rival Mickey Cohen was also questioned but, unlike the low-profile Dragna, this flamboyant mobster's more publicised business dealings opened him up to charges of tax evasion, for which he was jailed for four years and his armoured Cadillac confiscated. The conviction was a credit to the Gangster Squad, who had gleaned much of the evidence from his former bodyguard, Neal Hawkins, who, unbeknown to Cohen, had long been their paid informant.

It was unfortunate for Mickey Cohen that he had not heeded his old friend Bugsy Siegel's advice – for the tax rap was the same offence that had led to the imprisonment of his former Chicago boss Al Capone two decades earlier. Further charges for tax evasion were brought against Cohen and in 1961 he was again locked up, this time for 14 years. While in Alcatraz he survived a murder attempt by a fellow inmate wielding an iron bar. He was freed in 1972 and soon diagnosed with stomach cancer. Mickey Cohen was 62 when he died in his sleep in 1976.

CHAPTER 6

CROONERS, CUBA, KENNEDY AND THE STAR-STRUCK DONS

A curious bond has always existed between the Mafia and top entertainers, film stars and even politicians. Perhaps there is a parallel between living 'life on the edge' as a famous celebrity and as an infamous gangster. Many major figures have happily risked being tainted by their connections with the Mafia. For some, it has paid off. For others, the price has been high.

Best known among those accused of 'supping with the Devil' was Frank Sinatra. He freely admitted that he has known mobsters – but every time anything more than that was suggested he reached into his writ drawer. Right up until his death in 1998, the word's most famous singing star denied Mafia involvement. But was Sinatra being perfectly Frank? We shall see.

As entertainers of his era knew, it was impossible to play the clubs and not come into contact with organised crime. The Mafia backed or owned the venues, providing glamorous centres for money laundering, liquor sales, gambling and prostitution. Sinatra would have known many Italian criminals from an early age. Mob boss Meyer Lansky was said to be an acquaintance of Sinatra's parents. Guarino 'Willie' Moretti, the bald, wise-cracking Mafia boss of North Jersey, was one of his neighbours.

An under-boss of the Genovese family and a cousin of Frank Costello, Moretti became friends with the then unknown singer in the 1930s. Sinatra's first wife, Nancy Barbato, was a cousin of a Moretti associate. Moretti helped Sinatra get bookings in New Jersey clubs in return for kickbacks. He also became acquainted with comedians Dean Martin and Jerry Lewis – and the pair, along with Sinatra and comedian Milton Berle, performed at the wedding of Moretti's daughter.

Sinatra had signed a recording contract with band leader Tommy Dorsey in 1939 but within a few years had achieved nationwide stardom and wanted to wriggle out of it. Dorsey refused to release him, so Sinatra asked Moretti for help. The Mafioso's method of 'negotiating' was to jam a gun barrel down Dorsey's throat and threaten to kill him. It was a convincing argument; the band leader sold the contract to Sinatra for one dollar.

When the singer moved to California, he became a friend of former hitman and now the West Coast boss, 'Bugsy' Siegel. Sinatra and his friend Phil Silvers (TV's Sergeant Bilko) were enthralled by him, according to Silvers' wife, who never forgot 'the awe Frank had in his voice when he talked about him'. She recalled: 'He wanted to emulate Bugsy. He'd brag about what Bugsy had done and how many people he'd killed. Sometimes he'd argue about whether Bugsy preferred to shoot his victims or simply chop them up with axes.'

In February 1947 Sinatra stayed at the Miami mansion of his friends, the Fischetti family, cousins of Al Capone, before flying with Joseph 'Joe Fisher' Fischetti to Cuba for his most blatant walk on the wild side with the Mob. The notorious Havana summit of top US gangsters was under way, presided over by Godfather 'Lucky' Luciano. They all saw Sinatra sing, but he presented their subsequent meeting afterwards as pure coincidence. After the trip, he told Hollywood columnist Hedda Hopper that he had 'dropped by a casino one night and was asked if I'd mind meeting a few people. I couldn't refuse. One happened to be Lucky Luciano. I sat down at a table for about fifteen minutes then went back to my hotel. When such innocent acts are so distorted, you can't win.'

In 1950 a US Senate Select Committeee looking into organised crime began an investigation known as the Kefauver hearings, named after its chairman, Senator Estes Kefauver. In drawing up preliminary evidence, Frank Sinatra was called to account. His lawyers negotiated a private hearing for the sake of his career, but when summoned, 'he looked like a lost kitten, drawn, frightened to death,' said Joseph Nellis, the committee's lawyer. Asked about the Fischettis, he said he barely knew them. But his innocent explanation of the brief Cuban meeting with the mobsters was shattered when Nellis revealed photographs of Sinatra with his arm around Luciano on the hotel balcony in Havana and of the pair at a nightclub surrounded by bottles and girls.

The committee presented him with a list of known mobsters and asked whether he knew any of them. 'Just to say hello,' he replied, adding: 'Surely you're not going to put me on television and ruin me just because I know a lot of people?' He was lucky, because they did not. They let him off the hook.

Yet 12 years later, in 1962, Sinatra was named in a 12-page memorandum from the US Justice Department as being pals with a dozen of America's top gangsters. Some of them, the document stated, even knew his ex-directory telephone number. Here are the Men of Honour with whom Ol' Blue Eyes was linked:

LUCKY LUCIANO, Mafia legend, as mentioned above. Likewise, JOE FISCHETTI, cousin of Al Capone and one of three brothers who were all major Chicago and Las Vegas gambling tsars. Brother Charles was one of Capone's most violent cohorts and brother Rocco was a lesser hood. JIMMY 'THE WEASEL' FRATIANNO, confessed hitman turned informer. A family boss in Los Angeles, he was pictured with Sinatra at a theatre the Mob bled dry. RAYMOND PATRIARCA, Mafia boss in Boston co-owned a racetrack with Sinatra – the reason a Senate Crime Investigating Committee subpoenaed the singer. LOUIS 'DOME' PACELLA, a capo in the Genovese crime family, who chose to go to jail for eight months rather than answer a question about his 'long and close' friendship with Sinatra. They were 'like brothers', said a witness. JOSEPH GAMBINO, GREGORY DE PALMA, RICHARD 'NERVES' FUSCO and SALVATORE SPATOLA, all members of the Gambino crime family, with whom he was pictured in a notorious 1976 photograph. CARLO GAMBINO, steely-eyed head of America's largest crime family, on whom Marlon Brando's character in *The Godfather* was modelled. He was also pictured with Sinatra. PAUL CASTELLANO, successor to Gambino, who was gunned down on a Manhattan street in 1985. He and Sinatra were photographed together at a theatre in suburban New York that the Mob controlled.

The closest gangland figure to Sinatra was SAM GIANCANA, head of the Chicago Mob. Sinatra co-owned a Nevada gambling palace, the Cal-Neva Resort, with him. Judith Exner, who claimed she slept with President John F. Kennedy and Giancana (of which more later), said the singer introduced her to the don. Giancana's daughter Antoinette was livid over Sinatra's official denial of any friendship with her father. 'They'd organised shows together,' she said. 'They'd eaten at the same table. They'd hugged and kissed each other like long-lost friends whenever they met.' FBI records supported her story.

And what of two other names on the list of Sinatra's oldest buddies: 'BUGSY' SIEGEL and 'WILLIE' MORETTI? Siegel, who had been so admired by the rising star, was 'rubbed out' in a bloody execution – his death sentence discussed at the very same Cuba summit that Sinatra had graced in 1947. Moretti lasted some years longer – which was unique in Mafia history because of the way he behaved when called to testify at the aforementioned Kefauver hearings in 1950.

While other mobsters – Meyer Lansky, Mickey Cohen and Frank Costello among them – refused to testify before the Kefauver committee by repeatedly invoking the Fifth Amendment, Moretti was the only one who cooperated.

Although he didn't give away too many secrets, he overplayed his role – playing to the cameras, joking and chatting with the committee, the senators and public breaking out in laughter at his wise-guy comments. However, the joker was violating the Mafia code of silence.

A contract was placed on him by the Commission and a few months later, in October 1951, he was blasted to death as he lunched at a New Jersey restaurant. More than 5,000 mourners attended his funeral. In a Mafia trial 12 years later, a government witness, Joe Valachi, described a conversation with Vito Genovese about the murder, in which the Mafia Godfather said he had been concerned that Moretti was becoming deranged through syphilis. Valachi testified: 'It was supposedly a mercy killing because he was sick. Genovese told me, "The Lord have mercy on his soul, he's losing his mind".'

So some won, some lost. Sinatra was among the former. The Italian crime families helped launch his career, promoted it and Frank sang for his supper at Mafia venues. In *The Godfather*, one of author Mario Puzo's more gory storylines involves the flagging career of a singer being restored when he gets an important film part – thanks to a horse's head left as a warning in the movie producer's bed. It is probably a coincidence (and, in this case, it almost certainly is a coincidence) that Frank Sinatra's flagging career was relaunched when he unexpectedly got the part of Private Angelo Maggio in the 1953 movie *From Here to Eternity*.

But there were other ways in which the Mob helped him out, and vice versa. In his 2013 autobiography, *My Way*, singer Paul Anka, who wrote that song for Sinatra and remained a friend for 30 years, told how the star would act as a bagman for the Mafia. He was once stopped carrying a briefcase through

Customs containing $3 million in cash, said Anka – 'They eventually stopped using him because he always got caught.' It had already been noted by the FBI that when Sinatra turned up at the 1947 Havana summit to sing for 'Lucky' Luciano, he uncharacteristically carried his own heavy suitcase through the airport. Paul Anka also told how when Sinatra played Las Vegas – both on stage and at the gaming tables – his casino owning associates would give him $50,000 worth of chips and allow him to keep the winnings.

Italians love song and Italian-American hoodlums just adore singers, so Sinatra is not the only one who has been linked to the Mob. His 'Rat Pack' pals Dean Martin and Sammy Davis Junior performed at Sam Giancana's nightclub. Other great entertainers of the day who starred there included Tony Bennett, Eddie Fisher, Frankie Laine and Jimmy 'Schnozzle' Durante.

The 'Schnozz' was an especially close friend of Giancana. 'That wonderful man loved my mother and treated her like a queen, and he adored Sam,' said the Mafioso's daughter. Another star, Phyllis McGuire of the singing McGuire Sisters, was even closer – she and Giancana became lovers.

Godfather film actor James Caan proved to be close to a real-life Mafia godfather when he turned up at the 1999 trial of the notoriously violent Colombo crime family. His aim was 'to give moral support' to his long-time friend Andy 'Mush' Russo, who was a real-life godfather to Caan's son, Scott. He offered to stand bail for Russo. He also greeted accused Colombo family boss Carmine 'The Snake' Persico with a kiss on the cheek.

Another Hollywood star linked to the Mafia was the greatest screen goddess of her age, possibly of all time. But just how close Marilyn Monroe was to gangland has only come to light in recent years. And her fellow players in this murky game were Frank Sinatra, Mafia boss Sam Giancana and the President of the United States.

For it is now reasonably established that Monroe spent her last day alive in an angry confrontation with the Mafia boss. She had flown from Los Angeles to Nevada in Frank Sinatra's private plane and was staying at the singer's mountain retreat on the banks of Lake Tahoe, next to the Mafia-owned Cal-Neva Lodge hotel. There, Giancana – with whom she was allegedly in love – tried to persuade her not to go public about her affair with President John F. Kennedy and with his younger brother Robert, the Attorney General. She apparently refused to be silenced and, returning to her Hollywood home, she was found dead the following day, 5 August 1962, supposedly of a drugs overdose.

Neither of the Kennedy brothers had been suitably secretive in their extra-marital activities. They had both been Monroe's lovers and, in her developing state of depression and nervous disorder, it was thought that she might make public some of their indiscretions. Such stories, which were no more than rumours at the time of her death, have since become common currency.

In 1981 a reformed criminal, Ronald 'Sonny' Gibson, wrote a book, *Mafia Kingpin*, in which he made some startling new allegations. Gibson said that while working for the Mob, he had been told that Marilyn had been murdered by a Mafia hitman. J. Edgar Hoover, he said, had been furious about the actress's affairs with the Kennedys, whom he hated, so the Mafia had taken upon themselves the task of silencing her as a means of repaying favours done for them by the FBI.

Gibson is not alone in his assertion that Marilyn died not because she had swallowed an overdose of barbiturates but because drugs had been injected into her. Even top pathologists who investigated the case have since gone into print to say the same.

Then in 2011 an extraordinary tape-recording emerged that, for the first time, placed Marilyn with Sam Giancana on her last day alive. On the tape, made by the star's late make-up artist George Masters before his death in 1988, it is claimed that Monroe was besotted with the Mafia boss. But Giancana, having shared her favours with both Kennedys, feared that she was about to go public about her scandalous affairs.

In the recordings, Masters says: 'The night before she died, the last time I saw her, was in Lake Tahoe at the Cal-Neva Lodge. She was there with Sam Giancana, who was the head of the Mafia.' Masters flew back to Los Angeles with her and dropped Monroe off at her home that night. Her naked body was later found on her bed and it was assumed she had killed herself with sleeping pills.

But 50 years after her death, a 2012 bombshell book, *Marilyn At Rainbow's End*, claimed finally to reveal how the 36-year-old star had died. Investigative author Darwin Porter, who knew the star, says five Mafia hoodlums murdered her under orders from Sam Giancana. But Porter believes Robert Kennedy, who secretly visited Marilyn hours before she died, had a lot to do with her death. 'Of course Bobby didn't do it himself,' he said. 'He was a very smart man. Sam Giancana also had the motive to kill her – she was threatening to blow the lid off his operations. But it also begs the question, did someone pay him to murder Marilyn? And if someone did pay him, the only person I can think of is a Kennedy.'

Distraught at being used and then abandoned by both Kennedys, Marilyn had told friends she was going to call a press conference to reveal all of her affairs. The vulnerable star, who was overdosing on drugs and alcohol, intended to expose the Mafia's secrets too.

Porter, who first met Marilyn as a teenager, said that like her occasional lover Frank Sinatra she had become entangled in the Mafia – in her case, after bedding Giancana's henchman Johnny Roselli. President Kennedy also got caught up with the Mafia in sharing a lover, Judith Campbell Exner, with Giancana. In the months before her death, pill-popping Marilyn became more erratic, says Porter. A secret visit from Bobby Kennedy ended in a screaming match and further threats to bring down the Kennedy clan. Finally, someone – Porter does not say who – put a contract on the world's biggest female star.

According to the author, ex-lover Roselli called at Marilyn's house at 10pm on 4 August, leaving the door unlocked so that five hitmen could sneak in. She was rendered unconscious with a chloroform-soaked washcloth, then her limp body removed to the guest cottage in her garden, where the thugs stripped her and administered an enema of barbiturates. 'Giancana had ordered that her body was not to be bruised,' says Porter. His account is convincing. 'I went to see Marilyn's surviving friends, many were dying and had nothing to lose by finally telling the truth,' he says.

The theory that the Mafia might have killed Marilyn Monroe to satisfy or protect John or Robert Kennedy seems pretty far-fetched. Particularly as, for many years, the Mafia had its own 'Number One public enemy' – the Kennedy clan itself. The feud went back half a century to the days when, according to mobsters' stories, the Kennedy patriarch, Joseph, made a fortune from the profits of Prohibition whiskey illegally imported from Ireland to Boston. In 1927 one of the Irish cargoes was hijacked by the Mob and 11 smugglers were killed in the shoot-out. It was, believe the Mafia, the start of a long campaign, instigated by Joseph Kennedy and continued by his children – principally John, who became President of the United States, and Robert, who became Attorney General.

Bobby Kennedy was responsible for pursuing Teamsters union boss Jimmy Hoffa to jail in the US Justice Department's relentless drive to crush Mafia influence within the organised labour movement. It was elder brother John who, as President, failed to give full backing to the disastrous Bay of Pigs invasion attempt of Cuba, planned by the CIA with Mafia assistance.

Years later, after the assassination of both men, the question was being asked: was the Mafia linked with the killing of the President in 1963? At one time, such a question would have been unthinkable. But when dealing with the Mafia, the unthinkable often becomes perfectly feasible. That was what happened in 1979 when a committee set up by the US House of Representatives suggested it was likely that a contract killer was involved in the assassination that shocked the world, in Dallas, Texas, on 22 November 1963. After a $3 million investigation lasting two years, the committee's experts reported: 'An individual crime leader or a small combination of leaders might have participated in a conspiracy to assassinate President Kennedy.'

The report went on to name the 'most likely family bosses of organised crime to have participated in such a unilateral assassination plan' – Carlos Marcello, of New Orleans, and Santos Trafficante, of Miami – although both men issued strong denials of any involvement.

Lee Harvey Oswald, who is presumed to have fired the shots that killed the President, certainly had links, far from tenuous, with underworld figures. So had Jack Ruby, the man who gunned down Oswald before the latter could be brought to court.

Oswald's connection was through his uncle, Charles Murret, and an acquaintance, David Ferrie, both of whom worked for Carlos Marcello. The investigative committee described Murret, who died in 1964, as 'a top deputy for a top man in Marcello's gambling apparatus'. Murret took Oswald under his wing when his nephew moved from Dallas to New Orleans in 1963, treating him like a son and giving him a home and a job in his book-making business.

David Ferrie also worked for Marcello, as a pilot. He had flown him back to the US after Robert Kennedy deported him to Guatemala in 1961. Ferrie also had secret connections with the CIA and had trained pilots who later took part in the Bay of Pigs invasion. Oswald's New Orleans work address in 1963 was the same as Ferrie's and Oswald was in the same air club in which Ferrie was a pilot.

Such evidence, quoted in the House of Representatives committee's report, is circumstantial, but judged alongside the evidence linking Oswald's executioner Jack Ruby, to the Mafia, the conspiracy theory becomes stronger. Club owner Ruby's connections with underworld figures were well established. His telephone records showed that he had been in contact with Mob personalities in Miami, New Orleans and Chicago. He had visited Santos Trafficante. And on 21 November, the day before Kennedy's death, Ruby was seen drinking with a friend of pilot David Ferrie.

To this day, no one knows who was pulling the strings but all the evidence points to Ruby's public execution of Oswald being a certain way of keeping him quiet and preventing him naming accomplices during his trial. Ruby's own life would not have been of high account; he died in prison shortly afterwards of cancer.

Ruby's connection with Santos Trafficante brings the amazing web full circle. When Meyer Lansky, 'Lucky' Luciano and their associates ran the Havana hotel and casino business under corrupt Cuban dictator Fulgencio Batista, Trafficante was a small cog in the business. Fidel Castro overthrew the Batista regime in 1959 and threw the Mob's men either into jail or out of the country. Among them was Trafficante – whose pilot, David Ferrie, also worked for the CIA. And this might not have been a coincidence.

It had long been the ambition of the CIA and a group of big business interests to overthrow Castro and return Cuba to 'democratic' and capitalist rule. Equally, the US government wanted to remove the communist threat from the Caribbean. The Mafia's motives were more pragmatic: it wanted to restore its interests in Cuba's profitable tourist, gambling and vice industries, with acquiescent officials and politicians susceptible to bribes.

There had already been various plots to bring down Castro. And the CIA and the Mafia had often worked together successfully, even launching joint military operations before and during the allied invasion of Sicily during World War Two. A similar link-up made sound sense in the organising of the Bay of Pigs invasion, in which 1,400 Cuban exiles launched a botched attack on the south coast of Cuba on 17 April 1961.

The invasion was a debacle. It had been authorised by previous President Dwight D. Eisenhower in 1960 and John F. Kennedy had been briefed on it by the CIA. But the military support that the rag-tag army of Cubans, the CIA and the Mafia had hoped for never materialised. It was a humiliation – and President Kennedy was blamed.

So a President who was popular with the general public was less so with certain elements in the Secret Service and the underworld. The Mafia, of course, never forgives or forgets. Neither had the CIA any reason to thank him. The FBI did not look kindly on the President either. The Bureau's chief, J. Edgar Hoover, had long been hampered by the Kennedy brothers in his autocratic handling of the agency's affairs. Attorney General Robert, with White House backing, clipped the wings of the all-powerful Hoover and earned himself an unforgiving enemy. Hoover's agents collected every scrap of information about the private lives of every leading politician – and in the Kennedys' case, the files bulged with scandal.

So when Marilyn Monroe died in 1962 and Jack Kennedy in 1963 (and when Robert Kennedy was also assassinated in 1968) conspiracy theories instantly flew. And the link was always the Mafia … the experts at carrying out contracts through 'third parties'. Did the mobsters with 'friends in high places' murder Monroe and the President? The theories sound preposterous – until one realises that there's nothing more preposterous than the US government and the Mafia collaborating in the invasion of another country. When it comes to the Mafia, the 'impossible' often happens.

CHAPTER 7

DEATH OF GODFATHERS – ONE PEACEFULLY, ONE IN A HAIL OF BULLETS

Carlo Gambino was the inspiration for the character of Il Capo di Tutti Capi (The Boss of All Bosses) in the movie *The Godfather*. Under the iron rule of this frail old man, the Mafia flourished through the post-war years. And thanks to his low-profile management of the Mob, by 1976 when Gambino died peacefully in his bed at the age of 73, the Mafia had apparently vanished into the woodwork.

His predecessor as Capo di Tutti Capi, Salvatore Maranzano, had attempted the transformation of the Mafia from a public killing machine to a quietly corrupt corporation way back in 1931. But if Maranzano had first voiced the new philosophy and Meyer Lansky later espoused it, then Carlo Gambino perfected it.

Gambino, born in Sicily in 1902, sailed to the US and entered illegally to join up with his relatives in the New York crime family headed by his brother-in-law, Paul Castellano. He began carrying out murder contracts while still in his teens and at the age of 19 became a 'made man' and was inducted into La Cosa Nostra. Between the world wars he followed the traditional criminal path of bootlegging, illegal gambling, protection racketeering, extortion and loan-sharking.

Unlike many of his contemporaries, Carlo Gambino chose to stay low-profile. He lived modestly in Brooklyn. At the age of 30 he married his first cousin and they raised three sons and a daughter. His trademark was his meek physical demeanour, accented by a hawk's beak nose, and his polite, paternalistic manner. He preferred to work things out with his rivals but would not hesitate to have someone 'clipped' when they stood in his way. The most public of his many contracted 'hits' was that of Masseria family boss Guiseppe, ordered by Gambino and Luciano in 1931.

In 1937 Gambino was arrested and convicted of tax evasion but got off with a suspended sentence. World War Two was a gold mine for him. He became a millionaire by bribing city officials for ration stamps, which he then sold on the black market. After the war, the softly-spoken Gambino forged an unlikely alliance with the murderous Albert Anastasia and together they planned the overthrow of New York's Mangano family. Its leader, Vincent Mangano, vanished in 1951 in what was assumed to be a killing arranged by Anastasia and Gambino. In 1956 Anastasia appointed Gambino his under-boss. He didn't serve his master for long; the following year he ordered the barber's shop assassination of Anastasia. One of Anastasia's loyalists, James Squillante, followed his boss to the grave in 1960. Carlo Gambino now set about consolidating his power base.

In 1962 his eldest son Thomas married the daughter of fellow Mob boss Gaetano Lucchese in a union not only of two young people but of two burgeoning crime families. Rackets throughout New York were carved up between the 'amico nostra' – literally 'friends of ours'.

After surviving his main rivals – Joe Bonanno was ousted by 'The Commission', Vito Genovese died of a heart attack and Tommy Lucchese of a brain tumor – Carlo Gambino became all powerful. Quietly, throughout the Sixties and into the Seventies, he built an empire that operated in New York, Chicago, Boston, Miami, Los Angeles, San Francisco and Las Vegas.

The Gambino family – with names like Carmine 'Wagon Wheels' Fatico, Carmine 'The Doctor' Lombardozzi, Joseph 'Joe Piney' Armone, Armand 'Tommy' Rava, Joseph Biondo, Aniello 'Mr Neil' Dellacroce and Joseph Riccobono – had between 500 and 800 'soldiers' operating a $500 million-a-year business.

The Gambinos became the dominant family in Manhattan. They ran the Longshoremen's union, thereby controlling all goods entering New York by ship. The unions at the city's airports were also under their influence. However, Godfather Carlo avoided the lucrative but high-profile drugs trade. His warning 'Deal and Die' meant a death sentence to any family member dealing in heroin or cocaine.

It was a strangely moral stance for someone who had ordered the deaths of an untold number of enemies. Thomas Eboli was one murder attributed to him. The drug racketeer owed Gambino $4 million and, when he failed to repay, was sprayed with bullets from a passing truck as he sat in his car in Brooklyn in 1972. The same year, the Godfather's 29-year-old nephew 'Manny' Gambino was kidnapped and, despite a ransom being paid, murdered. Irish mobster James McBratney was suspected of being one of the kidnappers and the order went out for him to die slowly and painfully, in a manner befitting his crime against Carlo Gambino. The three-man hit squad, including a new protégé named John Gotti, found their man in a Staten Island tavern and, perhaps fortunately for him, was swiftly dispatched when he tried to flee.

Carmine 'Mimi' Scialo's end was less swift. A member of the Colombo family, the drunken Scialo verbally abused Carlo Gambino in a restaurant in 1974. Gambino remained calm, as he always did, and uttered not a word in retaliation. Soon afterwards, however, Scialo's body was found at a Brooklyn social club – semi-encased in the cement floor.

There were many challenges to Gambino's authority, particularly as he became old and frail, but he survived them all. While the Mafia had supposedly abolished the title of 'Boss of Bosses', Gambino's position afforded him all the powers such a title would have carried. He was the undisputed head of the largest, wealthiest and most powerful crime family in the country and was the leader of the Commission, a position only previously held by 'Lucky' Luciano.

Carlo Gambino died of a heart attack in October 1976 at the age of 74. He had given explicit orders that his brother-in-law and cousin, Paul Castellano, take over the family. But many of his associates and underlings believed his loyal under-boss Neil Dellacroce should have had the top job. The dissension split the family in two.

Gambino's legacy was not what he had hoped. His mission to transform the Mafia from a high-profile killing machine into an invisible corporate entity remained incomplete. In fact, the Seventies and early Eighties saw some of the most public instances of Mafia violence. Over the same period, ordinary Americans received, through police crackdowns, media investigative reporting and a few revelatory court cases, an insight into how little had changed in the murderous minds of the Mafiosi.

The most sensational example of this was a very public assassination that had been set in motion by Carlo Gambino himself. Shortly before he died, the ailing Godfather had happily given his seal of approval to the elimination of a deadly rival. It was vengeance from beyond the grave that remained outstanding for three years until the contract was finally executed on a man who had boasted: 'No one will ever kill me, they wouldn't dare.'

Carmine 'Cigar' or 'Lilo' Galante, who saw himself as the new Godfather following Gambino's death, was a brutal, old-time Mafioso of the Bonanno family. In his youth, he had been a vicious triggerman, carrying out contracts in grisly fashion many times. But now he was to become the target. His brazen bid to become Godfather and seize control of the New York narcotics market had angered other Syndicate leaders. And his aim of rubbing out all gangland opposition was drawing unwelcome attention from US lawmakers.

In July 1979 Galante was finishing lunch on the patio of Joe and Mary's Italian restaurant on Brooklyn's Knickerbocker Avenue. He had enjoyed a plate of spaghetti and meatballs with side orders of salad and fruit. Dining with him were Leonard Coppola, a Bonanno capo, and restaurant owner Giuseppe Turano, a cousin who was also a Bonanno soldier. Also sitting at the table were Galante's Sicilian bodyguards, Baldesarre 'Baldo' Amato and Cesare 'Tall Guy' Bonventre.

The cigar-chewing mobster was sipping his sixth glass of

Chianti as two black limousines drew up outside. He looked to his bodyguards – but they had set him up for the contract murder. Three men, neatly dressed but wearing ski masks, strolled calmly from the cars into the eating-house and opened fire with a whole arsenal of shotguns and automatic weapons. They didn't even give their quarry time to scream. The 69-year-old mobster tried to rise from his chair but was cut down in a hail of bullets. He died with his cigar still grotesquely clenched between his teeth. His two associates were also killed. As the gunmen sped off, the bodyguards walked away unharmed.

The Galante assassination was a Mafia 'classic'. The contract had been farmed out by the Commission to friendly Mafiosi in Connecticut, who provided the killers as a favour. This is a Cosa Nostra trademark. To confuse the authorities and hostile gangsters alike, the actual executioners are often 'imported' from out of town. The trail is sometimes covered once again when those who put out the original contract have the executioners rubbed out afterwards. Dead men tell no tales.

A string of murders during that period of modern history horrified an American public who believed such violence had ended in the lawless Twenties and Thirties. The headlines, however, proved that the Mafia's rules had not changed. In short, it is difficult to join the organisation unless, of course, you're close family. Getting out, though, is very easy indeed: you become dead.

The typical Mafia execution remains a few clean bullet holes in the head. Unwanted personnel, even Godfathers, are disposed of in this fashion. But there are nastier ways of disposing of the greedy, the talkative, the disloyal and the rebellious. By Mafia tradition, those undesirables were killed slowly and painfully. Some were garrotted, others cut to pieces with chainsaws or crushed to death in various ways.

Quite often, a cryptic message would accompany the rubout. A traitor's genitals would be cut off and stuffed in the corpse's mouth, for instance. In 1961 Giuseppe 'Joe' Profaci, founder of what is now known as the Colombo family, put out a contract on a member of a rival gang. Ten days after hitman Joseph 'Jelly' Gioielli disappeared, his bosses, the Gallo brothers, received the man's clothes wrapped around a fish. Translation: 'Jelly sleeps with the fishes'.

Joseph 'Crazy Joe' Gallo had been celebrating his 43rd birthday with a slap-up meal at famous Umberto's New York Clam House when he was 'clipped' in 1972. When he assassinated Gallo, the lone gunman – later revealed to be out-of-state hitman Frank 'The Irishman' Sheeran – broke an unwritten Mafia rule: you don't blow a man away in front of his family. With him at the restaurant that night were his bride of three weeks, former dental assistant Sina Essary, and her ten-year-old daughter Lisa, as well as Gallo's sister and a number of friends.

The furious gun battle spilled into the street, leaving Gallo, New York's most feared hitman, dead and his bodyguard, Peter 'The Greek' Diapioulas, wounded. The Gallo brothers had been responsible for shooting down rival don Joe Colombo at an Italian-American rally at New York's Columbus Circle a year earlier. At least a dozen men died in the ensuing feud between Gallo and Colombo factions of the old Joe Profaci family.

The violence was not restricted to New York. In Chicago, the infamous Momo 'Sam' Giancana was executed in 1975 by three hoods who burst into the kitchen of his suburban home. The 67-year-old was shot in the mouth, with another five bullets to the neck.

In Kansas City, the Spero brothers were wiped out one by one during their ten-year war with the reigning Civella gang. Nick was executed in 1974 and stuffed into the boot of his car. Michael was gunned down in a bar five years later. Joseph was wounded at that time but died when an explosion tore apart his warehouse in 1980. Carl was shot in the back when his brother Mike died. Paralysed, he carried on the war from a wheelchair, but in 1984, as he was rolling towards his specially adapted car, the Civella boys blew up the whole parking lot.

The decade was marked by a rash of arsons at Mafia-owned restaurants in Pennsylvania, Delaware and New York. In the smouldering ruins of Giuseppe's Pizza joint in Philadelphia one day in 1977, police discovered two charred bodies. One was still recognisable: Vincenzo Fiordilino, a Bonanno capo from New York. How had he come to die in a Philadelphia cafe? Police pieced together the story. Fiordilino and his friend had just brought 200 gallons of petrol into the kitchen, intending to start a blaze, but the pilot light ignited it before the two could get out.

Vincent Papa, a Colombo capo who made himself a legend when he stole $100 million worth of drugs from the police in 1972, was stabbed to death in the exercise yard of the Atlanta Penitentiary six years later. That daring robbery became a smash-hit movie, *The French Connection*. But Papa had begun to parade himself. It's called 'showboating' and if you do it within the Mafia, it usually gets you killed.

James Eppolito, a Gambino lieutenant, was running a bogus charity so successfully that the then president's wife, Rosalynn Carter, endorsed it with an appearance in 1979. A picture of the two together appeared in newspapers and Eppolito had extra copies made, which he passed around among friends and business associates. Two weeks later he was dead. Hitmen Roy DeMeo and Richard DiNome had orders from the top. Then they, too, were rubbed out.

One age-old Mafia rule always applies: the old must make way for the young. Many stooping, white-haired dons, like Carmen Galante, seemed to forget that. And so, usually with the thumbs-up from the other bosses in the Commission, the Mob 'retires' its oldsters. A pension is out of the question.

Philadelphia chieftain Angelo Bruno was 69 when he got his 'retirement' in 1980. He was shot through the back of the head as he sat in a friend's car outside his home. The body of an associate believed responsible for the murder was found a month later stuffed in a plastic bag, shot 14 times and littered with $20 bills torn in half, the Mafia sign that he had committed a greedy act.

Bruno's successor in Philadelphia was Philip 'Chicken Man' Testa. His reign lasted exactly a year. He was blown to bits when a bomb, set off by radio control, shattered his home. Three years later his 28-year-old son Salvatore, who had vowed vengeance on the perpetrators, was himself blown away with two bullets to the back of the head.

The seven-year war between the Philadelphia Mob and the Bonannos and Gambinos in New York claimed the lives of no fewer than 209 members from the three families. It felt like a replay of the territorial wars of the Twenties.

Frank Piccolo, allied to the Gambino clan, was Connecticut's most powerful mobster until the police nabbed him. He was due to stand trial for attempting to extort money from singers Wayne Newton and Lola Falana over a Las Vegas investment that had gone sour. Piccolo was the boss but he was also an embarrassment. Like Galante and others, 58-year-old

Piccolo was now dead weight. Shadowed by his colleagues for days, he collapsed in a spray of bullets as he made a call from a public payphone in 1981. The three carbine-toting hoods then made their getaway in a van, chased by police and a handful of very brave local citizens. The van turned into a long wooded driveway near the home of two Piccolo henchmen, brothers Gustav and Francis 'Fat Frannie' Curcio, where the pursuers lost it. It had been the classic *Godfather* movie-type execution.

It seems that food and death often go hand in hand for the men of the Mafia. They dine and they die. Sometimes, like Carmine Galante, they die after their spaghetti and meatballs. Other times, like Carlo Gambino's successor Paul Castellano, they die before they dine. The seven torpedoes who gunned down Castellano just before Christmas 1985 hissed Sicilian curses at him as they fired. Castellano, who had been on his way to dinner at Manhattan's Sparks Steak House died on an empty stomach. Killed with him was his bodyguard and would-be second-in-command, Thomas Bilotti.

Mafiosi are hit as an example to others. If their lives were ever spared, then the Cosa Nostra would disintegrate as each man looked to his own enrichment, rather than the Syndicate's.

The men who do the dirty work have no conscience. Time and again it is apparent when they talk about it, as in the case of two US government witnesses of the time. Luigi Ronsisvalle, a New York hitman working for the Bonanno family, told a court that he killed 13 people, the first when he was just 18 years old. 'That was a job,' he said. 'I no feel ashamed.' Apparently the only thing he regretted was pushing heroin 'which destroys hundreds and thousands of young American generations'.

Another 'squealer', Aladena 'Jimmy the Weasel' Fratianno, a Cleveland mobster who became acting head of the Los Angeles crime family, confessed to 11 murders but said he felt no emotion. One of the contracts was on his best friend, Frank 'The Bomp' Bompensiero, the most feared Mafia hitman in Southern California for more than 30 years. Killing fellow mobsters was Bompensiero's specialty and his reward from the Los Angeles Mafia was to be made boss of San Diego. In 1977, however, it was discovered that 'The Bomp' had been an FBI informer for a decade. 'The Weasel' had no hesitation in organising the execution of his friend, and the 71-year-old hulking hood was gunned down outside his home by another hired hitman from out of town.

Afterwards 'The Weasel' Fratianno became an FBI informant himself and later gained a measure of fame – or infamy – by writing about the Mafia and giving TV interviews. He revealed the sort of casual language used in the course of a contract killing. 'You know that fucking Bomp,' said his killer, 'he shit his pants when he saw me with the piece [gun]. He tried to give me a hard time.' Fratianno wondered: 'How tough a time can a guy with four slugs in his head give you?'

Like so many of his callous cousins in the Mafia, 'The Weasel' saw killing as no more than a bit of 'business', sometimes even a joke. He said during a television documentary in 1991 that Bompensiero 'had buried more bones than could be found in the brontosaurus room of the Museum of Natural History'.

CHAPTER 8

UNION MOBSTERS WHO CONTROLLED THE LIVES OF MILLIONS

Labour racketeering has always been one of the Mafia's fundamental sources of profit, power and influence. With 75,000 union branches in the US, many maintaining their own benefit funds, the labour market provides a rich source for organised criminal groups to manipulate, plundering their pension, welfare, and health funds. This exploitation also costs the American public millions of dollars each year through increased labour costs that are eventually passed on to consumers.

'The historical involvement of La Cosa Nostra in labour racketeering has been thoroughly documented,' says a current FBI report, which points to a century of corruption within the nation's major unions.

Early last century, the unions were manipulated by New York mobster Jacob 'Little Augie' Orgen, whose labour rackets earned him a huge fortune until his death at the hands of gunmen in 1927. Such Mafia notables as Albert Anastasia, Vito Genovese, Meyer Lansky and Lucky Luciano all took lessons from Orgen in those early days. By the following era, the web of corruption had spread nationwide. FBI files show that more than one-third of the 58 Mafiosi arrested in 1957 at the famous Apalachin Conference in New York listed their employment as 'labor' or 'labor-management relations'.

Three major US Senate investigations have documented La Cosa Nostra involvement. One of these, the McClellan Committee in the late-1950s, found systemic racketeering in both the International Brotherhood of Teamsters and the Hotel Employees and Restaurant Employees International Union. In the early 1980s Gambino family boss Paul Castellano was overheard saying: 'Our job is to run the unions.' In 1986 the President's Council on Organized Crime reported that the Mafia dominated five major unions.

Principal among them was the Teamsters. For if 'Little Augie' Orgen's century-old operation was the training ground for union corruption, the finishing school was that of Jimmy Hoffa, notorious leader of America's giant transport union. No labour force has been infiltrated to a more infamous degree than the Teamsters.

The Jimmy Hoffa story is one of legend – and explains in a way how a corrupt but flamboyant figure can be presented as that curiously American animal: a tainted folk hero. Pint-sized Hoffa, for instance, was known as the 'biggest little guy in the USA'. His firebrand exploits were lovingly reported by the media, and the reason for the fascination is not hard to fathom. The trade union bigshot fought the Kennedys, courted the Mafia, stole workers' millions, was imprisoned, courted Richard Nixon, did battle with the Mafia, won back the workers and split the unions. And then in 1975 he suddenly vanished.

So what happened? Was he turned into glue? Ground up in a mincer? Compacted in a garbage plant? Cemented into a bridge? Squashed inside a junked car? Fed to Florida's alligators? Or could he perhaps still be alive? It was many years before the truth about his fate emerged, and it wasn't pretty. But even on the day of his disappearance, all of America knew instantly that foul play was afoot. There was no question: Hoffa had been murdered. He'd had it coming …

The aptly named James Riddle Hoffa was born in poverty on 14 February 1913. In the tough Depression era, he worked his way up from a docker's job to become president of America's largest and most powerful trade union, the International Brotherhood of Teamsters. Anything that moved around America, by truck, ship or rail, involved this union. And anything that involved the union also involved the Mafia. Under the direction of Hoffa from his Detroit headquarters, the Teamsters changed from being a disorganised rabble into a major force. Even the Michigan State Police joined Hoffa's union. All employees and employers alike paid into the enormous Teamsters' pension fund, which was mercilessly milked by Hoffa's Mob supporters. Attorney General Robert Kennedy pursued Hoffa and his fellow officials with a vengeance but he was never able to nail him for the web of fraud he had spun.

Hoffa had been arrested 23 times but somehow no significant charges ever stuck. The 5ft 5in hothead boasted that he had 'a record as long as your arm' but in fact he had been fined only twice – a paltry $10 and $1,000 – and had never been to jail. Hoffa's luck finally began to run out in 1964 when he received an eight-year sentence for jury tampering. That same year he was given an additional five-year sentence for defrauding the Teamsters' pension fund of $2 million. A string of appeals failed and he eventually went to prison in 1967.

Astonishingly, for a cheat who had stolen their hard-earned funds, Hoffa was still a hero with his fanatically loyal union members. And from inside prison, he continued to influence the union's affairs. He had planned for a weak 'caretaker', his Detroit deputy Frank Fitzsimmons, to head the Teamsters while he was in jail. Fitzsimmons, however, wanted power in his own right. He failed to follow the orders relayed to him from inside a prison cell. Meanwhile, Hoffa seethed.

In December 1971, after his parole appeal had been rejected for the third time, Hoffa was suddenly freed – his sentence surprisingly commuted by President Richard Nixon. The union boss had served only 58 months of his 13-year sentence. There was a catch to the Nixon deal, however, in that Hoffa was barred from union activities until 1980. That just happened to coincide with the end of Fitzsimmons' term of office. Despite being freed from jail on the President's direct orders, Hoffa complained publicly that Nixon had conspired with Fitzsimmons to betray him. Hoffa was particularly upset because he had promised Nixon the endorsement of the Teamsters and other unions in his 1972 election.

But why would the President get involved at all? For money, said the Phoenix-based *Arizona Republic* newspaper, which in 1979 published the diary of Mafia paymaster Edward 'Marty' Buccieri, who was murdered in 1975. Handed to the FBI by convicted hitman Gerald Denono, the diary itemised $28 million of illegal financial transactions in a 15-month period between 1972 and 1973. The diary, which named Nixon aides Bob Haldeman, Charles Colson and John Ehrlichman, catalogued half a million dollars of Mafia funds going directly to the President of the United States.

Out of prison, Hoffa desperately tried to wrest control of the Teamsters away from Frank Fitzsimmons. He told his old supporters: 'I know the union business upside down, around and over. The members are interested in how many bucks they can make – I get them for them.' Where persuasion failed, violence began to have an effect. The union was torn apart by civil war. The Teamsters' Detroit office was machine-gunned, an official's boat was blown up, another official was blinded by a shotgun, other union activists were beaten up, and the union-owned car of Fitzsimmons' son Dickie, a local branch official, was dynamited. Although Dickie Fitzsimmons survived because he had stopped for a drink in a bar, the attack was obviously the last straw for the anti-Hoffa forces.

On 30 July 1975, exactly three weeks after the bomb attack, Jimmy Hoffa vanished. That evening, 62-year-old Hoffa took a phone call and told his wife Josephine that he was going out. He drove from his suburban home in Lake Orion, 45 miles north of Detroit, to the Machus Red Fox restaurant in Bloomfield township. There, he had a dinner date with two Mafia hoodlums: Anthony Giacolone and Anthony 'Tony Pro' Provenzano. Neither turned up at the restaurant – but Hoffa did, and was abducted somewhere in the street outside.

One witness saw him in what may have been the last moments of his life. By chance, the witness drew up alongside a brand new maroon Mercury car outside the restaurant and for a few seconds saw what everyone believes was the abduction. He recognised Hoffa as one of four passengers: he was leaning forward, shouting at the driver, and he had his hand behind his back, perhaps tied. The witness identified the driver from 'mugshot' files as being Charles 'Chuckie' O'Brien, Hoffa's own foster son. Raised by the Teamsters' chief, Chuckie had become his bodyguard and personal assistant. Hauled in by police, he vehemently proclaimed his innocence. The maroon Mercury was, however, tracked down by the FBI. Sniffer dogs picked up Hoffa's scent on the back seat – and in the trunk.

Both Giacolone and Provenzano made sure they had alibis for the night in question. Indeed 'Tony Pro' was conspicuously at his home in New Jersey the day he was supposed to be meeting Hoffa for dinner. Giacolone was a simple Detroit hood. But Provenzano, a former amateur boxer, was a member of the Mafia family of Vito Genovese, as well as being a local leader of the Teamsters in Union City, New Jersey. Hoffa and 'Tony Pro' bore a fierce hatred for one another. They had been close friends and allies, but during a term they shared at the federal penitentiary in Lewisburg, Pennsylvania, they fell out.

Although 'Tony Pro' almost certainly knew Hoffa's fate, the contract must have come from a much higher authority. Mafia boss Rosario 'Big Man Russell' Bufalino, head of the relatively small but influential Northeastern Pennsylvania crime family, is reputed to have ordered Hoffa's death. The accepted theory is that the Mob's operation to extort money from employers and to siphon off the union's pension funds was working so effectively under Fitzsimmons that they didn't want Hoffa returning to ruin it all.

After his abduction, the FBI launched the biggest manhunt in its history and continued to keep open the file on Hoffa's disappearance. But not a single arrest was ever made and no evidence was ever found of Hoffa's body. Was Provenzano the master-hitman? We shall never know. Two years after Hoffa's disappearance, Provenzano was given a life sentence for the murder of another Teamsters' official. In 1988 he died in prison, aged 71. After jail terms for extortion and attempted murder, boss man Bufalino died, aged 90, in 1994. Hoffa's wife died in 1980 after a long illness. His children, James and Barbara, continued to fight to have the FBI release files on the case that they believed could solve the mystery.

Hoffa may have known that he was a target. Just before he vanished, he drew out a million dollars in cash. Although this raised speculation that he might still be alive and on the run, his family and the police remained convinced that he was dead. And while it was uncertain who had ordered the killing, no one was in any doubt that it was a Mafia contract.

Over the ensuing years, dozens of criminals, from mobsters to fraudsters, have come up with 'revelations' about the slaying and the disposal of Hoffa's body. Here are a few of them: Hoffa's corpse was mixed into the concrete used to construct the New York Giants' football stadium in East Rutherford, New Jersey. The body was encased in the foundation of a public works garage in Cadillac, Michigan. His remains were buried at the bottom of a swimming pool in Bloomfield Hills, Michigan. The body was ground up and dumped in a Florida swamp. It was crushed in an automobile compactor at Central Sanitation Services in Hamtramck, Michigan. His corpse was put into a 55-gallon steel drum and carted away in a Gateway Transportation truck. His remains were disintegrated at a fat-rendering plant. He was buried under the helipad at the Sheraton Savannah Resort Hotel, which at the time of his disappearance was owned by the Teamsters. His body was placed in a steel drum and buried in a toxic waste site in Jersey City, New Jersey.

An intriguing report of Hoffa's death came in 1995 when an un-named ex-convict appeared on TV and, after taking a lie detector test, described his part in the murder. He said he had been a Mafia hitman but was suffering from emphysema and wanted to set the record straight before he died. This was his story:

I was in Federal Prison in Atlanta, about to be paroled. A person from a known Southern family contacted me and told me the contract would pay $25,000. This was too much money. Normal work was ten grand, that was the going rate, sometimes 15. I was flown to Detroit, and taken to a junkyard. In the office there I met three men, one of them was known to me as 'Sally Bugs'. As soon as I saw Jimmy [Hoffa], I knew who he was. He wasn't a tall man, but he was well built. Five of us including Jimmy got into a panelled truck. Sal drove and we took off. I didn't know where we were going because we were never told anything. We drove all the way from Detroit to Chicago's Lake Michigan. Jimmy was gagged with tape and they drugged him with a hypodermic to keep him quiet.

Nevertheless, during the trip Hoffa recognised 'Sally Bugs' as Salvatore Briguglio, a hood within the New Jersey Teamsters, who would be killed a year later in New York's Little Italy while working for 'Tony Pro' Provenzano. The hitman continued:

Jimmy refused a shot of whiskey, cursed at Sally Bugs and offered half a million dollars to call off the hit. It was refused, of course. At that point I think he realised that this was the end of the line. As darkness came we got into a yacht and motored to what looked like a Navy pier. Sal ordered us to strip Jimmy down naked. He never asked for mercy – I had to admire the guy for that. He wasn't afraid; he copped no pleas. He didn't beg for anything from us. Under the seat were these pigs of lead somewhat like what are used in a Linotype. They were strapped with tape to each of his legs and he was dropped over the side. When the bubbles stopped coming up, we up the anchor, start the motor and head back to shore.

Couldn't they just have shot him? 'One of the things a mechanic does is give the customer what he wants. That was the way the customer wanted it and this was the way it was done.' The anonymous hitman then paid a final tribute to the man he had helped murder: 'I've clipped people who'd beg and plead and say, Take pity on my family, and that kinda thing. Not him. He was a man's man – tough as nails.'

Another hitman who claimed to have been present at the Hoffa murder was Richard Leonard 'The Iceman' Kuklinski, a New Jersey contract killer who earned his nickname from his knack of disguising the time of his victims's death by placing their corpses in a freezer. Before his own death in 2006, Kuklinski cooperated in a book, *The Iceman: Confessions of a Mafia Contract Killer*, in which he said he had stabbed Hoffa with a hunting knife, after which his body was placed in a 55-gallon drum and set on fire. He was allowed to burn for 'a half hour or so' before the drum was welded shut and buried in a junkyard. Later the drum was dug up, placed in the trunk of a car which was compacted to a 4ft by 2ft cube and sold as scrap metal.

The most convincing of the many versions of Jimmy Hoffa's

death, however, was that of yet another hitman, one of 'Big Man Russell' Bufalino's lieutenants, Frank 'The Irishman' Sheeran, who implicated Bufalino, Provenzano and Briguglio in the killing. Sheeran was certainly an authority on Mafia assassinations, being named by the then US attorney Rudy Giuliani as one of only two non-Italians on the list of 26 top mobsters. In the final months of his life, Sheeran poured his heart out to a former prosecutor turned author, Charles Brandt. He died in 2003, aged 83, six weeks after reading the finished manuscript – and after having the writer drive him to a priest to receive his final confession.

Sheeran, who was 6ft 4in with a fair Irish complexion, told the author how he carried out a previous contract, on Joseph 'Crazy Joe' Gallo at Umberto's Clam House in New York's Little Italy. 'I don't look like a Mafia shooter,' said Sheeran. 'I look like a broken-down truck driver with a cap on, coming to use the bathroom.' Gallo's death, in front of his wife and young daughter, had until then remained a mystery.

'The Irishman', who served as a Teamster boss in Wilmington, Delaware, became a close confidante of Hoffa, but when he got the order to assassinate his old friend, he knew he had no choice. It was a case of kill on command or die for disobedience. He told Brandt how he lured Hoffa into an empty house and shot him twice in the back of the head. Brandt called his book *I Heard You Paint Houses* – the first words Hoffa uttered to Sheeran. The phrase was Mob slang for a killer, as in splattering blood over floors and walls. Sheeran replied that he was also a carpenter – Mafia-speak for someone who disposes of bodies. But because a second Mafia squad actually disposed of Hoffa's body, even Sheeran could not solve the mystery of where 'the biggest little guy in the USA' is buried.

CHAPTER 9

THE MAFIA'S NEMESIS ... AND HOW TERRORISM TOOK THE HEAT OFF

Nowadays the transformation of the Mafia is complete. Thanks to a new class of crooks with business brains, those migrant Mafiosi have swapped their humble working garb for slick suits and a sickening veneer of corporate 'respectability'. But at least they no longer shed each other's blood on the streets. Three factors have changed the face of the modern Mafia in the United States of America: high-tech evidence gathering, low-life supergrasses and one amazing lawman, who was the Mafia's nemesis.

He was Rudolph William Louis Giuliani, federal prosecutor in the war on organised crime before becoming Mayor of New York City. The single most devastating enemy the Mob has ever encountered, 'Rudy' Giuliani would have died a thousand deaths had all the threats against him been carried out. He has always shrugged them off, even using the best ones in the speeches he gave to prove that his side was winning! 'They can threaten all they want,' he said, as he cracked down on organised crime in the mid-Eighties. 'I believe in telling the Mob that nothing will deter me.'

His passionate pursuit of mobsters stems from a hatred of the Mafia by his father, a bar owner in Brooklyn, where 'Rudy' was born in 1944. Appointed 'gangbuster' by President Ronald Reagan, Giuliani drew up a massive Cosa Nostra chart detailing every single tentacle nationwide and hung it in his office. He then managed to coordinate decades of investigation by hundreds of FBI agents, city and state police forces. Then, with a force of 130 attorneys in America's largest federal prosecutor's office, he launched an uncompromising war against the Godfathers. 'Until a few years ago, law enforcement tactics were directed against individual Mafia members,' he explained. 'More recently, the FBI went after the Mr. Bigs. I just took it a logical stage further, and went for the board of directors governing all the Mafia families. It makes sense. You don't cut off the tail or the toes of the monster – you cut the head.'

Accordingly, armed with law books instead of a service revolver, Giuliani personally oversaw hundreds of top Mafiosi frogmarched into court, some of them sent to jail for a long stretch. In what was termed 'The Mafia Commission Trial', which ran from February 1985 to November 1986, he indicted 11 organised crime figures, including the heads of New York's 'Five Families' – Genovese, Bonanno, Lucchese, Gambino and Colombo. He utilised the Racketeer Influenced and Corrupt Organizations Act (known as the RICO Act) which allows for the leaders of a Syndicate to be tried for the crimes which they ordered others to carry out. Under this federal law, the Godfathers were convicted of charges including extortion, labour racketeering and murder for hire. Eight defendants were found guilty on all counts and subsequently sentenced on 13 January 1987 to hundreds of years imprisonment.

Time magazine quoted Giuliani as saying, 'Our approach was to wipe out the Five Families', and credited his success in so doing as 'the most significant assault on the infrastructure of organised crime since the high command of the Chicago Mafia was swept away in 1943.' Guiliani was congratulated by President Reagan and was given a special reward by the Italian government for his help in cleaning up some of the Mafia mess in their country.

A second significant reason for the Godfathers' downfall over this period was that the computer age had made the Mafia miserably outdated. Founded on an almost feudal system of overlords and chieftains, enforcers and soldiers, La Cosa Nostra managed to maintain a hold over a frightened public for longer than most oppressive governments ever did. But one area the Mob were tardy in entering, and one that has caused it most damage, is electronics. While the torpedoes were still out on the streets offering 'protection', the law enforcers were learning about the newest sophisticated eavesdropping devices.

Taking lessons from the CIA, local police forces and the FBI tooled up with the sensitive micro-technology used by spies. They planted bugs in the homes, cars and offices of top Mafiosi, including Gambino leader 'Big Paul' Castellano, Lucchese gang boss Antonio 'Tony Ducks' Corallo and Genovese captain Matty 'The Horse' Ianiello. When Paul Castellano had a new home built in 1979 – an opulently tacky replica of the White House in exclusive Todt Hill, Staten Island

– he demanded plush fittings but also got a couple he didn't order. In the ensuing years, his conversations were picked up by FBI bugs and mentioned in evidence as his trial opened.

Unfortunately for Castellano, he felt so superior as head of the Gambinos, America's most powerful crime family at the time, that he constantly bad-mouthed the other Godfathers who sat on the Commission. When transcripts of the tapes were released, as required by law, his fellow members went ballistic. An FBI agent was quoted as saying: 'The other bosses had never liked the arrogant Castellano but now they detested the man with a passion. Those tapes probably did more to seal his fate than anything else. It certainly gave one of his ambitious underlings, John Gotti, the excuse to eliminate his boss.

On 16 December 1985, while on $3 million bail from The Mafia Commission Trial, Castellano was driven by his equally unpopular underboss, 46-year-old Thomas Bilotti, to Manhattan's Sparks Steak House, where a hit team of four gunmen were waiting, with Gotti and his close friend Sammy Gravano observing the scene from a car across the street. Castellano and Bilotti were shot several times.

In releasing the Castellano tapes, the FBI had not intended to cause the 70-year-old Godfather's death, only to turn the Commission members against each other – to divide and conquer. The tactic was already working successfully by the time of the hit on Castellano. The Feds had placed a bug under the bed of Castellano's bitter rival for the position of Godfather, Gambino enforcer Aniello 'Mr. O'Neil' Dellacroce, as he lay dying in a New York hospital. Lung cancer and diabetes got him two weeks before the bullets of his followers got Castellano. But during the last two months of 71-year-old

Dellacroce's life, dozens of mobsters visited the hospital to pay their respects to the departing don – and to broadcast details about family business.

A little electronic device was somehow affixed behind the car dashboard of another don, Tony 'Ducks' Corallo. The 73-year-old head of the Lucchese family earned his nickname because of an uncanny knack throughout his life of dodging arrest and prosecution. But this time he'd forgotten to duck. His conversations with his driver and capo, Salvatore Avellino, were picked up by the bug and recorded by agents tailing the car from a distance. For four months the little transmitter spewed out fantastically detailed information about the inner workings of the Cosa Nostra, with names and places and specifics on the rackets that Tony 'Ducks' and the others were running. The case against Corallo was also built on 80 other bugging devices and 90 telephone wiretaps that picked up his many indiscretions. In 1986 he was found guilty and sent to prison, where he died in 2000.

Another transmitter was planted in the car of Colombo mobster Ralph Scopo, a 56-year-old former cement workers' union boss. Yet another went into a Brooklyn restaurant used by the family's acting boss, 48-year-old Gennaro 'Jerry Lang' Langella. Both of those detailed the widespread corruption in the construction and restaurant industries.

Key evidence in the trial against 66-year-old Matthew 'The Horse' Ianiello consisted of 7,000 tape and video recordings of him and his cronies at work. They were made by hidden transmitters planted by the Feds in Ianiello's New York offices and proved beyond doubt that 'The Horse' was the secret proprietor of five restaurants and topless bars from which he skimmed millions of dollars. He had denied ownership.

When government agents were investigating Mob control of the waterfront, they planted four dozen bugs in strategic spots, thereby obtaining 146 indictments and 118 convictions. Union president Anthony Scotto had one in his fancy desk, which picked him up vociferously complaining that his rake-off hadn't come in on time. Bizarrely, additional secret tapes were acquired by an FBI couple posing as lovers aboard a yacht.

Apart from transmitters, the FBI made extensive use of telephone taps to secure vital evidence. The mobsters often spoke in code while on their own phones but were more open when sneaking out to public payphones. But they got lazy and would use the same ones time and again. The lawmen noted them and put wiretaps on them too. In the mid-1980s, the FBI taped more than 7,000 hours of evidence in less than two years. With bugs and phone taps and the use of a dedicated Washington computer that cost $4 million a year to operate, the FBI nailed such Mafia overlords as Carlos 'Little Man' Marcello of New Orleans, Nick Civella of Kansas City and Russell Buffalino of Pennsylvania.

But the most publicly dramatic success of the entire war against the Mafia was the nailing of the brutal Godfather who ascended to the head of the Gambino family after the brilliantly executed killing of 'Big Paul' Castellano. After that putsch, John Gotti, 46, became an overnight underworld star, glorying in his nickname: 'The Dapper Don'.

Born in Brooklyn to dirt-poor Italian immigrants on 27 October 1940, Gotti became a teenage street fighter, whose first arrest was in 1958 for burglary. When he was 22 he was accepted as a part-time soldier by the Gambinos, who put him onto gambling and construction union matters. In this role, he met Salvatore Gravano, nicknamed 'Sammy the Bull' because of his muscular frame. Gravano came from the same background but lacked Gotti's ambition. As the latter rose up the ranks, Gravano was happy to be a loyal underboss. So blindly subservient was he that he would later say: 'John Gotti was my master and I was his dog. When he said "Bite", I bit.' But the dog was later to turn on his master in the most sensational manner.

Gotti took the faithful 'Sammy the Bull' with him as he climbed the Mafia command ladder over three decades. His first conviction, for unlawful entry, was in 1966. The next year, he headed a Mafia crew that used phoney passes to get into New York's JFK Airport and hijack a truckload of electronic equipment. Four days later they did it again, this time taking a truck full of women's clothing. They were nabbed and he served three years in prison. In 1973 Gotti and two others shot to death another mobster in a Staten Island bar. Charged, he plea-bargained for attempted manslaughter and served two of his four years. When he came out, he became a capo, heading a particularly tough crew of seven soldiers, and set out to make his way to the top.

Gotti's principal loyalty was to Gambino family enforcer Aniello Dellacroce, the Number Two to Paul Castellano. But when the popular Dellacroce died in December 1985, Castellano instead chose his bodyguard, 45-year-old Thomas Bilotti. By eliminating both of them, Gotti ended up the new Godfather.

To his admirers, the new Capo di Tutti Cappi was a generous guy who kept the drug-dealing scum away from ordinary, decent folk. Every year, he held a fireworks display on America's Fourth of July Independence Day, releasing thousands of dollars worth of rockets to the delight of the neighbourhood.

On the street, the 'Dapper Don', in his $4,000 silk suits and his pure cashmere coat, would acknowledge the respectful greetings of well-wishers as he made his way to the Ravenite Social Club, a nondescript tenement in the heart of Little Italy. It was behind these doors, armoured and alarmed, that the Godfather held court – and the veneer of the philanthropist was dropped. This was the office of the Godfather. Gambling, corruption, liquour sales, prostitution, drugs and murder were his business and he did it well. So well, in fact, that he earned another title; the FBI called him the 'Teflon Don' as no indictment they threw at him ever stuck.

Gotti's film star looks made him a celebrity far beyond New York's Italian community. The subject of awe-struck media profiles, he lived in an impressive house in suburbia. He had a wife, Victoria, a married daughter and a grown-up son, John. His other son, Frank, had been just 12 in 1980 when he rode his bicycle out from between two parked cars and was killed instantly. It was a complete accident. The horrified driver of the vehicle was Gotti's neighbour, John Favara, who four months later disappeared for good. Witnesses saw him being hit over the head with a board and then bundled by two men into a van. Informers told police that Gotti, eaten up with hatred, had the neighbour brought to a disused warehouse, where he personally cut the man to pieces with a chainsaw.

Gotti never forgot disfavour, and one of those doomed to find out the hard way was Wilfred 'Willie Boy' Johnson, a low-level soldier in Gotti's crew who later turned FBI informant. 'Willie Boy' had been living under an assumed name in Brooklyn ever since his testimony led to the convictions of several Mob figures, not least of all Gotti's brother Gene, subsequently sentenced to 22 years for heroin trafficking. One morning in August 1988, as 'Willie Boy' left home to go to work on a construction site, three hitmen stepped out of the stolen car and riddled him with 14 bullet holes. The main triggerman was 'Sammy the Bull' Gravano.

In 1985 Gotti was accused of assaulting a repairman and robbing him of $325 in a petty argument over a parking space. As soon as the repairman learned who Gotti was, he checked into a hospital and said he had developed amnesia. The charges had to be dropped. A year later, Gotti was accused of running a racketeering enterprise and hit with three charges including murder. He beat the rap. In 1992 he made it a hat-trick when jurors ruled he did not order the bungled contract-killing of a union official who wasn't paying his dues. But it was the loyal, psychotic lieutenant 'Sammy the Bull' who did most of the dirty work. On his own admission, by the late Eighties he had become kill-crazy and committed so many murders that he actually forgot many of them.

On 11 December 1990 FBI agents and New York City detectives swooped on the Ravenite social club and arrested Gotti and Gravano. Although this was the fourth indictment since Gotti's bloody rise to leadership, it was the first time he was charged with the murders of Castellano and Bilotti. At this time, the prosecution was relying on dozens of wiretaps and on the hearsay evidence of informants, including Philip Leonetti, former underboss of the Philadelphia crime family, who had since become a government witness. Leonetti was prepared to testify that Gotti had bragged about Castellano's execution while at a meeting of Philadelphia crime leaders. But the FBI suddenly knew they had a cast-iron case – when, hardly able to believe their luck, 'Sammy the Bull' Gravato, who had only served time in the past for low-level offences like hijacking and theft, offered to become the highest ranking informer in criminal history. It transpired that Sammy, who was tipped to be the heir apparent to the Gambino family, had a dread of ending his days in prison.

Gotti was denied bail. In Brooklyn Federal Courthouse, Judge Leo Glasser prudently pointed out: 'There are no conditions of release that will reasonably assure the safety of any person in the community.' In the spectacular trial that followed, through March and April 1992, Gravato took the stand to testify against John Gotti and his Mafia empire. Methodically confessing to all the murders ordered by Gotti, he squirmed under the gaze of the Godfather's steely eyes and knew that he would forever be a marked man. In return for his testimony, Sammy could expect leniency for his own crimes – but it would be a life spent looking over his shoulder.

Increasingly, the defiant Gotti failed to hide his arrogant attitude and Judge Glasser once had to clear the jury from the courtroom before angrily warning the defendant: 'Mr. Gotti, this is addressed to you. If you want to continue to remain at this trial and at that table, I am going to direct you to stop making comments which can be heard in this courtroom, and gestures which are designed to comment upon the character of the United States attorney. I will have you removed from the courtroom. You will watch this trial on a television screen downstairs. I am not going to tell you that again.'

Gotti's defence was slim. 'What happened to it?' he complained to his team. 'I should have put on a little song and dance.' Finally, after tantrums and screaming matches in court, and two bomb explosions outside, the prosecution summed up by damning the 'Dapper Don' as leader of the Gambino family and stating: 'Murder is the heart and soul of this enterprise.'

On 23 June 1992, Gotti wore his handmade silk suit for the last time as he was sentenced to life in prison without parole for ordering at least five murders and on 49 counts of racketeering. Going down with him was another underboss, Frank 'Frankie Loc' Locascio, a 59-year-old henchman also nailed by Gravano's testimony. Outside court, a riot broke out, allegedly organised by John 'Junior' Gotti, who had hired 12 buses to bring 1,000 flag-waving demonstrators to the courthouse. Eight police officers were injured. In 1997 Judge Glasser dismissed the fourth and final of Gotti's bids for a retrial. The 'Dapper Don' was destined to die behind bars.

That same year, Gotti's ex-underboss Gravano, freed after his own reduced five-year sentence, made his last appearance as a government witness by testifying against Genovese family boss Vincent 'the Chin' Gigante, known as 'the Oddfather' because he had for years feigned insanity to avoid prosecution. By then, Gravano was living the high life. The man who had admitted taking part in 19 murders had published a book, with a movie spin-off. He was a celebrity. But 'Sammy the Bull' could not stay clean. In 2000 he and his son were arrested for conspiring with Israeli mobsters to distribute the drug Ecstasy. The following year, they appeared in the same Brooklyn Federal Courthouse, where he had testified against John Gotti. A further trial was held in Arizona, where Gravano was also involved in a statewide drugs ring. He was jailed for 20 years. His belated incarceration pleased the families of many of his murdered victims, angry that he had been treated so leniently by the government. But his ticket to freedom had by then encouraged a wave of other Mafia members to become government witnesses.

John 'Junior' Gotti continued to run the family but his reign was short-lived. In 1999 he was jailed and forfeited $1.5 million after being found guilty of extortion, loansharking, gambling, mortgage fraud and tax evasion. Two of Gotti Senior's brothers and a nephew were also subsequently arrested. The 'Dapper Don' himself died in jail of cancer on 10 June 2002.

So where does that leave the most pervasive criminal organisation the world has ever known? Where today are the descendants of the Italian street gangs of a century ago, of the gun-toting gangsters of the Thirties, of the Murder Inc. mobsters of the Fifties and of the silk-suited Dons of recent times? Certainly the money they made didn't just evaporate. The billions that vanished from the public purse as the cost of organised crime in America is now largely laundered into legitimate businesses. And the pot still grows. The difference is that instead of seeing blood on the streets, the American public suffers a secret 'taxation' by the Mafia blood-suckers, the cost of whose criminal enterprises is reckoned to be well over a trillion dollars a year.

When legendary Mob mogul Meyer Lansky boasted in the Fifties, 'We're bigger than US Steel', most people thought he was exaggerating. Today the Mafia's turnover is bigger than the economies of many countries. America's over-stretched crime fighters know that the reason people tend not to hear much about the Italian Mafia anymore is because they are doing what they were always supposed to do: operating in secrecy.

That does not mean they're not still active. Selwyn Raab, an investigative journalist who covered the Mafia for 25 years at *The New York Times*, has highlighted their steady move into commercial and financial crime, which he says reflects 'the Cosa Nostra's Darwinian survival adaptability'. In his excellent book, *Five Families*, Raab writes: 'Despite pronouncements of unabated vigilance, law enforcement's efforts against the traditional crime families are unmistakably in a downward cycle. State prosecutors and police forces, confronting terrorism as well as violent crime pressures and budget restraints, show less zeal than previously to engage the Mob'.

FBI director Robert Mueller said as much in September 2003, two years after the 9/11 attacks on New York's Twin Towers, when he asked the public to accept that, with the agency's new focus on counter-terrorism, 'please recognise that we can't do everything'. But the notion that 9/11 dimmed the Mafia's intent soon proved deluded. Members of New York's Lucchese family were found guilty of extorting pay-offs from a company engaged in the removal of debris from the World Trade Center. And the rival Bonanno family tried unsuccessfully to steal scrap metal from the ruins of the Twin Towers.

So any romantic view of the Mafia as just another episode in America's sometimes violent past is fallacious. Attorney and law professor George Robert Blakey, the principal author of the RICO Act that put so many gangsters in prison, warned: 'We don't win a war against the Mob; all we can do is contain it. Keeping a boxer down is easier than knocking him down a second time. By withdrawing resources, we'll just have to go back and complete the job at a larger cost.'

CHAPTER 10

AN UNHOLY ALLIANCE BETWEEN WARTIME VILLAINS

Gangsters elsewhere in the world tend not to have quite the same 'glamorous' image as American mobsters. Maybe it's in the names. It's difficult to compete with the anti-heroes of previous chapters, like 'Bugsy' Siegel, 'Lucky' Luciano, Jimmy 'The Weasel' Fratianno, Carmine 'Wagon Wheels' Fatico or Jack 'Machine Gun' McGurn. Britain's underworld is nowadays short of descriptive nicknames – but it wasn't always like that.

A little short of a century ago, Britain's underworld boasted quaint characters like gems thief Joseph 'Cammie' Grizzard and drugs smugglers 'Brilliant' Chang and 'Sess' Miyakawa. There were hard men like 'Jew Jack the Chopper King', 'Wassie' Newman, 'Dodger' Mullins and 'Razzle Dazzle' Dalziel. Through the Twenties and Thirties, Soho was controlled by vice king 'Papa' Pasquale and North London was terrorised by

Darby Sabini, labelled by the Press as 'Britain's leading gangster'. South of the Thames lurked the Elephant and Castle Mob, while in the Midlands the Brummagen Boys held sway. A famous cat burglar of the day was a man named 'Ruby' Sparks, aided by his getaway driver, a beauty known only as the 'Bobbed Hair Bandit'.

Prostitution was big business between the wars, the principal racketeers usually being immigrants – Latvian 'Red Max' Kessel, Frenchman Casimere Micheletti and Spaniard Juan Castanar, with their henchmen Charlie 'the Acrobat' and 'Mad Emile' Berthier. After World War Two the three Messina Brothers, of mixed Sicilian, Maltese and Egyptian descent, took over the London vice trade. Their best night's business was on VE Day 1945 when, it was faithfully recorded, one girl alone serviced 49 revellers.

But among all these exotically named villains of the past were two hoodlums who stood out as masters of post-war gangland: Jack 'Spot' Comer and William 'Billy' Hill. They were, at different times, close friends and bitter rivals. And both claimed the title 'King of the Underworld'.

There are differing versions of how Spot gained his nickname of which he was so proud. As a youth, he was constantly getting into 'a spot of bother'. Later in life, as a protection-racket enforcer, he was always 'on the spot' to sort out trouble from rivals. Or it might have been because of the mole on his face. The son of Polish Jews who had come to Britain in the 1890s, Spot was born Jacob Comacho in Whitechapel, in London's East End, on 12 April 1912. The name he used changed to Colmore, then Comer, then simply Jack Spot. He gained an early reputation as a street fighter and, with anti-Semitism rife in the Thirties, was paid retainers by

Jewish shopkeepers, stallholders and illegal bookmakers to protect them from thugs. He became a local hero when in 1936 he helped East-Enders break up a march through the area by Sir Oswald Mosley's fascist Blackshirts. But by then, Spot was combining community protection with full-scale protection rackets, concentrating on the illicit gambling clubs that flourished both in the East End and the more lucrative West End of London.

His criminal career was interrupted in 1940 when Spot and some of his cronies were conscripted into the Army. For three years he fought the system and, avoiding any sort of military action, was discharged as mentally unstable. He returned to the East End to find his parents dead and much of his home territory devastated by the Blitz. Spot tried to pick up his old business but after an attack on a rival led to a warrant for his arrest, he fled to Leeds, then the black market capital of the North. There he worked as a minder around Leeds and Newcastle, helping other gangsters beat or intimidate businessmen out of their nightclubs, gambling dens or racecourse pitches. He returned to London enriched and set himself up in offices in the West End.

According to Scotland Yard Inspector Leonard 'Nipper' Read: 'Spot epitomised everything about the old-time Mafia-style gangster. He always looked the part. Immaculately dressed, wearing a brown fedora hat, he would come out of his flat every morning and cross the road to the barbers where he would be given a shave and a hair trim. Then he would march down the Edgware Road receiving the accolades of the local business owners, and take his usual table in the Cumberland Hotel, where he would receive 'guests' in much the same way as Don Corleone did in *The Godfather*.'

But Spot had his eyes on rackets further afield. Before World War Two, an Italian gang, the Sabini Brothers, controlled racecourse rackets, setting up the Bookmakers Protection Association. During the war, the Sabinis were interned like other Anglo-Italians and their absence from the tracks allowed other Mobs to move in. Spot, more ruthless and violent than most, gained a near monopoly on the business after pitched battles with rival outfits, which were harassed and attacked with knives, bottles, and machetes.

Spot's own favourite weapon was the cutthroat razor. 'My brother was a barber,' he once said, 'and I used to get my nice sharp razors from him.' Taped at one end, they would be used by Spot and his growing gang to 'chiv' thugs who tried to muscle in on his territory – although, he boasted, 'I'd make sure never to cut them through the jugular vein. I didn't want to be done for murder, did I?'

Spot's major rivals for the racecourse protection business were the White family, who controlled major southern courses including Ascot, Epsom and Brighton. Their leader, Harry White, had taken over these courses from the Sabinis and was not now going to offer them on a plate to Spot's Mob. He soon changed his mind. According to a newspaper report of the time: 'Harry White's fear of Spot began in January 1947 in a club in Sackville Street, off Piccadilly. He was drinking with one of his henchmen and racehorse trainer Tim O'Sullivan. Spot walked in with ten thugs, went straight up to Harry and said, You're Yiddified – meaning he was anti-Jewish. White denied it. He said, I have Jewish people among my best friends. Spot wouldn't listen and hit him with a bottle. As White collapsed in a pool of blood, the rest of Spot's men attacked O'Sullivan and the third man. O'Sullivan was beaten unconscious and pushed into an open fire. The other man was slashed with razors and stabbed in the stomach.'

The White family were finally routed in a very public battle at Harringay Arena, six months later – after which, Spot later revealed, he was pulled in by a chief superintendent at Scotland Yard and given a warning that gang warfare in the city would not be tolerated. Spot said: 'I called the heavy mob together at once. I said, "We've got to pack it up, so get rid of the ironmongery." We collected all the Stens, the grenades, revolvers, pistols and ammunition, loaded them onto a lorry and dumped the whole lot into the Thames.'

Spot was now running a lucrative gambling club in Aldgate, a protection racket among the West End clubs and was making a fortune from the races. More fancifully, he also saw himself as 'the Robin Hood of the East End', travelling to Leeds, Manchester or Glasgow to beat up villains who threatened Jewish businesses. He even claimed that rabbis would advise their frightened people to call for his services.

Spot's career almost ended when he organised a £1.25 million gold bullion robbery at Heathrow Airport in July 1948. After coshing security guards, his ten-man gang were pounced on by police, who arrested eight of them. Spot escaped. So did 'Franny' Daniels – by clinging to the underside of a Black Maria, crawling away only when it reached the police station.

In 1949 Spot, believing he needed a tough enforcer to hold his crime empire together, went into partnership with Billy Hill, a notorious hard-man whose eyes were said to be 'like black glass'. Hill, the son of a Covent Garden 'fence', had committed his first stabbing at the age of 14 in 1925. He was a house burglar while still in his teens and graduated to smash-and-grab raids targeting furriers and jewellers in the Thirties.

Jack Spot once praised Hill as 'an out-and-out thief and a very good one – and very good safe blower, too.'

During London's wartime blackout, Hill's gang expanded their business into black marketeering and providing false documents for deserting soldiers. He also cooperated with Spot in West End protection rackets. After the war, Hill went on the run following a warehouse robbery and fled to South Africa, where he briefly ran a gambling club in South Johannesburg. There, his reputation was enhanced when he silenced a rival by slicing him from head to toe with a razor, leaving the man needing 100 stitches. Arrested by South African police, he jumped bail and returned to Britain, where he gave himself up and was sent to jail.

On his release in 1949, Jack Spot was waiting outside the gates of Wandsworth Prison, southwest London, to offer him a partnership. The two gang leaders settled down as 'businessmen', living well on the proceeds of their rackets in West London. They left the vice trade to the Maltese Messina Brothers, who ran Soho's sex industry. Spot concentrated on his gaming and racecourse 'protection'. Hill was more adventurous, though. In 1952 he stole £287,000 (the equivalent of more than £6 million today) in used banknotes from a Post Office van in Paddington and in 1954 he organised a £45,000 gold bullion heist in Holborn. In neither case was any of the money recovered.

Hill also funded a drug smuggling operation from Morocco, where he owned a nightclub. It was run by his wife, an ex-prostitute known as 'Gipsy' Riley. He had fallen for her after his release from prison, and when her ex-pimp, 'Belgian Johnny', tried to force her back on the streets, he cornered him in a restaurant and carved his face to shreds. Hill later described his expert use of the razor-sharp knife he usually carried: 'I was always careful to draw my knife down on the face, never across or upwards. Always down. So that if the knife slips you don't cut an artery. After all, chivving is chivving, but cutting an artery is usually murder. Only mugs do murder.'

Both Spot and Hill were planning their retirement by 1953 – the same year that they met a pair of violent young East End twins, Ronnie and Reginald Kray. The old and new guard got involved in a few joint enterprises before Spot and Hill fell out. Each of them was keen to be recognised as 'King of the Underworld' and the crunch came when Billy Hill achieved celebrity status first.

In September 1954 'The Amazing Confessions of Billy Hill' were serialised in *The People* newspaper. The newspaper's renowned crime man Duncan Webb had ghosted Hill's biography, immodestly titled *Boss of Britain's Underworld*, in which Hill was described as 'a crook, a villain, a thief, a thug' – but also strangely as 'a genius and a kind and tolerant man'. In his memoirs, Hill boasted of organising the bullion robbery in Holborn the previous year and spoke of his 1952 Paddington mailbag heist.

Jack Spot was furious. Spot blamed not only Hill but also Duncan Webb for the unwelcome publicity about the gang's previous crimes. He invited Webb to a pub meeting and beat him up with a knuckleduster; he also retaliated by giving his own version of events to the Press. He said: 'I made Billy Hill. He wrote to me when he was in jail, wanted me to help him. Then he got to be top over me. If it wasn't for me he'd never have got there. I should have shot Billy Hill, I really should.'

A string of court appearances followed as Spot tried in vain to reassert his authority. For the attack on Webb, he was fined a modest £50 for grievous bodily harm. For an unprovoked attack on another rival, his ex-bodyguard Albert Dimes, Spot was charged with instigating the affray, attempting to pervert the course of justice and with perjury. With off-course betting about to be legalised and suffering mass defections of his troops to Hill, Spot faced bankruptcy.

But Billy Hill was not yet finished with him. One night in May 1956 Jack and his wife Rita were strolling outside their Bayswater home when they were attacked by a gang armed with coshes, knives and razors. Spot needed 78 stitches and a blood transfusion. He knew his assailants but refused to name them. Rita, however, gave evidence and three of them – all Hill henchmen, including the feared 'Mad' Frankie Fraser – were sentenced to seven years' imprisonment.

Following the murderous street attack, Spot moved to Ireland in fear of his former partner. Hill briefly prospered as a Kray mentor but sank into depression and died alone at the age of 73 in 1984. Spot, who described Hill as 'the richest man in the graveyard', died, aged 83, in 1996. Their 'manors' had long been taken over. For just as those self-styled 'Kings of the Underworld' had fought their way to the top, so younger, hungrier and more vicious figures arose to fill the void created by their downfall.

CHAPTER 11

THE GANGLAND CURSE OF THE CRUEL KRAYS

In a reign of terror that marred the memory of the 'Swinging Sixties', Ronnie and Reggie Kray became the most notorious gangland bosses of London's underworld. The twins' merciless violence silenced rivals and bred respect by fear. Their tight control of the East End also, oddly, earned them local loyalty, some regarding them as 'Robin Hood' characters who maintained gangland peace and kept the seedy streets safe.

In their heyday, they were photographed with the famous, fêted by showbiz personalities and were generous in their support of charities. They were also feared like no other criminals of the time. In every way, they were a British version of America's Thirties' gangsters, whose exploits they studied and copied slavishly.

Ronnie and Reggie were born on 17 October 1933, at Hoxton in the East End of London. Ronnie was the elder;

Reggie arrived 45 minutes later. They also had an older brother, Charles. The boys had Jewish, Irish and Romany blood in their veins. Their father Charles, who was 25 at the time of the twins' birth, was a dealer in old cloth, silver and gold. Their mother Violet was just 21. Shortly before the outbreak of World War Two, the family moved a brief distance to one of the toughest, most run-down areas of Bethnal Green, soon to become even more dilapidated, thanks to visits from the Luftwaffe. Ronnie and Reggie became known as the Terrible Twins because of their love of fighting, at first with fists and later with bicycle chains and flick-knives.

By the age of 16, they were carrying guns. A year later, they made their first appearance in court. They were accused of seriously beating up a 16-year-old rival but the case was dismissed for lack of evidence.

The boys were fighters in every sense. At 17, they became professional boxers and it looked at that stage as if their route to the top would be via the ring. They had been taught their pugilistic skills by brother Charlie, who had joined the Royal Navy and won a reputation as a forces boxer. When on leave, he hung a canvas kit bag from a ceiling of their home and let the twins use it as a punch bag.

In the spring of 1952 the twins received their call-up papers for National Service and joined the Royal Fusiliers. But only a few hours into their Army careers, Ronnie punched the recruiting corporal on the nose. Their subsequent military service was remarkable for their violence, serious trouble with the military authorities and periods in custody. Following dishonourable discharge in 1954, they went into the 'protection' business. If a bookmaker, store or club owner wanted to ensure 'troublemakers' did not target his establishment, a weekly payment to the twins would do the trick. As the easy money rolled in, so their gang of collectors grew. Their territory covered the East End and much of North London. They founded their own clubs, at first in the East End, where a sports hall provided a front for their rackets, and later in fashionable Knightsbridge, where the West End found the pair a rough-and-ready attraction.

Ronnie, who was known as 'the Colonel', had a brutal and unstable nature which Reggie, 'the Quiet One' with a good business brain, tried to keep under control. Still operating from their modest home in Vallance Road, known locally as 'Fort Vallance', the Krays could be magnanimous, loyal and charming. They could also be frighteningly, unpredictably brutal – a trait mainly initiated by Ronnie, who would egg his brother on to prove himself by being as tough as his twin.

The swaggering Ronnie was in trouble with the law again in 1955 when he shot a man in the leg. Ronnie had gone to confront the victim, a local dock worker, who was demanding his money back from a car dealer, who was paying the twins for 'protection'. By the time Ronnie tracked him down, the docker had changed his mind and wanted to keep the car – but Ronnie shot him anyway. He was subsequently arrested and picked out at an identity parade but avoided being charged by claiming he was Reggie, thus making nonsense of the evidence.

The following year, Ronnie was re-arrested and this time convicted. He received a three-year sentence for stabbing a man with a bayonet in a raid on a rival gang's territory. Having Ronnie locked up was, ironically, good news for the Krays' businesses. In his brother's absence, Reggie expanded the rackets and sought new clubs in which to invest.

But inside prison, Ronnie's dangerous instability became

apparent. He grew obsessively fearful that someone was trying to kill him – he even had to be shown his own reflection in a mirror to prove he was still in one piece. Finally, in December 1957, after receiving news that a favourite aunt had died, Ronnie went berserk. He spent a night in a straitjacket and the following morning was certified insane and sent to a mental hospital.

Long Hill psychiatric unit in leafy Epsom, Surrey, was no high-security prison. One Sunday, Reggie paid a visit and swapped clothes with his brother. When Ronnie was safely away, Reggie owned up to the stunt but was not prosecuted. Ronnie remained free for some weeks, during which time his sense of bravado induced him to make surprise calls on East End pubs to taunt the police. But his strange state of mind worried his family and, after a suicide attempt, they allowed the police to recapture him and he was returned to prison. After further treatment, he was deemed fit to be released in the spring of 1958.

Now the duo could enjoy the riches that Reggie had been accumulating while his brother was 'inside'. Reggie had a good business brain and the family's commercial enterprises had flourished during Ronnie's spell in jail. There was the original Double R Club in Bow, a new club in Stratford, a car sales business and even an illegal gambling club a stone's throw away from Bow police station. But the unpredictable Ronnie was far from cured and no one knew it better than Reggie, who realised that a return to heavy-handed gangsterism would be bad for business.

The pair argued about the running of their 'firm', but when in 1960 Reggie was jailed for 18 months for demanding money with menaces, it was his brother's turn to have a free hand at the family business. Ronnie took a contract from the notorious slum landlord of the time, Peter Rachman. The Krays' hoodlums would guard Rachman's rent collectors in return for a healthy commission. The result was not only added riches for Ronnie but an introduction to a more upmarket circle of acquaintances. His new Knightsbridge club, Esmerelda's Barn, became a favourite rendezvous for sportspeople and entertainers like world heavyweight champion Rocky Marciano, singer Judy Garland and film stars George Raft and Diana Dors.

Esmerelda's Barn also became a haven for young men willing to sell their bodies – a clientele encouraged by Ronnie, who was by now openly homosexual. Reggie was otherwise inclined. After being freed from prison in 1961, he fell for a 16-year-old East End girl, Frances Shea, whom he married in 1965. Tragically, she suffered Reggie's strange way of life for just two years before committing suicide.

The brothers' lifestyles were now widely different. Ronnie veered towards his 'Swinging Sixties' West End friends while Reggie returned to his East End roots. Suffering the strain of his failed marriage, Reggie seemed no longer able to control the Al Capone fantasy world of brother Ronnie, and the reputation of the Krays became even more brutal in the second half of the Sixties. There were beatings, brandings and knifings. One former friend who drunkenly insulted Ronnie needed 70 stitches to face wounds. There were also at least three unsuccessful attempts on the Krays' lives, and Ronnie took to sleeping with a gun under his pillow.

In December 1965 the Krays felt they needed the protection of an especially violent bodyguard, Frank Mitchell, known as 'the Mad Axeman', whom Ronnie had met in

Wandsworth Prison back in 1956. Mitchell was now in top-security Dartmoor Prison – from which the twins helped him escape. They supplied him with a flat as a hiding place but eventually found him not only violent but unstable. He disappeared. The Krays were subsequently cleared of his murder but the body was never found. Another member of 'the Firm', Freddie Foreman, later revealed that Mitchell was shot and his corpse dumped at sea.

The main reason for springing Mitchell had been a flare-up of warfare between the Krays and rival gangsters Charles and Eddie Richardson, based in South London but intent on muscling in on West End protection rackets. George Cornell, a small-time 'heavy' working for the Richardsons, had allegedly upset Ronnie Kray by calling him 'a big fat poof'. One March evening in 1966 Cornell strayed into Kray territory and was perched on a stool in Whitechapel's Blind Beggar pub when Ronnie arrived with two henchmen. Cornell remarked: 'Well, look what the dog's brought in!' Ronnie walked calmly to the bar and, as he later described, 'put a gun at his head, looked him in the eyes and pulled the trigger. His body fell off the stool and I walked out.' Later he justified the murder by saying: 'Cornell was vermin. He was a drunkard and a bully. He was simply nothing. I done the Earth a favour ridding it of him.'

The following year, Reggie made his own violent contribution to the murder statistics. By then, the brothers' business had expanded to drugs and pornography, areas that did not endear them to their traditional East End friends. Ronnie's homosexual proclivities were the talk of their 'manor', quite apart from his now obvious paranoia. Meanwhile, the more moderate Reggie had taken to drink since his wife's suicide, and when fired up with alcohol, he would take pot-shots at the legs of people who offended him.

The Krays were becoming bad news. Their instability was damaging their image as reliable 'protection' racketeers. To restore their reputation, they decided to hold a very public test of their 150-strong gang's loyalty – a meaningless murder. The victim was to be Jack 'The Hat' McVitie, so called because of the hat he wore to hide his baldness. McVitie's crime was to owe the brothers £500 and to have insulted them in their absence during a drunken binge. Four of the Krays' men lured McVitie to a 'party' in a borrowed house in Stoke Newington, where Ronnie, Reggie and two henchmen lay in wait. As their victim entered, he realised his impending fate and turned to flee.

Ronnie pinned him against a wall and told him: 'Come on, Jack, be a man.' McVitie said: 'I will be a man but I don't want to die like one.' Ronnie led him into a basement room, where the killing became near farcical. As McVitie walked through the door, Reggie pointed a pistol at his head and pulled the trigger. But the gun did not fire. Ronnie then picked up a carving knife and thrust it at McVitie's back but it failed to pierce his thick coat. McVitie made a dash for the window. He dived through, only to be grabbed by his feet and hauled back in. Ronnie pinioned his arms from behind and screamed at his brother: 'Kill him, Reg! Do it. Don't stop now!' Reggie picked up the knife and stabbed his pleading victim in the face and then through the throat. The knife passed through his gullet and pinned him to the floor. McVitie's body was never found.

The twins planned three more 'hits' – the first steps in their formation of a 'Murder Incorporated' style organisation along the lines of the American model. A witness at an Old Bailey trial was to be killed by a crossbow or a syringe of cyanide. A Maltese club owner was to have his car bombed. A gambler who owed money to a Kray associate in Las Vegas was also to be eliminated.

However, a Scotland Yard team led by Detective Superintendent Leonard 'Nipper' Read was now watching every move the gang made. Read's case against the Krays was not strong but he knew that unless the twins were safely behind bars, prospective witnesses would suffer 'loss of memory' or would simply vanish. Then the police got lucky. A Kray associate was stopped while about to board a plane from Glasgow to London. He was carrying four sticks of dynamite, presumably destined for the Maltese club-owner's car. Detectives raided his home and found the crossbow and briefcase complete with poisonous syringe.

On the night of 8 May 1968 Ronnie and Reggie went drinking at the Old Horn pub in Bethnal Green. They continued on to the Astor Club in fashionable Berkeley Square, Reggie having brought along a young lady while Ronnie enjoyed the company of a young man. They all returned to their mother's new council flat in Shoreditch at four in the morning. An hour later, at dawn, Read's men used a sledgehammer to open the door of the apartment – a particularly startling awakening for the boyfriend in Ronnie's bed.

The twins were charged with the murders of George Cornell and Jack McVitie. Eight other members of their 'firm', including their brother Charlie, were charged with various lesser crimes. The twins pleaded not guilty but after a sensational 39-day trial at the Old Bailey, they were jailed for life with a recommendation that they should serve no less than 30 years. They were 35 years of age when the trial ended on 8

March 1969, which meant that they would be pensioners before they ever had the chance of being released.

Ronnie and Reggie were sent to separate top-security prisons. In 1972 they were briefly reunited at Parkhurst jail on the Isle of Wight. But in 1979 Ronnie was again certified and sent to Broadmoor hospital for the criminally insane. Reggie found his sentence harder to take than his brother. He was classified as a Category A prisoner: highly dangerous and liable to escape. Shadowed at all times by two prison officers, his movements were monitored and his visits were screened and limited. While of Category A status, no parole board could consider his case. All his appeals fell on deaf ears. In 1982 he unsuccessfully attempted suicide by cutting his wrists.

Ronnie was luckier in his time behind bars. Being an inmate of Broadmoor, he was allowed more privileges than his brother. He received visits from old East End associates and from showbusiness and sporting friends. They brought him parcels of food from Harrods – smoked salmon and game pie – and classical records for the hi-fi in his cell. He also had a colour television set.

The brutal twin would regale visitors with details of his exploits in the days when he and his brother wrote headlines in blood. In 1983 the self-justifying gangster told a visiting journalist: 'We never hurt ordinary members of the public. We only took money off other villains and gave a bundle of that away to decent people who were on hard times. I look back on those days and naturally remember the good times. Then people could take ladies into pubs with them without the risk of their being insulted. Old people didn't get mugged either. It couldn't have happened when we were looking after the East End.'

Of life in Broadmoor, he said: 'There are some really bad ones in here. But they are all some mother's sons – and that's where the heartbreak is. Because no matter what they've done or how they've been, the mothers don't stop coming and don't stop loving them. When I see these mums, I feel really sorry for them having to come here.'

In 1982 the twins' strongest link with the outside world ended. Their most constant visitor, their mother Violet, died one week before her 73rd birthday. Violet Kray had become an East End legend in her own right and is said to have been the only person on earth who had any control over her boys. Ronnie and Reggie were allowed out for a day to attend her funeral, which was turned into a star-studded East End occasion.

Reggie said after his return to Parkhurst jail: 'It's so lonely without visits from our mum. They were always the best ones. I shall miss her so much. Through the funeral, Ronnie and I were handcuffed to police officers who must have been 6ft 3in tall. But they needn't have worried. Violence is not part of my life anymore. I get angry when I read about the way things are in the East End nowadays. Like those attacks on old ladies. Years ago, if we saw an old lady we would help her across the road and wish her goodnight. Now they rape 80-year-old women and kill them for their pension. It makes me sick.'

Of the hopelessness of life in jail, he said: 'You can so easily give up after these years. They have passed quickly. But it is only when I see the youngsters come in here that I realise what a terrible waste of life it is.'

It was a lesson that the Kray brothers had not fully learned, however. Elder brother Charlie Kray had been released from prison in 1975 after serving seven years. But he was back in jail in 1997 after a police sting proved his part in a conspiracy to smuggle cocaine worth £69million. He died of natural causes in prison on 4 April 2000.

Five years earlier, Charlie had been on hand to comfort brother Reggie when the latter was allowed out of prison to attend the funeral of Ronnie Kray, who was 61 when he died on 17 March 1995 after collapsing on his ward at Broadmoor mental hospital.

The last of the Kray brothers to pass into history was Reggie. Aged 66 and suffering from inoperable bladder cancer, he was freed on compassionate grounds in September 2000 and moved from Wayland Prison, Norfolk, to a Norwich hospital. There, he invited a BBC TV crew to interview him, and surprised them by confessing to a previously unknown murder. Although he did not name the victim, it was thought to be Edward 'Mad Teddy' Smith, who had been missing since 1967. Explaining why he murdered Jack 'The Hat' McVitie, he said he thought him 'very uncouth and vexatious to the spirit'. During the one-hour documentary Kray refused to give a fulsome apology for his violent behaviour. He said: 'It is very difficult to apologise in some cases but not in others. I suppose if I've been a bit too violent over the years I make some apologies about it, but there's little I can do about it now, so again it's no good reflecting back. It's pointless, negative.'

In the final days of his life, he booked into the bridal suite of a local hotel with his wife Roberta, whom he had married in jail in 1997. She maintained a bedside vigil until his death ten days later on 1 October 2000. He was finally reunited with his twin, being buried alongside Ronnie in Chingford Mount Cemetery.

In the media circus that followed Reggie's death, his lawyer Mark Goldstein described the Krays as 'icons of the twentieth century'. A less florid epitaph would have been the words of the Old Bailey judge, Mr Justice Melford Stevenson, in sentencing them in 1969, when he told them with scornful understatement: 'In my view society has earned a rest from your activities.'

CHAPTER 12

THE TERRIBLE RETRIBUTION OF THE TORTURE GANG

The Krays and their rival gangsters the Richardsons vied with each other for the reputation of being the most monstrous merchants of terror in London. But whereas the Krays, on the north side of the Thames, were infamous for meting out instant vengeance, the Richardson gang, based south of the river, were masters of a slower punishment. Known as the 'Torture Gang', their notoriety stems from the penalties for those who fell foul of them, which included beatings, electric shock treatment, extracting teeth with pliers and removing toes with bolt cutters. An added speciality was the use of a building tool called a 'Spitmatic' to pin their enemies to the floor with six-inch nails.

Charles Richardson, born in 1934, and brother Edward, two years younger, were raised in Camberwell, Southeast London, where their mother ran a sweet shop. Their father was a feckless rag-and-bone man, who disappeared when the boys were in their teens, leaving the family penniless. Charlie was sent to an approved school at the age of 14, escaping at one time to go on a burglary spree. Released from the school at 16, he acquired a horse and cart and went 'totting' for scrap metal. He and Eddie were seen as no more than petty thieves.

But along the way, they built up a string of businesses – some legitimate, others not – throughout South London. Charlie specialised in scrap metal but also ran furniture and fancy goods firms. Eddie operated fruit machines and ran a wholesale chemists' supply company. But these were fronts for their more profitable lines of trade – fraud, theft, 'protection' rackets and receiving stolen goods.

The pair had good business brains and it is a tragedy that they did not concentrate on their legitimate businesses because they could have been comfortably off without ever breaking the law. But that was not their style. Eddie's fruit machine business, for instance, was more successful than most in the same line. The reason was simple: if a pub or club owner was offered one of Eddie's machines, he would be wise to accept. If not, he knew his premises would be broken into and vandalised or quite openly smashed up by 'heavies' in broad daylight.

Their most masterful moneymaking strokes, however, involved what were known as 'long firms', whereby goods would be ordered and quickly sold – then both the goods and the firm would vanish. A company would be set up under a Richardson nominee and begin trading perfectly legitimately. Goods would be ordered from suppliers and paid for promptly, so creating a good credit rating. After a few months' operation, massive orders would be placed on credit with the suppliers. The goods would be quickly sold, the Richardsons would pocket the money, and the company would seemingly evaporate into thin air.

By the age of 30, the Richardsons were millionaires. Charlie, who married a local girl called Margaret with whom he had five children, lived in a large house in Camberwell. He had a smart office in Mayfair's Park Lane from which he ran a company with interests in mining. But his real powerbase lay south of the river, in the offices of Peckford Scrap Metal, of New Church Road, Camberwell. It was here that people whom the brothers believed had crossed them were brought in for 'questioning'.

The Richardsons' activities were supported by a team of brutal enforcers who ensured that those tempted to complain would think again. The brothers also had a number of bent coppers in their pocket who would immediately alert them if anyone went to the police to 'grass them up'. Charles was once arrested for receiving stolen goods but police had to drop the charge for lack of witnesses. They kept a careful watch on the gang's activities, however, and in 1965 they got an insight into the full horrors of their methods for keeping order and repaying old scores. In July of that year, one of the gang's victims walked into a South London police station and related a horrific story of how he had been tortured by the Richardsons.

The sadistic punishments at these kangaroo courts were equally meted out by Charlie and Eddie. Sick with fear, the victims would be hauled in by gang enforcers and tried before Eddie and the others in a mock court. Then the punishments were ordered – anything from beatings to more fearsome forms of torture. Men were whipped, burned with cigarettes, had their teeth pulled out with pliers, were nailed to the floor, had their toes removed by bolt cutters, and leaped in agony from the effects of electric shocks. Afterwards, if the victims were too badly injured, they would be taken to a struck-off doctor to be patched up.

A favourite tool in these interrogations was a former Army field telephone, a device that had its own electrical generator. The terminals would be attached to the victim's body and a gang member – usually either 'Mad' Frankie Fraser or another thug named Roy Hall – would frantically crank the handle. In one session, the electrodes attached to the feet of a victim were failing to deliver the desired level of pain. Charlie Richardson called for some orange squash. He wasn't thirsty – the drink was poured over the prisoner's feet to increase the flow of current. The screams of agony began again.

As the Richardsons' empire grew, their swaggering subordinates often came into contact with their rivals in the Kray gang. At a Christmas party in a club in 1965, fighting broke out after Richardson gang member George Cornell called Ronnie Kray a 'fat poof'. Three months later the feud worsened when the two sides fought with guns and bayonets at a Catford nightclub for which the Richardsons were providing security. An associate of the Krays was shot dead and Frankie Fraser was wounded in the thigh. The following evening, Cornell wandered off his 'manor' and was shot dead in the Blind Beggar pub, Whitechapel, by Ronnie Kray.

The Richardson gang was now in trouble, with Cornell dead and two other leading members behind bars. 'Mad' Frankie had been cleared of the Catford club murder but he and Eddie Richardson were both jailed for five years for affray. The end came when two people talked – one in England, the other at a murder trial 5,600 miles away in South Africa.

In Britain, businessman James Taggart went to police to

reveal that he had been tortured by Charlie Richardson and Frankie Fraser because his company owed a gang member £1,200. Taggart said his two torturers had used fists, boots and a metal pole to beat him for nearly nine hours, only pausing to order themselves some light refreshment of beer and sandwiches. Afterwards the victim, who had been stripped naked and trussed to a chair, was made to clean up the blood-spattered room with his own underpants.

Also in 1965, mineral prospector Thomas Waldeck was shot dead on the doorstep of his home in Johannesburg. Lawrence 'Johnny' Bradbury, a former barrow boy who lived in Peckham, South London, was arrested and confessed to being the getaway driver. But what was Bradbury doing in South Africa and why would he want Waldeck dead? It transpired that Bradbury had known Charlie Richardson since their schooldays together and that he had been leaned on by the gangster to take part in the 'hit'. The murdered man had been Richardson's business partner in a mining company but they had fallen out.

Facing the death sentence at his trial for murder, Bradbury cracked and told the court that Richardson was a major gangland boss, who had made him take part in the murder through fear – at one time holding him over a bar counter while someone slashed his arm with a broken bottle. Bradbury was sentenced to death, later commuted to life. Back in London, Richardson responded with hurt bewilderment: 'I was amazed at what happened at the trial,' he said. 'There is no reason on earth why I should want him killed.'

British detectives flew out to speak to Bradbury in May 1966 and discovered that the murdered man had owed the Richardsons a considerable sum of money. Two months later, in a series of dawn raids, most of the gang's key members were seized in one of the most carefully planned operations in police history – significantly led not by the Scotland Yard chiefs but by a force from outside the city.

The following year, in the first major 'supergrass' trial of its kind, several witnesses came forward on the promise of immunity and new identities. The court heard from so many of Richardson's victims that the trial became known as the 'Torture Case'. The evidence was horrific, plentiful and persuasive. One man told how he had been attacked outside a pub then driven to Camberwell, where Charlie had placed a gun on a table and ordered him to be stripped. Then Frankie Fraser appeared with a pair of pliers. 'He put them into my mouth and started to try to pull out my teeth,' said the witness, 'but he slipped and pulled a lump of my gum out instead.' He was then beaten before Richardson held an electric fire against his genitals. Cigarettes were applied to his arms and chest. He was then wrapped in tarpaulin, 'taken for a ride' and dumped. After all that, Eddie Richardson apologised to him – saying they'd made a mistake and had got the wrong man.

Another victim described how he was invited to Camberwell for a chat about the whereabouts of someone Charlie was hunting. 'He came up and stuck a thumb in each of my eyes and ordered me to take my shoes and socks off,' the winess told the court. 'Leads were attached to my toes and I got some violent shocks.' Richardson then plunged a knife through his foot and into the floor beneath.

Yet another witness told the court that he had had his toes broken with pliers. Afterwards he could hear the screams of another man being tortured. One businessman said when he heard that Richardson wanted to speak to him he fled to

Heathrow but was so terrified that he was unable to form the words to buy an air ticket.

The Old Bailey trial began in April 1967. Despite an attempt to bribe a juror, Charlie was found guilty of grievous bodily harm, demanding money with menaces and robbery with violence. He was jailed for 25 years, while Eddie had another ten years added to his existing sentence. Six other gang members were also jailed. The judge, Mr Justice Lawton, told the Richardsons: 'You terrorised those who crossed your path in a way that was vicious, sadistic and a disgrace to society. One is ashamed to think one lives in a society that contains men like you. You must be prevented from committing further crime. It must be made clear that all those who set themselves up as gang leaders will be struck down, as you have been struck down.'

Like the Kray brothers, Charles Richardson was later to issue an apologia for his crimes. He said: 'The men I was involved with were professional swindlers. I was only trying to get my own money back. I feel sick about the way I have been portrayed. I'm a scapegoat. I got 25 years for grievous bodily harm and not one of them needed an aspirin.'

He was also at pains to deny stories that had emerged about his links with the South African secret service, BOSS – and there was even talk of an attempt to bug the telephone of British Prime Minister Harold Wilson. Richardson told the *Sunday Times* in 1983 that his links with South Africa and the shadowy BOSS had been an embarrassment to the British government. 'I was a pawn,' he said. 'The bigger a criminal the British made me out to be, the more leverage they could apply on the South Africans for having used me. Most business is pressure and blackmail, isn't it? I never tapped Harold Wilson's phone. It could have been done but it wasn't. But people here got very upset about that. They wanted to get rid of me for as long as possible.'

A vociferous campaign for his early release was launched by Charlie Richardson's family and friends, backed by parole board reports stating that he was no longer a danger to society. They fell on deaf ears. In 1980 he walked out of an open prison and went on the run for almost a year, supposedly to campaign for his early release as a 'reformed citizen'. He even dressed up as Father Christmas and handed out presents at a children's party. When he finally gave himself up and returned to prison, he was allowed out on a day-release scheme to work with the disabled.

In 1983, anticipating his early release within a year or two, he was allowed home for a long, quiet weekend to prepare himself for life again on the outside. A preview of the lifestyle befitting one of the biggest ex-crooks in London was revealed when he was collected at the gates of Coldingley open prison, Berkshire, by a Rolls-Royce. He was driven home for a family reunion, then treated his relatives, including his freed brother Eddie, to a champagne lunch. Over the following days, the festivities continued at pubs and clubs in Southeast London, where members of the public thronged the bars to pay their respects to the villain. 'Look around you,' he told reporters. 'I love these people and they love me. I get 200 Christmas cards a year in jail – that's what a bad man I am.'

Charles Richardson was finally freed from prison in July 1984. It was Eddie's turn to go back inside when in 1990 he was given another long stretch for his involvement in a £70 million cocaine and cannabis heist. He was sentenced to 35 years but released after 12. In later years, the brothers who once ruled half a city fell out. They became estranged after Eddie accused Charlie of 'ripping him off' over business deals during Eddie's time in prison.

Charlie Richardson, 78, died in a Kent hospital in September 2012 with his wife and five children at his bedside. He contracted blood poisoning following a gall bladder complaint. His brother Eddie said: 'I haven't spoken to him in years. I can't say he was a good father, but he was a father. He leaves a big family behind him.'

CHAPTER 13

'ONE DARE TOUCH US – WE'VE MORE GUNS THAN THE POLICE'

When the crime empires of the Krays and the Richardsons began to crumble, a power vacuum existed – but not for long. South of the Thames, in old Richardson territory, the Arif family, of Turkish-Cypriot origin, came to prominence. Meanwhile, in North London, the Krays' 'manor' became the stamping ground of the now notorious Adams family.

The Arifs were considered the leading crime family in the capital throughout the late 1980s. Although Dennis, Mehmet, and Dogan Arif – three of seven brothers – had been feared names in the London underworld since the Sixties, the clan first hit the headlines in 1983 when Dogan was acquitted of taking part in a bogus arms deal to swindle the Iranian regime of Ayatollah Khomeini out of £34 million. As author James Morton says in his book, *Gangland International*: 'The British criminal had now seriously entered the international market.'

The Arifs are known to have been involved in racketeering, drug smuggling, armed robbery and murders. In the Nineties, they launched a decade-long gang war with the rival Brindle family, which resulted in at least eight deaths. In September 1990 a Brindle associate, Stephen Dalligan, was wounded after being shot seven times by Ahmet 'Abbi' Abdullah, a Turkish gunmen working for the Arifs. The following March, Abdullah was shot in a South London betting shop by two men. Brothers Anthony and Patrick Brindle were charged with the murder but later acquitted at the Old Bailey. In August 1991 David Brindle was shot in a Walworth pub by two men who burst in and sprayed the bar with bullets, yelling: 'This is for Abbi.' One of the assassins was said to have been hired hitman James Moody, a former Richardson minder who had been on the run since escaping from jail 12 years earlier. In revenge for David Brindle's death, in June 1993 a gunman walked into a Hackney pub, coolly ordered a drink, then turned to Moody and shot him four times.

While they were waging their turf war with the Brindles, the police mounted a huge undercover operation against the Arifs, leading to the conviction and imprisonment of most of the leadership, including various family members.

In 1990 Dennis and Mehmet Arif tried to steal £1 million from a security van near Reigate, Surrey – but the Flying Squad had been tipped off and were waiting for them. The gang were armed with two revolvers, a 12-bore Browning shotgun, a self-loading Colt and a Browning pistol. In the gun battle that followed, Arif henchman Kenny Baker was shot dead as he tried to open fire on officers. Mehmet was shot by police but survived. The two brothers were jailed for a total of 40 years. In 1999 Bekir Arif, known as 'The Duke', was convicted of conspiracy to supply 100 kilograms of heroin worth £12.5 million and was given a 23-year prison sentence.

The family's 'godfather', Dogan Arif, was jailed for seven years in 1990 for conspiring to supply £8 million worth of marijuana. He continued to control the family's operations from inside prison – and on his release, from his £2 million villa in Northern Cyprus, which has no extradition treaty with Britain. Police are certain that, even from abroad or behind bars, it was business as usual for the family. A senior cop who has worked on the Arifs case was reported as saying: 'They are one of the most awesome gangs of villains ever seen in London. You write them off at your peril.'

While the Arifs continued to exert a malign influence from their Southeast London power base, once the domain of the Richardsons, across the Thames in former Kray territory lurked the silently sinister Adams family. Unlike the violent twins, their modern-day successors in the London underworld never sought notoriety. But they got it anyway.

The story of their amazing power emerged when the gang's leader Terence 'Terry' Adams was jailed for seven years in 2007 for the relatively minor offence of money laundering. It emerged then that the charge was the tip of a monstrous iceberg, for the gang was reportedly the most powerful criminal organisation in the UK. The Adams family, or the 'A-Team' as they liked to be known, have been linked to more than 25 murders as well as a string of rackets including armed robbery, fraud, drug trafficking and extortion – racking up estimated profits of £200 million.

The gang was formed around 1980 by Terry, with his brothers Sean 'Tommy' Adams as a brutal enforcer and Patrick 'Patsy' Adams as the finance expert. Of Irish parentage and initially based in London's Clerkenwell, the family (there were 11 siblings in all) expanded from petty extortion of market traders into a vast racketeering and drug trafficking empire throughout the capital and beyond, with links to Spain and South America. By 1990 they were so feared they could 'franchise' the Adams name so lesser criminals could say they were working for them.

When police raided Terry Adams' home near Barnet, North London, in 2003, they found antiques worth £500,000 and tens of thousands of pounds hidden in a shoebox. More money was salted away in secret bank accounts to go with the cars, yachts and a home in Cyprus. Bugs later placed in the house in a unique MI5 operation caught the gangster sounding like Marlon Brando in *The Godfather*.

In one tape, recorded in 1997, Adams was heard discussing a dispute over a missing £50,000. He told a 'financial adviser', jeweller Saul 'Solly' Nahome: 'Let Simon give the geezer a good hiding ... tell him to use the family name.' In another conversation, Adams said: 'When I hit someone with something I do them damage.' In a third, he told how he dealt with a row over cash. He said: 'A hundred grand it was, Dan, or 80 grand, and I went "crack". On my baby's life, Dan, his kneecap came right out there – all white, Dan, all bone and white.'

He wasn't boasting. The Adams family made it to the top of the criminal hierarchy by ruthless brutality against anyone who stood in their way, and although the brothers were never charged with any killings, the culture of violence that developed on the periphery of the gang was frightening, with numerous associates and rivals said to have met brutal ends. At the height of their power in the early Nineties, the Adams family were in charge of most of the cannabis, ecstasy and cocaine coming into the capital. They recruited Afro-Caribbean members to add manpower and used them to murder rivals and informants. They also built up links with Jamaican crack cocaine Yardie groups and with the Colombian cocaine cartels. The money made was laundered through various corrupt financiers, accountants, lawyers and other professionals, and subsequently invested in property and other legitimate businesses.

Terry's favoured laundering method was to set up sham companies, for which he claimed to work as a 'business consultant'. Some of his illicit income was spent on his £2 million home, furnished with antiques and paintings. He spent £78,000 remodelling the garden. He and his wife Ruth bought a series of top-of the-range cars. Their daughter, Skye, was privately educated and they also bought her a Mercedes sports car. Adams himself had a luxury yacht.

But it was not all plain sailing. Patrick Adams had been jailed for seven years for armed robbery in the 1970s. And in 1998 brother Tommy, who had previously been acquitted of handling the proceeds of a bullion robbery, was jailed for seven-and-a-half years for masterminding an £8 million hashish smuggling operation. When a judge ordered that he surrender some of his profits or face a further five years, his wife turned up twice to the court, carrying £500,000 in cash inside a briefcase on each occasion.

Terry Adams himself was finally caged in 2007. He had been arrested four years earlier and charged with money laundering, tax evasion and handling stolen goods but was released on £1 million bail. At the Old Bailey in February 2007 he pleaded guilty to a sample charge of conspiracy to launder £1.1 million

– an offence reminiscent of Al Capone's arrest for tax evasion in the 1930s. Prosecuting barrister Andrew Mitchell QC described him as 'one of the country's most feared and revered organised criminals' and added: 'He comes with a pedigree, as one of a family whose name had a currency all of its own in the underworld. A hallmark of his career was his ability to keep his evidential distance from any of the violence and other crimes from which he undoubtedly profited.' Sentencing Adams to seven years' imprisonment, Judge Timothy Pontius told him: 'Your plea demonstrates that you have a fertile, cunning and imaginative mind capable of sophisticated, complex and dishonest financial manipulation.'

His wife Ruth was also subject to the money-laundering charges but these were 'left on the file'. Ordered to repay £750,000 of legal fees from the trial, the marital home was sold but Ruth was allowed to keep part of the value. When Terry, then aged 56, was released from prison on parole halfway through his sentence in June 2010, he went on a spending spree – in defiance of a court order (known as a Financial Reporting Order) aimed at preventing criminals profiting from hidden riches.

In August 2011 City of Westminster Magistrates heard that Adams had enjoyed, among other treats, a £2,200 gold Cartier watch, a £2,000 gym membership, £7,000 cosmetic dentistry and a £7,500 Harley Street facelift. A scowling Terry was sent straight back to jail to serve the rest of his sentence, completed in 2013.

Despite the frightening reputations of the Arif family and the Adams brothers, Britain today has no single crime czar, godfather, or 'Mr Big'. There is, for instance, no single national organisation that controls the distribution of narcotics, which nowadays are key to the funding of almost every major crime.

In the Northwest and Northeast of England, the supply of drugs is often through bouncers who operate in pubs and clubs. The doormen allow only their own dealers into the premises or are paid a percentage from freelance traffickers. In Newcastle the fierce rivalry between different groups of bouncers has led to a number of shootings. Every city has its own gangs, although none has occupied such a powerful position as, for instance, the legendary Krays. Instead there is a proliferation of outfits across the country controlling small patches of the UK with specialist interests.

Sharing the South London patch with larger families like the Arifs are the crack-dealing gangs. On the other side of the Thames, in Adams' territory, are the North London forgery gangs. Newcastle upon Tyne is traditionally the home of protection racketeers. In the 1920s Sheffield was known as 'Little Chicago'. More recently its gang warfare has been dictated by postcodes, the S3 and S4 gangs becoming locked in a vendetta that resulted in bloodshed on the streets. In Birmingham, the recent threats to law and order have been from juvenile gangland, where guns are a fashion accessory and shootings take place in broad daylight. A drive-by shooting with a machine-gun that killed innocent bystanders at a New Year's Eve party in 2013 shocked the nation. In Glasgow, savage blade attacks typify the street violence. In 2005 the World Health Organisation designated the city the murder capital of Europe. Overall, Scotland has the second highest murder rate in Western Europe (after Finland), the main cause being over-use of alcohol and drugs. Glasgow suffers about 70 killings each year, much of the violence blamed on gangs vying to control the city's drugs trade. The WHO added that 'a culture of young men carrying knives' also played a part.

In Liverpool, the city's fortunes were determined by the docks, which allowed local criminals to play a part on the international stage. Merseyside is one centre where, unlike other provincial towns mentioned above, a criminal 'Mr Big' did emerge in recent years – the infamous Curtis 'Cocky' Warren, whose drugs gang saw millions of pounds passing through the city in the Nineties. Warren is the only known criminal to make it into The Sunday Times Rich List through his very public role as a mastermind of Britain's £2 billion-a-year cocaine business.

Warren, a mugger and robber from the age of 11 and a drug dealer while still in his teens, became by the 1980s a trusted client of Colombian cocaine cartels, Turkish heroin traders and Spanish marijuana suppliers, a reputation that enabled him to get vast quantities of drugs on credit. After a 1993 trial for smuggling £250 million of cocaine, at which he was acquitted on a technicality, he is said to have told Customs officers: 'I'm off to spend my £87 million from the first shipment and you can't fucking touch me.'

As Merseyside turf wars worsened in the mid-Nineties, Warren switched his gang's operations to Sassenheim in Holland. But when Dutch police intercepted £125 million worth of drugs he was smuggling into the country in 1996, he was jailed for 12 years. Three years later, while in Holland's Hoorn prison, he kicked another inmate to death and earned himself an extra four years for manslaughter. In 2005 Dutch authorities charged him with continuing to run his smuggling business from his jail cell but the case was dropped because of insufficient evidence.

Meanwhile, in Warren's absence, gang rivalry was causing chaos in Liverpool. In 2004 the biggest explosions in mainland Britain since the IRA ceasefire were the result of a drugs cartel faction planting car bombs outside two Liverpool police stations in a bid to stop a major investigation. It was a power struggle that resulted in the death of another drugs boss, former Warren associate Colin 'King Cocaine' Smith, who was gunned down as he left a Merseyside gym in 2007.

On his release from prison in Holland, Warren returned to his Merseyside 'manor' to resume his role as 'King of Coke'. He did not stay free for long. In 2009 the 46-year-old faced a Jersey court and was jailed for 13 years for trying to smuggle £1 million of cannabis into the Channel Islands – for him, a minor consignment which he had described as 'just a little starter' to get himself re-established. But even from prison, Warren's tentacles still stretched around the globe, according to police. One officer on the case said: 'Cocky needs only a mobile phone to communicate with his gang on the outside for him to operate a £300 million-a-year smuggling business from his cell.' The retribution that looked as if it would have most effect on the cocky crime lord, however, was a more subtle attack on his empire – using court orders seeking to confiscate all his ill-gotten assets.

Like Liverpool, Manchester has long had a deep-rooted gang culture, often creating national headlines in recent years. The so-called Quality Street Gang ruled the city for three decades from the Sixties through to the Eighties. The QSG, as it became known, tended to get the unjustifiable blame for every crime in the city, although the members of this loose-knit organisation were certainly behind a number of well-executed robberies and major drug importation. The thriving

Manchester club scene was entirely dominated by the QSG. However, the gang's influence began to fade in the mid-Eighties after two violent robbers turned supergrass, leading to a special police squad conducting a string of raids across the region that netted a healthy haul of crooks and booty.

The QSG's successors have certainly not faded from view, for there is nothing secretive about Manchester's scary Noonan family. They court celebrity status and have become reality television stars by openly boasting about their lives of crime. Led by brothers Domenyk and Desmond, the family starred in fly-on-the-wall TV documentaries that revealed their gloating roles in one of the UK's most notorious crime families. (The series *At Home With The Noonans*, presented by investigative journalist Donal MacIntyre, was screened on TV's Crime and Investigation Network.)

There are 14 Noonan siblings who all have names beginning with the letter D. Raised in Manchester's Cheetham Hill area, it is claimed their mother once burned their home down in a bid to move up the council housing list. The Noonans worked as bouncers at the city's notorious Hacienda nightclub. When they had trouble with another gang, they raided the rivals' pub. Wielding shotguns and machetes, they chopped the head off their guard dog off and placed it on the pool table, warning them: 'Next time it will be human.'

The family's burly boss, Domenyk Noonan, has more than 40 convictions for armed robbery, assaulting police, attacks on prison officers, deception, firearms and fraud. While in Manchester's Strangeways jail, he changed his name to Dominic Lattlay Fottfoy – in homage to one of his father's sayings: 'Look After Those That Look After You, Fuck Off Those That Fuck Off You.' When he last appeared gloatingly on television in 2012, the 48-year-old had spent 22 years in prison – and, for that particular 'starring role', he was interviewed behind bars.

Older brother 'Dessie', an enforcer linked to dozens of armed robberies and several murders, was knifed to death in 2005. He was found slumped in the street close to his home in the Chorlton district, having made a last phone call to tell his wife he was dying. Shortly before his murder, aged 46, he appeared in a TV documentary, *A Very British Gangster*, and at first denied police reports that he had carried out 25 murders. But when asked how many people he had actually killed, his brother Domenyk butted in to say it was 24 – before 'Dessie' held up seven fingers indicating that the true figure was 27. 'Dessie' Noonan then boasted ominously: 'No one would dare touch us. If they did there would be serious fireworks. I've got a bigger army than the police. We have got more guns than the police, silly buggers. We're strong and we've got strong people around us. People know that. If they think they can take one of us out and that's the end of it, then they're silly people, fucking silly people.'

However, in September 2012, the violent Noonans were warned they would never again be untouchable after one of the family, Domenyk's nephew 25-year-old Damien, was jailed for abduction, torture and plotting to flood the streets of Manchester with a banned dance drug. He and two accomplices were each jailed for six years and nine months at Preston Crown Court. The court heard that the gang dragged a rival off the street and, in front of bystanders and children, beat, kicked and stamped on their victim. During his hour-long ordeal, their target was threatened with a blowtorch and told he would have his kneecaps shot off. Police found him still alive in the boot of Damien Noonan's car.

It has long been assumed that the sort of violence in which the Noonans and their ilk gloried would have faded from fashion as criminals enter the electronic age, in which money can be made and moved without a crook getting his hands dirty. That theory ignores the surge of foreign-influenced criminals in the UK. Since the late Seventies, as ethnic communities established themselves in Britain, a new type of organised criminal has emerged, the most obvious being the Chinese Triads and the Jamaican Yardies, each of which operates within its own communities, at times extremely violently.

Four separate Triad societies – 14K, Wo Shing Wo, Wo On Lock, San Yee On – are known to operate throughout the UK, with bases in every city where there is a large Chinese community. They make their money from drug trafficking, prostitution, credit card fraud, protection, extortion, gambling, counterfeiting, copyright piracy, money laundering and immigration. Police find it almost impossible to persuade witnesses to come forward because of brutal reprisals and intimidation. But in the Nineties, the problem of extortion, or 'tea money', became so severe within London's Chinatown that restaurant owners called on the government and police for help.

The influence of the Yardies has grown with the boom in crack cocaine, Jamaican gangs now controlling most of the supply in London, Manchester, Birmingham, Nottingham, Leeds and Bristol. Yardies use brutal tactics against rivals and a string of casual shootings, in which innocent bystanders were also killed, has brought their activities shockingly to public notice.

Home-grown young Asian gangs tend towards 'protection', car theft and credit-card fraud. Hell's Angels, who have about a dozen chapters in the UK, have been accused of firearms sales, drug trafficking and extortion. In Northern Ireland, despite the peace process, both Republican and Loyalist terrorist groups still raise funds through robbery, extortion, smuggling, gun running and ownership of drinking clubs.

An investigation by the BBC's prestigious *Panorama* programme in 2013 found a 'ghost community' of 600,000 illegal immigrants, many of whom operate in criminal gangs. It pointed out that whereas once most serious crime was down to indigenous 'firms' like the Krays or the Richardsons, now drug smuggling, people trafficking, prostitution, robbery and fraud are all being carried out under the auspices of gangs whose homelands are overseas. Gangsters from abroad now operating in Britain include, of course, the Italian Mafia, principally involved in financial crime. There are also elements of the Japanese Yakuza, of Vietnamese, Kurdish and Turkish drugs gangs and West African fraudsters.

But it is crimes committed by EU nationals that have more than trebled in just five years, according to *Panorama*. The TV report estimated that more than 1,000 gangs of Eastern Bloc nationals were operating in Britain, netting £30 million a year. The specialities of these migrants are street begging and cashpoint scams, with Romanians responsible for 92 per cent of all ATM fraud in Britain, according to police figures. One of the most notorious examples was Gheorge Banu, who in 2005 was ringleader of a gang who used fake ATM machines to record financial details in order to steal £643,000 from customers' accounts. A judge had already asked for his deportation after a previous conviction. Another Romanian fraudster, Adu Bunu, was jailed for five years in 2008 after he was convicted of cloning more than 2,000 cards, which allowed him to steal more than £1 million. Instead of giving his baby son toys to play with, Bunu presented him with a mountain of stolen banknotes. The cost of accommodating Eastern European crooks like him in British prisons was reckoned in 2013 to be almost £100 million a year – and rising.

In March 2013, authorities in Europe arrested 44 members of a global fraud network in a joint operation against a gang targeting victims in Britain and 15 other countries. Operation Pandora Storm successfully shut down illegal workshops producing card machine theft devices and involved 82 house searches in Romania and the UK.

A 2013 report by Financial Fraud Action, an organisation formed to fight plastic-card crime, reported that ATM thefts had trebled in a year, and that police intelligence suggested 90 per cent of such thefts had been linked to Romanian criminals.

An even greater threat, according to both police and NCIS, is the influx of criminals and vast sums of money from the former Soviet Union. The break-up of the USSR resulted in a sudden decline in law and order. The profits of organised crime there have been fed through the weakly-regulated banking system in the gangs' own countries. And here the once highly respected British financial services sector plays its part. It is conservatively estimated that £5 billion of criminally generated money enters the UK financial system each year. This enables foreign criminals to gain a foothold without stepping onto British soil.

As a senior legal academic, Dr Barry Rider of Cambridge University, warned: 'Official investigations have continued grossly to underestimate the ingenuity and resourcefulness of the British criminal classes. This is particularly so in regard to financial frauds and money-laundering.' And as a Home Affairs

Select Committee report concluded: 'Organised crime raises images of the Mafia or the Krays. But to confine concern to such relatively tightly organised groups would be to miss most of today's criminal activity – which, if more loosely organised, is nevertheless actually more threatening.'

CHAPTER 14

A CHUBBY MOBSTER'S MURDEROUS MAYHEM

Carl Anthony Williams, Australia's most notorious mobster, was about to name names. Fellow inmates at maximum-security Barwon prison learned that he was cooperating with police, detailing gangland killings of which he had intimate knowledge.

On the night of 19 April 2010, Williams phoned his lawyer to claim that he was being taunted by prisoners howling like dogs, a sign that his life was in danger. As the howling echoed throughout the prison, the drugs kingpin put the phone down in terror – and minutes later his skull was crushed with the metal stem of an exercise bike wielded by a fellow inmate.

Thus ended the career of Carl Williams, aged 39, the central character of a spate of rival gang murders that had terrorised the state of Victoria. The mobster had been serving a life sentence, with a minimum 35 years before parole, for ordering a string of contract killings.

Top left: Mafia financial whiz Meyer Lansky.

Top right: Chicago mobster Al 'Scarface' Capone at a football game in 1931.

Bottom left: George 'Bugs' Moran.

Bottom right: Jack 'Legs' Diamond arriving at a New York courthouse in 1931.

© *PA Photos*

Top: Benjamin 'Bugsy' Siegel, the handsome playboy mobster (*left*) and his glamorous one-time girlfriend Virginia Hall (*right*).

Bottom: Rudolph Giuliani (*left*), nemesis of the late twentieth century Mafia, and one of the men he helped to put behind bars, Tony 'Ducks' Corallo, head of the Lucchese family (*right*).

© PA Photo

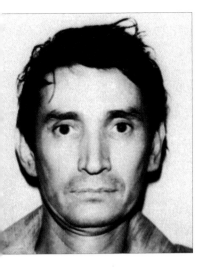
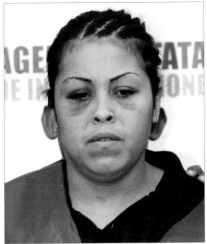

Top left: The birth of all Mexican drug cartels is traced to former Mexican Judicial Federal Police agent Miguel Angel Felix Gallardo, known as 'the Godfather'.

Top right: Maria Jimenez, nicknamed 'La Tosca', leader of a cell of the Zetas drug cartel.

Bottom: The Mexican Authorities frequently parade suspected members of Los Zetas in front of the media: the Army stand with 'El Loco' (*left*) and the 'Piracy Czar' (*right*) in 2012.

© *PA Photos*

Top left: The Richardsons' sinister scrapyard, where Charlie and Eddie brought people whom they suspected of crossing them in the 1960s.

Top right: Billy Hill, self-styled boss of the 1950s London underworld.

Left: Ronnie and Reggie Kray, child boxers before they became London's most notorious gangland bosses of the Swinging Sixties.

© PA Photo

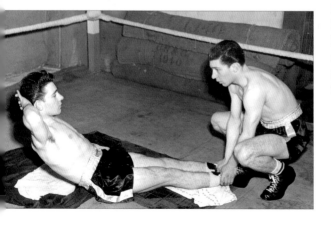

Top left: Members of the Bandidos bikie gang take the coffin of a colleague to a cemetery in Sydney.

Top right: Bandidos arrive in Ruegen, northern Germany, for the burial of one of their leaders.

Bottom: Members of Hells Angels, Nomads, Rebels, Bandidos and Comanchero Motorcycle Clubs in a rare moment of solidarity at the funeral of a bikie.

© *PA Photo*

Top left: Charismatic gang leader Charles Manson at his 1969 trial.

Top right: The bodies of Adolfo de Jesus Constanzo (*inset*), ringleader of a violent drug-trafficking cult, and cult member Martin Quintana.

Bottom: Children play next to graffiti with the initials of drug trafficking gang Comando Vermelho daubed on a favela wall in Rio de Janeiro.

Top left: Colombian drug kingpin Pablo Escobar.

Top right: Daniel 'El Loco' Barrera, the last of the great capos, being extradited from Colombia to the US.

Bottom left: A police officer stands guard next to Luis 'Don Lucho' Caicedo, associate of Barrera with whom he ran the El Dorado Cartel.

Bottom right: Vyacheslav Ivankov, accused of being a godfather of Russian organized crime that included narcotics, money laundering and prostitution and had made ties with the American Mafia and Colombian drug cartels.

© PA Photos

Top left: The National Police Agency holds a meeting on counter-measures against Japan's largest crime Syndicate, the Yamaguchi-gumi.

Top right: Tetsuya Shiroo, the former Yakuza member convicted of assassinating the mayor of Nagasaki.

Bottom left: Former member of Japan's Bosozoku biker gang showing off the team name and motto embroidered on his robe.

Bottom right: Sicilian Mafia leader Salvatore Riina in 1993. © PA Pho

Williams, born in Melbourne in October 1970, grew up in a culture of drug abuse. His elder brother Shane died of a heroin overdose. He married Roberta Mercieca, a convicted drug trafficker, with whom he had one daughter. Williams worked as a labourer and his wife ran a children's clothes shop.

His life of crime started with petty thefts. In 1990 he was fined AU$400 for handling stolen goods and failing to answer bail. Then in 1993 he was sentenced to 150 hours community service for criminal damage. But the drugs trade would become his main occupation.

In the 1990s the local manufacture of illegal pills had become a boom industry, to the extent that police described Melbourne as the 'amphetamine capital of Australia'. The gangs that ran this trade were also involved in protection rackets, nightclubs, prostitution, illegal gambling and armed robbery.

A special police unit, the Purana Task Force, was established to curb the inter-gang violence that exploded across the state of Victoria. And they soon established that Carl Williams was becoming the central figure among Melbourne's mobsters as he vied for power with rival crime families. These included: The Honoured Society, an Italian gang who controlled the city's vegetable markets; the Carlton Crew of Cosa Nostra expatriates; The Dockers, a group of Irish waterfront workers led by the Moran family; the Radev Gang, led by career criminal Nikolai 'the Russian' Radev; The Sunshine Crew led by Paul Kallipolitis, and of course the Williams family led by Carl and his father George.

The period that became known as 'the Melbourne Gangland Killings' began with the 1998 murder of a Carlton Crew chief by hitmen from The Dockers. Drive-by murders, suburban ambushes, workplace executions and even car bombings followed over the next few years. In October 1999 Carl Williams was shot in the stomach in the city's Gladstone Park but survived. Two members of the Moran family were present at the time but Williams told police he had blacked out and could not identify his assailants.

In June 2000 Williams ambushed Mark Moran outside his Aberfeldie home and shot him dead. Between 20 and 30 other shootings followed – putting paid to Nicolai Radev, Paul Kallipolitis and three more of the Moran family – but by now the net was tightening on Williams. In November 1999 Williams, his father and another associate were arrested and charged with the illegal possession of 250,000 amphetamine tablets after a raid on a Broadmeadows drug factory. The pills had a street value of $20 million.

The case never went to court, however, because of corruption allegations against detectives involved in the raid. Williams was re-arrested a year later but again granted bail while a corruption investigation ensued.

So it was not until 2004 that the crime kingpin received his first major jail sentence: seven years for drug trafficking. Two years later he was sentenced to 27 years for the murder of a drug dealer shot outside his home in front of his five-year-old son. The following year he received two 25-year sentences for the slayings of Mark Moran's stepfather Lewis and an associate. He also got a life term for the murder of Lewis Moran's son Jason and a money launderer named Mark Mallia.

Jason Moran's execution took place while in the driving seat of his van, with five young children watching from the back seat. Williams and seven henchmen who took him to a warehouse and tortured him into confessing where some laundered money was buried, kidnapped Mallia. His charred body was found by the Fire Brigade in a wheelie bin.

When in 2010 Carl Williams' skull was smashed with a metal bar, it was seen by many Australians as no more than fitting punishment for the man who had brought so much murderous mayhem to the streets of Melbourne.

The modern-day mobsters who terrorised Melbourne were merely the latest in the city's criminal history. Gangs like The Dockers, led by the Moran family in the Nineties, inherited their violent methods from the thugs who ran Melbourne's waterfront after World War Two. The notorious Painters and Dockers Union operated a Mafia-like system of control over goods that passed through the port. Major earners for the union bosses were hidden shipments of heroin and more recently cocaine. Once safely out of the docks, these illicit substances were passed across the road to the adjacent Melbourne Markets, whose fruit and vegetable vans provided a handy distribution system.

The history of criminal gangs goes furthest back in Sydney, the first urban settlement of the fledgling colony. Groups of dangerous vagabonds flourished in the waterfront Rocks district in the nineteenth century. The most notorious of these was a Mob called the 'Rocks Push' that dominated this area of Sydney from the 1870s to the 1890s. The gang was engaged in running warfare with other larrikin gangs of the time, such as the Straw Hat Push, the Glebe Push, the Argyle Cut Push, the Forty Thieves from Surry Hills and the Gibb Street Mob.

The gang names are evocative titles from an age that was hardly glamorous. And it was hardly surprising that a gang culture existed at that time in Australia's short history, for the country had been a penal colony within living memory, with some convicts still being transported (to Western Australia) until 1868.

Law-abiding Australians in the twenty-first century could be forgiven for thinking that criminals were still among the nation's less welcome imports.

Asian and Middle-Eastern gangs are now active in major cities. Following the fall of the Republic of Vietnam in 1975, refugees arrived in Australia and settled in Sydney's Cabramatta area, forming the 5T gang in the mid-Eighties. One of them was Tri Minh Tran, who rose to become leader of the 5T at the age of 14 in 1989. He was already well known to police. At the tender age of 11, he had been arrested for carrying a sawn-off shotgun, and during the next couple of years had been prime suspect in the murder of two rival gang members.

The 5T became dominant players in the heroin trade in Sydney's western suburbs, especially at street level, and were believed to be involved in the murder of John Newman, the Member for Cabramatta in the NSW State Parliament. Newman had been the target of numerous death threats from Asian gangs but did not seek police protection. In September 1994 he was shot and killed while outside his home with his fiancée, Lucy Wang. A local club owner, Phuong Ngo, who had run against Newman as a rival candidate, was convicted of the killing in 2001.

The murder of Tri Minh Tran in 1995 sparked a power struggle within 5T and by the turn of the century the organisation had broken up, replaced by rival mobs the Four Aces and Madonna's Boys. Although publicly not as violent as their predecessor, the new gangs managed a diverse criminal portfolio, profiting from drug importation and distribution, money laundering, human trafficking, and coercion of women into prostitution.

The scale of the drug trade in Australia was exposed in 2010 with the arrest of 14 members of a Vietnamese Syndicate in Victoria's biggest drugs bust, with the seizure of merchandise and assets worth $30 million. Police had swooped on 14 properties in Melbourne's inner northern and western suburbs following a ten-month Australian Crime Commission investigation dubbed Operation Sethra. In one Carlton apartment, allegedly used as a safehouse, they found a stash of heroin, almost $600,000 in cash and $50,000 in casino chips. A Keilor Downs house yielded 350g of heroin, $345,970 in cash and $54,500 in casino chips. The Syndicate had been using casinos' high-roller tables to launder drugs money. In court, prosecutors claimed that proceeds of the illicit trade had been used to buy property in Australia and Vietnam, including the purchase of a hotel for $2.8 million.

The Vietnamese have no monopoly on organised crime, of course, and since the 1990s it is Middle Eastern gangs that have caused crime-fighters most headaches. They are most prominent in Sydney, where police have been accused of going soft on gangs for fear of being accused of targeting ethnic minorities. But a string of drive-by shootings shocked authorities into action.

The most serious was an attack on Lakemba police station, in Sydney's south-west district, in November 1998. In the early hours of the morning, 17 shots were fired, bullets shattering the plate glass doors, with one punching a hole in a computer screen at head height. The attack was designed to deter cops from investigating a Lebanese gang named DK's Boys, after its founder Danny Karam. Formed only in the late 1990s, this brutal Mob was responsible for one of the bloodiest periods in NSW criminal history – a drugs gang that killed its own boss and set out to rule Sydney's nightlife district, Kings Cross.

Between July and December of 1998, the gang terrorised the inner city, committing four murders, at least 16 shootings and several knee-cappings. Their violence was for monopoly over the cocaine trade that raked in a fortune for Karam but much less for the young runners he used to distribute the drugs. In December 1998 his minions rebelled. As Karam sat in his car outside a Surry Hills safehouse, he was sprayed with bullets by gang members led by Michael Kanaan, a thug with a criminal history that includes three murders and four charges of GBH.

Kaanan was an immediate suspect in the drive-by shooting at Lakemba police station but he and fellow gang member Wassim El-Assaad were found not guilty by a court. A third man, Saleh Jamal, was later convicted. He had jumped bail when first accused of the shooting but was extradited from Lebanon in 2007 and jailed for nine years for another act of violence, the kneecapping of a rival in 1998. It was not until May 2010 that Jamal was found guilty of the police station attack and jailed for an additional 12 years. It was revealed that Jamal was so feared that police had to promise that four witnesses who testified against him would be given new identities. Although fellow gang member Michael Kanaan had been found not guilty of the Lakemba shooting, he won't be coming out of prison. For his other offences, he has three life terms to serve plus an additional 50 years at maximum security Goulburn Correctional Centre.

The final clampdown on DK's Boys and similar thugs came after New South Wales Police set up a special squad to tackle organised crime by Middle-Eastern gangs. The move was prompted by an extraordinary event in Sydney's recent history

– a huge public backlash against Arab gangsters who had been allowed to gain ground as police seemingly overlooked the crime wave, fearful of Internal Affairs investigations for targeting ethnic minorities.

Apparently unaware of growing public fury, the police were taken by surprise when, on Sunday 11 December 2005, a vast crowd gathered at Cronulla, singing and waving the national flag as they 'reclaimed' the beach. The so-called Cronulla Riots grew into a series of sectarian clashes and Mob violence that spread, over the next few nights, to other Sydney suburbs.

The fuse for this popular explosion of rage had been lit a week earlier when a group of volunteer surf lifesavers were assaulted by a band of young men of Arab appearance, with several other violent assaults occurring over the following days. By midday on 11 December about 5,000 people had gathered at Cronulla beach to protest against the spate of violence against locals. But fuelled by drink, some of the protesters turned to violence themselves, attacking a sunbather of Middle-Eastern origin. Similar assaults occurred elsewhere later that day. Retaliatory riots took place that night and on subsequent nights, resulting in extensive property damage and even attacks on police and ambulance crews. The riots forced NSW Premier Morris Iemma to promise a permanent Middle-Eastern Organised Crime Squad similar in vein to an existing Asian Crime Squad.

The riots might have tarnished Australia's image abroad – several countries issued travel warnings – but it also awoke police and politicians to the anger of ordinary Aussies in the face of unchecked gang warfare.

CHAPTER 15

'BIKIES' RIDE OUT...
INTO AN ALL-OUT WAR

On Australia's affluent East Coast, gang warfare has erupted between rival outfits across two states, conducted on high-powered machines by modern-day 'bikies'. The motorcycle-riding old guard is being supplanted by a violent new breed of steroid-pumped, amphetamine-taking young rebels, often of Middle Eastern or Eastern European descent. They shun leathers and straggly hair, preferring designer clothes and 'gansta' bling.

According to police, the feud between rival gangs is now a step away from an all-out war. The epicentre of the current outbreak of violence is Sydney, where there were more than 60 drive-by shootings in 2012 alone. Homes have been sprayed with bullets while children have slept inside.

Tensions in the city go back to an infamous massacre in 1984 when six bikers were shot dead in a pub car park and a teenage girl killed in the crossfire. Since the 1980s there have been about 100 biker killings across the country and 1,000 shootings. The most dramatic was the 2009 murder of a biker in the crowded main terminal of Sydney Airport. The scale of the problem was highlighted by police in a major crackdown on the gun-toting gangs – which, in Sydney alone, resulted in 555 people being arrested and 908 charges laid.

As well as an epidemic of violence centred on Sydney, New South Wales, there have been several related shootings in South Australia, Western Australia and Queensland. The main target of Sydney gangs is the lucrative drugs trade on Queensland's Gold Coast, where in April 2012 a tattooed gunman shot a rival and a woman bystander in the region's biggest shopping mall.

It is estimated there are 35 'outlaw' motorcycle groups in Australia with an inner circle of 3,500 fully 'patched' members and many thousands more followers. Among this assortment of bikie groups, a handful are especially powerful, some of them with international branches. Among them are the gangs profiled below – not a comprehensive list but one that reflects the sometimes typical, sometimes differing aspects, attitudes and histories of these Aussie outlaws.

Pre-eminent are the Bandidos, which the American FBI has identified as one of the 'world's Big Four' outlaw motorcycle gangs, with an estimated 210 chapters in 16 countries. Nineteen of these chapters are located across Australia, comprised of up to 400 members. The Bandidos' international origins go back to 1966 when it was formed by a Texan named Don Chambers. The Australian chapter was not founded until 1983, by Anthony Mark 'Snodgrass' Spencer, its first national president, following a split from the existing Comanchero Motorcycle Club. Its motto is: 'We are the people our parents warned us about'.

The Bandidos is one of the clubs that has actively recruited from ethnic groups in recent years. Wannabe members are called 'hangarounds' and the chapter president decides when they can become a 'prospect'. To become patched members, other full members must unanimously vote them in. Members wear leather or denim vests known as 'cuts' because the sleeves are cut off. The logo is a Mexican bandit.

The Bandidos are probably best known for their involvement in the Milperra Bikie Massacre on 2 September 1984 – a dramatic event related later in this chapter, and one that was a catalyst for significant changes to gun laws in New South Wales. Among the 30 convicted combatants, 'Snodgrass' Spencer took his own life in prison.

Over a decade later, in October 1997, it was thought the club had mellowed but a triple murder of three of the members prompted the National Crime Authority to wrap up a two-year investigation into the Bandidos, code-named 'Operation Panzer', during which two undercover detectives had infiltrated the Bandidos' operations in Ballarat, Victoria. State police raided properties in Ballarat, Geelong, Shepparton and Bendigo, while simultaneous raids took place in New South Wales, South Australia and Western Australia. Police seized more than $1 million worth of drugs – including cannabis, LSD, amphetamines and heroin – and weapons such as an AK-47 assault rifle and sawn-off shotguns. Nineteen people faced charges, including 13 Bandidos in Victoria.

The raids initially weakened the Bandidos but the club continued expanding in regional Victoria by taking over smaller rivals. Inter-gang feuding continued. In October 2008, Bandido member Ross Brand was shot dead while walking outside the gang's Geelong clubhouse. The rival Rebels motorcycle gang was blamed and affiliate John Bedson was convicted of the shooting and sentenced to 23 years in jail.

In New South Wales in March 2009, the 'sergeant at arms' of the Bandidos chapter in Parramatta, Mahmoud Dib, was arrested and charged with firearms offences by police investigating a string of drive-by shootings in Sydney. Police found a .45 calibre semi-automatic pistol that was loaded with seven bullets. Days before Dib's arrest, his family home was the scene of a wild shoot-out between members of the Bandidos and the rival Notorious gang in an ongoing feud with the latter Parramatta based bike group. In Queensland, enemy gangs in the Brisbane metropolitan area targeted Bandidos properties, the most serious incidents being two drive-by shootings at their Woolloongabba clubhouse and a Milton tattoo parlour in June 2012.

Among the Bandidos' main rivals are the Comancheros. Boasting roots that go back to Hispanic-American traders from New Mexico who made their living by dealing with the nomadic plains tribes in that state and neighbouring Texas. One of the oldest and smallest outlaw clubs in Australia, with a New South Wales membership of perhaps 100, its headquarters is in Sydney's western suburbs.

Club positions include president, commander, vice-president, sergeant-at-arms and secretary. Prospective members are 'nominees' and expected to obey the motto: 'If the president says jump, ask how high'. Titles are indicated in patches on the front of a vest or jacket, usually including the letters ACCA (Always Comanchero, Comanchero Always).

For almost a decade after its inception in 1966, the Comanchero Motorcycle Club kept to itself, shielding the public from boozy, violent behaviour within. Their founder,

Scotsman William George 'Jock' Ross, ruled the Sydney-based club with an iron fist, demanding members live by the club's rules of loyalty. It was the violation of this sacred law that sparked Australia's most infamous bikie battle, the 1984 'Milperra Massacre'.

After months of in-fighting, Ross's follower, Anthony 'Snodgrass' Spencer, defected from the Comancheros to start the first Australian chapter of the American group the Bandidos. His defection was seen as treason and on Father's Day 1984 the two bikie gangs squared off in Milperra's Viking Tavern car park, as families visiting a motorcycle swap meet ran for their lives. Four Comancheros, two Bandidos and an innocent bystander, 14-year-old Leanne Walters, died during a ten-minute gun battle that left at least 20 others injured. In a landmark trial lasting 14 months, nine men were found guilty of all seven murders and affray, while 21 others were found guilty of manslaughter and affray. Judge Adrian Roden, who presided over the trial, warned about the dangers of bikie culture. 'As patriotism can lead to jingoism, and mateship can lead to cronyism, so bikie club loyalty can lead to bikie club war,' he said. On appeal, all nine murder convictions were overturned and all those jailed were back on the streets in just over five years.

In the decade following the massacre, tensions between the Comancheros and the Bandidos simmered but both clubs were also careful not to further tarnish their image. However, like most outlaw gangs, the Comancheros continued to be involved in tit-for-tat violence over turf and power. In 1999 the body of Comanchero bikie Peter Ledger was found dumped in the driveway of his ex-wife's house. He had been tortured and beaten to death by Comancheros sergeant-at-arms Ian Clissold for selling a Harley-Davidson motorcycle against club rules. According to court papers, Clissold had been ordered to 'sort somebody out who had been causing a bit of trouble' and the beating 'went a bit too far'.

By the turn of the century, both police and public had become enraged by the growing abuses of the motorcycle gangs. But by then the main outlaw groups had already agreed to curb their public feuding – by creating a mafia-style 'crime Syndicate'. This loose association of the major players was formed not for altruistic reasons but to cut smaller clubs out of the lucrative drugs market. A 2000 police report into organised crime read: 'In early 1994, following the world trend, there was a meeting in Sydney between the major gangs where it was decided informally that the gangs in the country would adopt a similar stance to that already being set up by the rest of the OMCG (outlawed motorcycle gangs). It was agreed in principle that there would be a maximum of six gangs controlling Australia by the year 2000, hence the project being dubbed The Australia 2000 Pact'.

It appeared that the Comancheros may have been locked out of the drug market, as they were not included in the six powerful gangs vying for dominance. But they survived and the feuding continued. In 2001 their western Sydney headquarters in Erskine Park was fire-bombed, causing about $40,000 damage. The following years saw a spate of further fire-bombings, bashings and drive-by shootings culminating in the Sydney Airport shootings in March 2009. This time the feud, between the Comancheros and the Hells Angels, boiled over publicly with tragic consequences.

Comancheros president Mahmoud 'Mick' Hawi and four other members had boarded a flight from Melbourne to

Sydney. Hells Angels chapter president Derek Wainohu also happened to be on board. When the plane touched down, each gang called for reinforcements. The ensuing wild brawl in front of horrified travellers claimed the life of Anthony Zervas, the brother of a well-known Hells Angels member. Zervas suffered stab wounds and massive head injuries when he was attacked with bollards and kicked, punched and stomped on as he lay on the floor of the domestic terminal.

Fourteen people were charged over the murder, including Hawi who, just days after the attack launched a 'damage limitation' exercise, banning the wearing of Comanchero club colours and rallying of motorcycles in a bid to curb the escalating violence. But Hawi's call for calm among bikie gangs was ignored when the airport victims' Hells Angels brother, Peter Zervas, was also murdered – shot as he arrived at his mother's home nine days after the airport brawl. Police found Zervas leaning against his white car, which was left streaked with his blood.

More than two years after the airport brawl, Hawi was found guilty of murdering Anthony Zervas, while the 13 others were found not guilty. In the NSW Supreme Court, Zervas' mother Frederica Bromwich called out, 'No punishment is enough for the loss of my son' as Hawi was sentenced to a minimum of 21 years behind bars. Judge Robert Hulme said Hawi and his Comanchero colleagues had displayed 'a flagrant disregard' not only for the law, but also for the many witnesses 'in whose memories the incident will live long'. As a result of heightening violence, New South Wales Premier Nathan Rees announced that the state police's anti-gang squad would be boosted from 50 members to 125.

While the bikie wars raged on, the Comancheros grew ever

more powerful. Creating new chapters, the club has widened its membership to allow Middle Eastern and Islander members. From their Sydney base they expanded into South Australia and Victoria. The Spearmint Rhino strip club became a known Comanchero haunt in Melbourne, with the gang running three suburban clubhouses. At the helm of the South Australian expansion was former Hells Angel and founder of New Boys street gang Vince Focarelli, who has survived four attempts on his life. His 22-year-old son Giovanni was not so lucky.

The Hells Angels are undoubtedly the best known of all the bikie gangs. 'Treat me good, I'll treat you better; treat me bad, I'll treat you worse,' was the saying of Sonny Barger, founder of the Hells Angels, which was established in March 1948 and has since spread worldwide, with 230 chapters in 27 countries and a membership of around 3,500.

Australia is home to 14 chapters with around 250 members, the first having been granted their charters in Sydney and Melbourne in 1975. Keeping the public in the dark about the murkier side of the cult's activities, they expend a great deal of time and energy cultivating a positive image, raising money for charity and delivering Christmas toys to children. But many see this as a cloak behind which the gang practise a nonconformist and often violent lifestyle.

Violence has certainly bubbled to the surface in recent years, with friction between rival gangs exasperated by the Angels' renewed push into the glittering Gold Coast of southern Queensland. The holiday area's large transient population makes it an attractive destination for bikie gangs wanting to exploit lucrative criminal markets in drugs and prostitution. The NSW Hells Angels also control 'legitimate' businesses –

including gyms, tattoo parlours and a haulage company – and attempts have been made to spread these enterprises north of the Queensland border.

In 2012 two senior Sydney members were reported to be spearheading the campaign, both having been granted 'nomad' status, which meant they no longer belonged to any one chapter but could operate freely in rivals' territory. They chose the Gold Coast resort of Burleigh Heads as the base of the new chapter and settled in what was the heart of Bandido territory, within walking distance of the rivals' clubhouse.

The local police force was immediately on the alert, saying the tentative peace that had existed in the city now looked decidedly shaky. They feared the move would fuel tensions with the other 300 Gold Coast gangs – in particular, Bandidos, but also outfits known as Finks, Uhlans and Lone Wolf Club – that had long fought to stop Hells Angels from encroaching on their turf. 'This will not go down well,' said a police source. 'The Uhlans will probably do nothing but the Bandidos will have to react or be seen as weak.'

The front line switched to South Australia in November 2012 when fighting broke out between members of the Finks and Hells Angels at the 'Knees of Fury' Thai kick-boxing event in Adelaide. Worse was to come within a few days when a business owner in the city's Pooraka district was killed in an execution-style murder. Jason De Ieso, 33, was gunned down in front of terrified witnesses in his spray-painting workshop, where he specialised in hot cars and motorcycles. Finks bikies arrived at the scene soon after the shooting, with one suggesting it was one of their number, or a close associate, who had been killed. The police, in a move aimed at keeping a simmering bikie war off the streets of Adelaide during the

Christmas festivities, barred up to 80 known trouble-makers from every licensed venue in the state. The barring orders were to be for between three to six months and those caught breaching them could face a fine of up to $1,250.

In January 2013 a Hells Angel was killed and another man wounded in a shooting at the offices of a trucking company in Wetherill Park, Sydney. When police looked into the background of the victim, 45-year-old Zeljko Mitrovic, they found that, although he was a senior Hells Angel, he also had a network of friends in the Bandidos. He had been jailed in connection with a double murder in 1998. And he had been one of the confrontational Hells Angels members sent to Queensland's Burleigh Heads to found a new chapter there. The convoluted saga of the bikie gangs' feuding seemed to be summed up in the character of the victim of one single random slaying.

Another long-established Outlaw motorcycle club is the Coffin Cheaters but their approach is very different to the high-profile gangs such as the Hells Angels and Bandidos. Founded in Perth in 1970, the Cheaters' chapters have spread from Western Australia to Victoria, New South Wales and Queensland – as well as Asia and even Norway. They have between 200 to 300 members. To join, applicants must be blood relatives of existing members, hence the patch 'Blood in Blood Out'. For this reason, they have no 'prospects' (probationers). Neither do they claim any state territory, which is why their profile is lower than most of the major gangs.

Their mission statement runs: 'We only claim the ground we are standing on at any given time. We look for no trouble, but our history dictates that we do not hesitate to settle any. We do not want to be featured on TV, Gangland, the History Channel or anywhere else. Leave us alone and we will leave you alone. We do not participate or condone the use of or sale of guns, drugs or any illegal activity of any kind. We have stayed off the radar for 40-plus years'.

Australian Coffin Cheaters are most often seen on long-distance runs. They claim that these extensive road trips, undertaken in relatively small groups, are the sole reason for their existence. They have sought to demonstrate to the public that, although fiercely independent, they are honest and principled. Yet they are known to be one of the gangs that have spread their network into Asia, one of their strongest overseas chapters being in Indonesia. They own businesses in Kuta and have been seen in groups wearing their colours in clubs and bars. Other bikie gangs with a presence in Bali include the Bandidos and Rock Machine.

Nick Anticich, WA assistant police commissioner and the force's top bikie expert, confirmed the Cheaters had a local club in Bali and said gangs were 'expanding aggressively overseas, opening clubhouses and absorbing smaller clubs in other countries'. He added: 'Intelligence suggests local clubs are keen to build connections to some South-East Asian countries where amphetamines and the precursor chemicals needed to make them can be more easily obtained. There is also anecdotal information to suggest the interest in overseas countries may be to facilitate money laundering. The tough laws in Bali around drug dealing we believe provide a significant deterrent for members to engage in that activity – but we are not so confident that this deterrent exists in relation to the chemicals that can be used for drug manufacture.'

The Notorious gang reveal another dimension to bikie culture. It's a recently formed Middle Eastern group that has begun competing with established Australian gangs in a turf war for drug sales. Notorious was established in 2007 in Sydney by Alan Sarkis and senior members of the Nomads motorcycle gang after the latter's Parramatta branch was disbanded. They started to recruit youth of Middle Eastern and Islander backgrounds, aligning themselves with street gangs to boost numbers and challenge rivals, in particular Bandidos, Comancheros and Hells Angels.

Although considered to be an outlaw bikie club, its members don't all ride motorcycles. They are sometimes called 'Nike bikies', for wearing expensive trainers, fashionable T-shirts and being clean shaven, in contrast to the traditional bikie attire. The club emblem features a skull with a turban brandishing twin pistols and the words 'Original Gangster' along with the motto 'Only the dead see the end of war'.

Labelled as one of Australia's most dangerous gangs, the Notorious grew to between 150 and 200 members, with the usual criminal activities of drug trafficking, arms dealing, extortion, prostitution, money laundering, murder, assault, kidnapping and drive-by shootings. However, leader Alan Sarkis has denied any involvement his club may have with organised crime and repudiates feuding with other gangs. He claimed the club had a very strict policy on drugs – even though Notorious members as young as 14 have been charged with possession and drugs supply. In an interview with a Sydney newspaper, Sarkis said: 'Linking us to drugs or the drug trade is way out of line. We want to be acknowledged and respected as a motorcycle club, not as gangsters.' This protestation apparently did not wash with NSW police, who arrested key members in 2012 in a bid to close it down.

While Notorious considered themselves 'new blood', the Rebels are 'traditionalists'. Founded by Clint Jacks in 1969 with Brisbane as its heartland, the Rebels are by far the largest club in Australia, with around 2,000 members in 29 chapters. It also claims to be 'the biggest all big twin Harley-Davidson club in the world'.

The structure of the Rebels hierarchy is revealing as to how these gang leaders and their minions think of themselves. To quote from a membership website, the Rebels ranks are as follows. 'Head' is the boss/leader. When he is around everyone has to listen to him and take orders, and of course he is the most respected and most powerful when it comes to deciding. 'Second In Hand' is the underboss/co-leader, the acting head while the leader is not around. He's running everything in the gang and is in charge of recruitment. 'Rebel' is a made person, a high rank within the gang. This person must be respected by other members; he's adviser for higher ranks and teacher for lower ranks. 'Thug' is a half-made person, a regular member, active and respected, involved in everything in the club. 'Outlander' is a person who is around sometimes, under watch by other members; more respected within the club. 'Scum' is the lowest rank. It's the one who is outsider for the gang. He doesn't have the respect of other members and leaders.

It is significant that followers are proud to be called thugs and others are happy to be known as scum. Perhaps this acceptance of their roles is something to do with their leader, a colourful character named Alessio Emmanuel 'Alex' Vella. Born in Malta in 1954, Vella, who was one of the original founding members of the gang, is an ex-boxer known to his followers as the 'Maltese Falcon'.

Protesting that he was no more than an honest businessman

importing motorcycles, police raided Vella's Sydney suburban home in 1990 believing it to be a methamphetamine factory and found a $15,000 stash of marijuana, for possession of which he served a brief prison sentence. He has also been arrested, but not convicted, on other suspected crimes including stabbing two men and assaulting a woman. In 2008 he successfully sued the ANZ Bank for $2.7 million after accusing his former business partner, Tony Caradonna, of falsifying Vella's signature to re-mortgage three properties, including the Rebels' own clubhouse.

In 2009 Rebels members were the target of 49 coordinated dawn raids across Australia by 250 officers who swooped on homes in Western Australia, Queensland and South Australia. They seized drugs, including methamphetamine, heroin and cocaine, banned weapons, cash, child pornography, stolen vehicles and large amounts of stolen gold. Twenty-seven people were arrested, mainly on drug and weapons charges.

In 2011 New Zealand police announced that the Rebels were attempting to set up a chapter there, and that their introduction was not welcome. Some Australian Rebels members were deported. But not all the publicity surrounding the gang's activities has been adverse. Unexpected scenes were recorded in Canberra in 2012 when 800 bikies descended on the capital for the Rebels' National Run, the biggest in the club's history, with members arriving from as far afield as Western Australia and Tasmania. The 'shock' news was that everyone was well behaved! As the club's Canberra president, Wayne Clark, said: 'We were very happy with the behaviour of everyone. And we were very happy with the police assistance – they were great.'

Whereas gangs like the Rebels are capable of displaying their more peaceable natures, the Gipsy Jokers glory in their notoriety. An Outlaw motorcycle club that was originally formed in San Francisco, California, on April Fool's Day 1956, they are one of the most violent motorcycle gangs in both the US and in Australia, where they have 200 to 300 members. Gypsy Jokers MC Australia, established in 1969, has a high profile in state capitals Sydney, Perth, Adelaide and Brisbane as well as provincial Mt Gambier, Wadonga and Kalgoorlie. The club's colours feature a skull with the thirteenth tooth missing, which corresponds to the thirteenth letter of the alphabet: 'M' for marijuana. Their criminal activities include armed robbery, arson, drug trafficking, fraud, gun trafficking, homicide, identity theft and prostitution.

The Gypsy Jokers continued to hit the Australian headlines. Since the turn of the century, there have been charges of assault, unlawful possessions of large sums of cash, weapons and ammunition and attempted murder. In 2001 member Anthony 'Rooster' Perish and his brother Andrew (a Rebels follower) abducted a jailed drug dealer who was on a work release scheme. Believing the man, Terry Falconer, had previously murdered their grandparents, and also suspecting him of being a police informant, the Perish boys placed him in a sealed metal container, where he was asphyxiated. They then chopped up his body and disposed of it in the Hastings River, near Port Macquarie. It was 11 years before justice was meted out when, in April 2012, the brothers, along with a third man, were handed hefty jail sentences for the murder.

Another high-profile incident occurred in May 2009 when five members of the Jokers were involved in a drug-related shoot-out with another gang in Perth. Two were wounded and taken to hospital, one of whom was club president Leonard

Kirby. But the most savage act of violence and vengeance by the Gypsy Jokers was the infamous 2001 car bomb murder in Western Australia of an ex-detective.

On 1 September 2001 Detective Don Hancock, formerly of the Criminal Investigation Bureau, and also known as 'Silver Fox', was returning from a day out at Perth's Belmont racecourse when a massive bomb, planted under his car at the race meeting, was remotely detonated, killing him and his passenger, a bookmaker friend named Lou Lewis. The murder of the tough, popular detective, with 35 years service in the Perth force, caused a public outcry against the perpetrators, a faction of the Gipsy Jokers bike gang.

The case was not clear-cut, however. As investigations got underway, it became clear that Hancock, the son of a Kalgoorlie prospector, had tarnished his career by persistent allegations (since his death proven true) that he had doctored evidence in a notorious 1988 gold swindle case. It was at first thought that the murder was connected with these allegations but it became evident it was a clash he had with the Gypsy Jokers that got him killed.

After retiring as head of the Perth CIB, Hancock bought a pub in the hamlet of Ora Banda, about 50 kilometres from Kalgoorlie. In October 2000 several Gipsy Jokers entered the pub and badmouthed the barmaid, who was Hancock's daughter, after which he threw them out. Later that night, one of the bikies, William Grierson, was shot dead as he sat around the group's campfire. The Jokers believed Hancock was the killer. So, more significantly, did the police who came to investigate, though they had insufficient evidence to charge him.

Hancock remained free but the Jokers vowed vengeance.

They repeatedly bombed his pub and home, concealing the explosives before one attack in the coffin of a teenage boy. Hancock returned to Perth, where he kitted out his home with a high-tech security system. But the Jokers discovered his visits to the racetrack and, supposedly with the details of the bookie's car leaked by a Transport Department insider, they located it at Belmont and planted a package of ammonium nitrate under the passenger seat. It was remotely detonated by a mobile phone as Hancock drove away with his innocent friend.

In September 2003 a known bikie chief, Graeme Slater, sergeant-at-arms of the Jokers' Kalgoorlie chapter, was put on trial for Hancock's murder. The principal witness, however, was a minor gang member who had turned informant in return for a reduced sentence on another charge. He was deemed unreliable and Slater walked free, although local police superintendent Dave Caporn said afterwards: 'We considered that Slater was a dangerous criminal who committed violent crimes. We considered that he killed Don and Lou, but he's been found not guilty and we have to live with that decision.'

With more operation strike forces across Australia to target outlaw bikie activities, the gangs have been squeezed in recent years. In May 2008 South Australia passed what Premier Mike Rann proclaimed as 'the world's toughest anti-bikie laws'. In a blueprint for other states, the Rann Act put restrictions on clan gatherings, created a new law of 'criminal association' to isolate gang chiefs, made it more difficult for gang members to get bail, and created new offences of violent disorder, riot and affray.

But the dubious glamour of the outlaws on two wheels still attracts followers. Criminologists put the increase in bikie warfare down to recruits from street gangs, the waves of new migrants and young newcomers, often recruited in prison. They usually arrive with existing grudges – against family rivals, other cults and cultures or, all too often, society at large.

CHAPTER 16

TATTOOED AND TERRIFYING : THE KIWI CRIME WAVE

New Zealand's image is one of tranquility – a beautiful, peaceful, civilised country where citizens old and new have merged in an enviable semi-rural idyll. So it comes as a shock that the nation's population of four million has the highest ratio of gang members in the world. A police estimate puts the number of major gangs at 40, with more than 70,000 members.

According to a 2012 police report: 'These gangs have been involved in serious violence, selling and distributing drugs, possessing firearms and offensive weapons, and using intimidation and threatening tactics in pursuit of their criminal activities'. The problem in NZ's largest city, Auckland, has become so serious that some politicians have called for all gangs to be banned.

The gangs are mainly made up of Maori, Pacific and Polynesian communities who moved in the late 1950s from the countryside into the newly prospering towns hoping to find jobs and wealth. Instead, many of them claim, they found themselves socially excluded and deprived of the economic growth enjoyed by their white neighbours.

The result was the rise of ethnic-minority gangs that are now linked to drugs, theft, assault, rape and murder. Increasingly, they model themselves on Los Angeles street 'gangstas' and adopt the violent, drug-fuelled culture that goes with them.

Largest of the rival Maori-dominated gangs are the Mongrel Mob, Black Power, the Nomads, the Tribesmen and the Stormtroopers. They have similar hierarchical structures, with a president and a sergeant-at-arms leading so-called 'patched' members and 'unpatched' recruits.

To earn a 'patch' (a tattoo or a symbol sewn onto a jacket) a recruit must pass initiation tests ranging from drinking urine from a gumboot to committing a serious crime or even doing another member's time in jail. This explains the high percentage of gang members behind bars. Forty per cent of inmates at Auckland's Springhill prison are in a gang. Although only 15 per cent of NZ's population is Maori, they make up 50 per cent of the prison population.

One of the most violent gangs, the Mongrel Mob, was formed in Hawkes Bay in the late 1960s. Its name originated from comments made by a district judge who described a group of men up in front of him as 'nothing but a pack of mongrels.' Their territory is now nationwide, with a network of more than 30 chapters. There is even a branch in Auckland Maximum Security Prison.

Members wear principally red and are recognised by the bandanas they tie around their heavily tattooed faces. The tattoos and matching 'patches' often depict a swastika and their logo is a British Bulldog wearing a German army helmet. They greet each other with a shouted 'Sieg Heil!' Indeed, the Mongrel Mob's ditty runs:

> Born in a brothel
> Raised in a jail
> Proud to be a Mongrel
> Sieg f****** Heil

Pitched battles are a weekly occurrence between the Mongrel Mob and their deadly rivals, Black Power, which formed in the capital, Wellington, in the early Seventies. Their 'patch' of a closed black fist and the identifying blue scarves are now seen nationwide.

Attacks in recent years have included a gang member shot in the face – the retaliatory assault leaving a man stabbed in the face and another in the spine. Drive-by shooting victims have included a man blasted with a shotgun and a two-year-old child killed in crossfire. Gang sex, termed 'blocking', is a particularly vile practice. A teenager was murdered for refusing to have sex with a Mongrel member in 1987. The following year, a young woman was raped by 15 Mongrel Mobsters at one of their conventions.

The growth in drug use is now the most worrying trend, say police. The rituals of gang membership disguise the manufacture of illegal stimulants – particularly smokable methamphetamine (known as 'P' or 'Pure'). Three-quarters of raided laboratories making 'P' have been under the control of the gangs. Money from this illegal trade is laundered through legitimate tax-paying businesses such as nightclubs, massage parlours and sports fishing.

Now the growing threat is from Pacific Islands youth gangs as new generations of young islanders distant from home cultures have grouped together. They particularly model themselves on US style 'gangstas' and favour rap music, flashy jewellery and expensive cars, paid for by aggravated robbery, drug dealing and intimidation. By 2010 there were reckoned to be more than 50 such gangs with around 1,000 members in South Auckland alone, although many have nebulous memberships and exist for only short periods. In addition to these are the street gangs who mark their neighbourhood presence with graffiti. As their names often form three-letter acronyms, they are referred to by the police as 'ABC gangs' – such as Respect Samoan Pride (RSP), Killer Beez (KBZ) and Bud Smoking Thugs (BSTs).

'These gangs could be much worse than those we've seen in the past,' says sociologist Dr Jarrod Gilbert of the University of Canterbury. 'They want the trappings of success, the bling, the cars and fancy clothes – but their means to achieve that legitimately are blocked, and that leads inevitably to more profit-driven crime.'

Back in the 1970s, a government initiative had aimed to reduce youth gang recruitment by helping underachieving students make the move from education to employment and by providing recreational activities outside of school. The money pumped into the schemes may or may not have reduced anti-social offending but it ironically raised the standing of some gangs and made them more attractive to young prospects. The Prime Minister of the time, Robert Muldoon, was a strong advocate of these schemes and took a personal interest in the gangs, giving them a status they had not previously enjoyed. Negative publicity resulted in a sudden decision to close the gang support schemes in 1987 but at Muldoon's funeral in 1992 the regard for the premier from those quarters was revealed when Black Power members performed a haka in his honour.

Throwing taxpayers' money at the problem did not seem to work, as seems to have been proved by the growing power of the oldest established of these gangs, the King Cobras, who are heavily armed and were linked to eight murders over a two-year period during the early 2000s. The Cobras are a Central Auckland based gang who originated from an earlier group, the Polynesian Panthers, in the 1970s. Although mainly of island backgrounds, their ranks are not exclusive of other races. The Cobras' turf stretches from Auckland's Downtown area to the southern suburbs of Mangere and Papatoetoe.

A mainstay of their business surrounded the New Zealand peculiarity of so-called 'tinnie' houses which traditionally sell small amounts of cannabis wrapped in tinfoil, hence their name. Nowadays, however, a variety of other drugs may also be available through them. The houses are frequently run by gangs, using young prospects hoping for membership. If independently run, the 'tinnies' are hit with protection-money demands from the gangs. Busy operations are said to produce a daily income of up to $(NZ) 2,000.

In South Auckland in 2003 a notoriously brutal slaying took place at a 'tinnie' at Mangere, where a 15-year-old youth, Michael Heremaia, helped run the drugs den, hoping to work his way up to becoming a patched member one day. The teenager is believed to have blown the whistle on some of the senior gang members who had been stealing from the kitty – which is why a group of them visited the house with murder in mind. They were going to teach the boy a lesson – 'you don't nark on patched gang members,' said the state prosecutor in the subsequent trial at Auckland's High Court.

The vengeful King Cobras, one of whom had already vowed that he was going to kill someone that night, burst into the house, where they found a man sleeping on a couch, held him down and stabbed him in the chest. When young Michael Heremaia emerged from a bedroom, they turned on him, allowing the first victim to flee. One of the gang then held the boy against a wall while two others stabbed him more than 30 times. The knife went into his neck, his head, his chest and at times plunged right through his body. One of the Cobras, Ofisa Andrew Kopelani, who said he had waited outside in a getaway car until the very end of the slaying, told police that Michael's last words were: 'What did I do? What did I do?'

The sale of joints traded from 'tinnie' houses was on a small scale compared with the major narcotics business that has made the King Cobras so powerful. In 2009 members of the gang were involved in a multi-million dollar methamphetamine drug ring organised within Auckland maximum-security prison at Paremoremo. According to the summary of a police investigation, the drug trade, which involved both importing and manufacturing, was carried out under the noses of – and sometimes with the assistance of – prison officers, allowing some inmates to make fortunes and at least one allegedly to have become a millionaire.

In July 2010 police intelligence revealed that the King Cobras were tooling up with Tasers and specially silenced pistols in what threatened to become all-out war for control of the drug trade on Auckland's streets. This new threat brought in the Armed Offenders Squad, who used tear gas in dawn raids on two homes in their hunt for gang member Daniel Vae, wanted on three arrest warrants. He evaded them but the police uncovered Vae's patch, his methamphetamine gear, a Chinese-made Taser, a bulletproof vest and a specially adapted semi-automatic handgun. Vae was arrested a month later and pleaded guilty to possession of the Taser and firearm.

Following the raid, Detective Sergeant Callum McNeill, of Auckland Central's Organised Crime Unit, warned that the Cobras were increasingly arming themselves, their favoured weapon being a compact semi-automatic. He said: 'They can be concealed in a normal laptop bag so you could carry them around in the streets of Auckland and no one would know they are there. We are seeing them more and more on the streets. These are .22 rifles bought legally with licences. The crooks are getting their hands on them, taking off the stocks, putting on pistol grips, putting on bigger magazines, and cutting down the barrel and putting on a silencer.' Detective-sergeant McNeill said the gangsters were also increasingly tooling up with illegal Tasers that had been smuggled into the country from China, adding: 'We are concerned these guys are armed and ready for action.'

Just how pervasively lawless the New Zealand gangland scene has become was revealed in an Auckland court case in 2012. It ended with four King Cobra members and associates being jailed for kidnapping and assaulting two Asian men after a business arrangement turned sour. During the three-week trial, a jury heard how the underworld saga had begun two years earlier when a Chinese man, known as Han, engaged the King Cobras to track down a debtor, named as Johnson, who owed him $70,000. Han agreed to pay the gang $10,000 for their services.

The Cobras did indeed find their man but Johnson could

not pay Han, so he in turn was unable to pay the Cobras. Han was kidnapped and taken to a house in the Auckland inner suburb of Kingsland, where four of the gang were waiting: Joe Tie, Robert Logo, Ross Romana and Ofisa Andrew Kopelani, the driver in the 'tinnie' house slaying of 2003.

Fearing he was going to be tortured, Han rang a friend pretending he was raising the money but, speaking to him in Chinese, he was really calling for help. The friend, Jack Wu, sought out another senior Cobra to act as an intermediary and the pair turned up at the kidnap house. This enraged the gangsters, who punched and kicked Wu and Han. Ross Romana ordered them to pay half of the money the next day while Robert Logo, armed with a knife, threatened to cut off their fingers.

Again pretending to be raising funds from friends, the pair once more managed to raise the alarm. A Chinese speaking police officer called their mobile phones and they were able to explain their predicament and give their location. Police then arrested the men. In a subsequent court case, they were found guilty on multiple charges including kidnapping, blackmail and wounding. Romano, described as the 'leader of the pack', received the longest sentence, of six years. Kopelani, whose role in the group was said to be 'at the lowest end of the spectrum', was jailed for three.

Despite the involvement of Asians in that last case, Asian gangs have had a relatively small presence in New Zealand. But simply by their ethnic closeness and secretive nature, the full extent of their growth has probably been overlooked. By the late 1980s, police had identified Triad-type gangs – Hong Kong's Wo Group, Sun Yee On and Malaysia's Ah Kong – with involvement in drugs, prostitution, fraud, counterfeiting and extortion. A more recent arrival was the Big Circle Gang from China, who brought with them expertise in protection rackets, extortion, gambling, counterfeiting, kidnapping and drug trading.

Recently law enforcement agencies have detected alliances between the Asian gangs and home-grown gangs offering their services as 'enforcers'. But it is the introduction of international bikie cults that is likely to prove a more obvious cause of criminal behaviour, mainly inter-gang warfare. In 2011 Rebels Motorcycle Club patches were first sighted on bikies around the North island and the following year the Bandidos formed a chapter in Auckland.

It is this prominent display of gang membership that is often blamed for the public perception of the country as being in the grip of a crime wave. Since the turn of the century, the number of reported crimes has actually dropped, but visible and seemingly unchecked gangsterism has persuaded many New Zealanders to continue to believe that violent crime is out of control. Ministry of Justice statistics claim that the total number of offences in 2012 was the lowest since 1989, and gave the lowest crime rate per head of population since before electronic records were maintained.

A study undertaken for the Justice Ministry back in 2003 found that 83 per cent of New Zealanders held 'inaccurate and negative views about crime levels in society and wrongly believed' that crime was increasing. A more recent study in 2009 by Dr Michael Rowe, from Victoria University, found an overwhelming public belief that crime has got worse despite New Zealand's murder rate dropping by almost half in the previous 20 years. Reflecting the depth of this perception, only 57 per cent of citizens reported feeling 'safe'. This means that despite New Zealand's international standing as a peaceful country with a high level of human development, its inhabitants feel no more secure than citizens of countries like Iran (55 per cent) and Lebanon (56 per cent) and not much safer than those in African countries such as Nigeria and Uganda (both 51 per cent).

In the knowledge that it is the high-visibility of gang crime that has fuelled this public feeling of insecurity, attempts to suppress the gangs had been stepped up since the Nineties, with the strengthening of laws specifically aimed at them. In 2008 a special police unit, the Organised and Financial Crime Agency of New Zealand, was established to disrupt their activities. The following year, the Criminal Proceeds (Recovery) Act gave police greater powers to seize the proceeds of crime and use the money to fund further policing efforts. At a local level, Wanganui District Council in 2009 passed a controversial bylaw banning gang patches in public places throughout the city, a move studied closely by other towns. It opened a debate about the wider ban on patches – and the potential for action from gangs against the law, like that taken against Wanganui councillors.

Moves for a national ban on patches on public premises were stepped up in late 2012 following an outcry about gang intimidation following the killing of a Rotorua schoolboy whose uniform was a colour associated with a rival gang. The death was in the constituency of National Party MP Todd McClay, who launched a campaign for the prohibition of patches from schools, hospitals and other government and local government buildings.

The MP sponsored the Prohibition of Gang Insignia in Government Premises Bill with the aim, he said, of 'focussing on the harm and significant misery that gangs cause throughout all communities and all parts of New Zealand'. He told Parliament: 'People feel intimidated by what they stand for and they feel intimidated every time they see them in their WINZ office [Work and Income centre], in council offices and in schools and hospitals around this country. I believe this bill is one step towards banning gangs in New Zealand. To gang members I say this: if you go to government premises with a patch, your government will not serve you. Instead, a policeman will and he will want to talk to you about all the nasty things you and your criminal mates have been involved in.'

Another MP, Richard Prosser of the NZ First party, was even more forthright, describing gang members as 'weak, sick, fat, unfit, drug-addled retards'.

The bill specified gangs that would be covered by the ban – including the Hells Angels, Mongrel Mob and Killer Beez – and said others that emerged with 'a common name or common identifying signs' that 'collectively promote, encourage, or engage in criminal activity' could be added.

In ensuing parliamentary hearings, the police union gave official backing for the ban. Police Association president Greg O'Connor said that in many places around the country the gang presence is 'real on the most vulnerable people'. He added: 'This bill, while no panacea, does give another tool to show that those who are vulnerable, those who are likely to be intimidated, will see gang members scuttling, [or] taking their patches off before they go into buildings.' However, the legislation was still being argued about a year later, with claims that it was inconsistent with the country's Bill of Rights.

How does New Zealand's gang culture look to an outsider – perhaps someone who has grown up with the notion of this beautiful land being the epitome of rural tranquility and peaceability? A BBC journalist, Rebecca Kesby, presented a shock report on the NZ phenomenon in 2012. She says: 'It's not just the swastika tattoos, the missing teeth and scars that make these men – and some women – frightening. The list of serious crimes many of them have been convicted of is also terrifying. And those are just the crimes the police know about.'

It is ironic that the Maoris, the indigenous people of New Zealand before the white man arrived two centuries ago, were persuaded to end their warlike ways and become settled and peaceful. The British governor, signing a treaty with their traditionally tattooed leaders in 1840, promised: 'We are one people.' Sadly, that can no longer be taken for granted.

CHAPTER 17

BLATANT PUBLIC FACE OF JAPAN'S UNDERWORLD

In Japan today there are two principal types of gang that make up the nation's criminal underworld: the old and the new, the Yakuza and the motorbikers.

The Yakuza can be traced back over 400 years and supposedly originated from Robin Hood-like characters who defended their villages against roving bandits. But their days of protecting the weak against the strong are long gone. They may be less well known than the Italian Mafia or the Chinese Triads but the Yakuza form one of the largest organised crime groups in the world. It is now a mighty and entrenched criminal network with 100,000 members operating in 22 crime Syndicates and raking in billions of pounds a year

Of the 22 Syndicates, the Sixth Yamaguchi-gumi is the largest and most infamous. It is named after its founder Harukichi Yamaguchi, with its origins tracing back to a loose labour union for dockworkers in Kobe before World War Two. There are 55,000 members divided between 850 clans directing their criminal operations that, from their headquarters in Kobe, have spread to Asia and the US. Over recent years, their oyabun (leader) has been Shinobu Tsukasa, also known as Kenichi Shinoda, whose leadership has seen an increase in membership and initiated expansion into Tokyo, traditionally not Yamaguchi turf. Yamaguchi-gumi are among the globe's wealthiest gangsters, bringing in billions of dollars a year from extortion, gambling, the sex industry, guns, drugs, real estate and construction kickback schemes. They are also involved in stock market manipulation and internet pornography.

The second largest Syndicate is the Sumiyoshi-kai, sometimes referred to as the Sumiyoshi-rengo, with an estimated 20,000 members divided into 277 clans. It differs structurally from the Yamaguchi-gumi, working more as a federation where the chain of command is more lax. Its current oyabun is Shigeo Nishiguchi.

Rare death sparks flew when the Sumiyoshi-kai felt their traditional base in Tokyo threatened by Yamaguchi-gumi expansion into the capital. One morning in January 2007, a senior Sumiyoshi member was shot in his car in Tokyo. Within hours the offices of the Yamaguchi-gumi were fired upon in retribution, bullets shattering the doors and windows. Police arrested two members of the Sumiyoshi-kai and raided their offices in a bid to halt the escalating gun violence, which is rare on the streets of Tokyo.

The Inagawa-kai is the third most significant Yakuza grouping with approximately 15,000 members divided into 313 clans. It has its base in the Tokyo-Yokohama area and was one of the first Yakuza families to expand its operations outside of Japan. Most of its members were drawn from the bakuto (traditional gamblers), and illegal gambling has long been the clan's main source of income. It has also expanded into such fields as drug trafficking, blackmail, extortion, and prostitution. The death of its oyabun, Yoshio Tsunoda, in February 2010 marked the beginning of what may be a shift in the structure of Japan's criminal community. Although he had been the group's formal head since only 2006, he had overseen a strategic shift towards greater cooperation with the Yamaguchi-gumi. According to security experts, his death destabilised the Japanese underworld, presaging another period of gang warfare.

Many Yakuza members can be recognised by their full body tattoos or missing fingers. Known as irezumi, the tattoos are still often 'hand poked' – that is, the ink is inserted beneath the skin using non-electrical, hand-made and hand-held tools with needles of sharpened bamboo or steel. The procedure is expensive and painful and can take years to complete. They are normally only displayed when playing cards (usually the traditional game of oicho-kabu, similar to blackjack) as they tend to keep them concealed in public with long-sleeved and high-necked shirts. When new members join, they are often required to remove their trousers as well and reveal any lower body tattoos. Yubitsume, or the cutting of one's finger, is a form of penance or apology. Upon a first offence, the transgressor must cut off the tip of his left little finger and give the severed portion to his boss. Sometimes an underboss may do this in penance to the oyabun if he wants to spare a member of his own gang from further retaliation.

As previously mentioned, public displays of violence are rare in Japan but an exception was when the Yakuza were linked to the cold-blooded killing of the mayor of Nagasaki, Iccho Itoh, in 2007. Police arrested Tetsuya Shiroo, a senior member of a gang affiliated to Yamaguchi-gum, who supposedly admitted the shooting. His motives, which have remained unclear, may have been political. Shiroo was sentenced to death but was subsequently spared the hangman's noose.

To curb their growing control not only of 'orthodox' criminal activities but also high-level corporate fraud, Japanese authorities are trying to choke the Yakuza's existence by starving them financially. A new law, the Organised Crime Exclusion Ordinance, was implemented in late 2011 to force businesses to stamp out Mob links, direct banks to safeguard against money-laundering, cut off loans to Mob-related companies and deny bank accounts to anyone with known gangster ties. In January 2012 Tokyo became the last of Japan's 47 prefectures to introduce local laws aimed at depriving crime Syndicates of income by targeting firms that knowingly do business with them. One of the main targets is the nation's multi-billion-construction industry, where the Yakuza have long run rampant by pressuring developers to pay 'protection' money or using front companies to win lucrative contracts. But their influence now reaches into almost every area of Japanese business life.

Ironically, one of the difficulties in clamping down on the Yakuza is their seeming openess. They are not an entirely secretive society like their counterparts, the Mafia and the Triads. Yakuza organisations often have an office with a plaque on the front door displaying their name or emblem. Yakuza leaders are the subject of fan magazines and their exploits are turned into comic books. The Inagawa-kai, for instance, exists openly, with offices opposite Tokyo's Ritz Carlton hotel. The death of Yoshio Tsunoda, who led the Inagawa-kai from 2006 to 2010, was widely featured in weekly magazines and Kazuo Uchibori, the de facto leader of the group, has done interviews with yakuza fanzines and appeared on their covers.

Yakuza often take part in local festivals, where they carry a shrine through the streets proudly showing off their elaborate tattoos. One Yakuza family even printed a monthly newsletter with details on prison inmates, weddings, funerals – and murders. The Syndicates also make very public their 'good works' for the community. It's good PR, of course. Their most publicised charitable efforts were in reaction to the Kobe earthquake in 1995 and the 2011 Tsunami, after which Yakuza families, particularly the Yamaguchi-gumi based in Kobe, mobilised to provide disaster relief. They hired helicopters and ran truck convoys of aid.

Until recently, the majority of Yakuza income came from protection rackets in shopping, entertainment and red-light districts. But drugs are the more recent growth industry. Owing to a strange moral code, some Syndicates, including the Yamaguchi-gumi, forbid members from trafficking. Others, like the Dojin-kai, are heavily involved, with arrests of their drug mules being made across the Far East. Other Syndicates are involved in people trafficking, usually of impoverished Filipino girls brought to Japan to work as prostitutes.

Yet because of their history as a legitimate feudal organisation and their support of extreme right-wing political groups, the Yakuza are though of by many Japanese as no more than a part of the nation's establishment. Disturbingly, an opinion poll found that one in ten adults believed that the Yakuza should be allowed to continue to flourish. Which, despite the government's latest crackdown, they do with impunity.

However, in 2006 in the city of Kurume, around 600 residents who had become exasperated at an explosion of gang warfare launched a court case to drive the gangsters out of town using a civil law that allowed them to challenge businesses that 'infringe on the right to live peacefully'. Kurume's problems began in May of that year when a long-time Dojin-kai boss, Seijiro Matsuo, suddenly announced his resignation. This sparked a war of succession with splinter group Kyushu Seido-kai that erupted in a busy shopping centre housing Dojin-kai's headquarters. Innocent families were caught in the crossfire as gunmen sprayed bullets from AK-47 rifles. In the most notorious episode in the feud, a gangster high on amphetamines walked into a hospital and pumped two bullets into an innocent man mistaken for a rival. The attacks snapped the patience of locals, who launched the legal action. The liberal *Asahi* newspaper reported: 'This is the first time that citizens have tried to expel the head office of a designated gangster organisation.' It praised efforts 'to drive the Yakuza into extinction' – though sadly, in the end, Japanese law favoured the rights of the Dojin-kai as tenants over the rights of the citizens of Kurume to live in peace.

Whereas the Yakuza stretch back 400 years to an age when they were considered folk heroes defending poverty-stricken peasants, the other principal style of Japanese gang has no pretensions to history or ideology.

'Motorbike gangs have been a huge part of Japanese culture for over half a century, threatening the obedient status quo of the nation since the end of World War Two,' according to international gangs expert and author Tony Thompson in his best-selling book *Outlaws*. He adds: 'Legend has it that the early gangs were formed by fearless Kamikaze pilots not "blessed" with the opportunity to die for their emperor and desperate for new kicks. They were joined by thousand of antisocial young punks who customised their bikes, removing the mufflers to maximise the ear-splitting revs, earning them the nickname kaminarizoku (thunder tribes).'

These motorbike gangs are different from most others around the world – in that they tend not to feud with one another but are wholeheartedly dedicated in a war against authority of all kinds. Their enemies are the police and the Establishment. They are known for their fast, reckless driving and complete disregard for traffic laws, and have been causing mayhem in inner cities since the 1950s. In many ways, these members of the 'thunder tribe', all under the age of 20, were no more than rowdy, rebellious youths who were too immature to be allowed to become members of Yakuza.

According to Tony Thompson, the main biker group, Bosozoku, reached peak strength following riots in Toyoma of 1972 and in Kobe four years later, when 10,000 youths joined forces and rampaged through the streets, burning, stoning and destroying anything that appeared to be connected to law enforcement. A cameraman who got in the way of a sabotaged police truck was killed. The happenings of that day gave the biker gang its name – bosozoku translates as 'violent running tribes'.

During their heyday, Bosozoku, with their instantly recognisable and intimidating leather, militaristic dress style, would strike fear into neighbourhoods. Their uniforms (tokko-fuku or 'special attack uniform') generally consisted of a jumpsuit, military jacket worn open with no shirt, baggy trousers and tall boots. To complete the look, the uniforms would be adorned with slogans, gang symbols, flags, and even swastikas. Favoured accessories included wrap-around sunglasses, hachimaki headbands, surgical masks and pompadour or punch-perm hairstyles. Female members, although less common, would dress in a similar manner, often sporting high-heeled boots, excessive make-up and dyed hair.

Reaching their peak in the Eighties and Nineties, the modern Bosozoku were infamous for their individual reckless driving and their intimidating mass rallies. Their bikes would be uniquely adapted, usually from a normal Japanese road bike but combined with parts of American choppers and British café racers. They would gather in their hundreds and drive slowly though suburbs, blocking traffic and waving imperial Japanese flags while creating an uproar with their illegally modified mufflers. As well as creating havoc on the roads, there were regular attacks on people and property, with gang members wielding metal pipes, baseball bats, swords and even Molotov cocktails.

The fightback against the biker gangs began in earnest in the 2000s. 'Anti-Boso' laws were introduced that took the worst elements off the streets, literally. By 2011, membership had fallen from an all-time high of 42,510 in 1982 to a new low of 9,064. With legislation giving powers to clamp down on groups of reckless bikers, the police were arresting 100,000 of them on traffic violations every year. The Bosozoku are hardly recognisable today. Gone is the tokko-fuku attire. To the shame of their violent forerunners, modern Bosos may well be seen on scooters – and some even wear safety helmets!

With the decline of the Bosozoku, bikers have looked overseas for fresh influences. The American Outlaws

Association in 2006 launched their first prospective chapter in Okinawa and by November of that year Japan had its first fully patched Outlaw chapter. While the old school were reduced to riding scooters, the new wave rumbled in on modified Harley-Davidsons.

CHAPTER 18

THE TRIADS A CHINESE MULT-BILLION POUND TAKE-AWAY

One of the largest, richest and most secretive criminal organisations on the planet owes its success to the British Empire. For when the so-called 'Black Societies' of mainland China were purged by the Communists 60 years ago, they found a new homeland in colonial Hong Kong. There in Britain's Far Eastern enclave, they flourished under the dreaded title given to them by their English-speaking hosts … the Triads.

This 'Oriental Mafia' grew so quickly with the help of the colony's corrupt cops that membership in Hong Kong alone topped 300,000. And having taken over the tiny island's underworld, the Triads exported their terror trade to Chinese communities across Southeast Asia and into the Chinatowns of Britain, Australia, New Zealand, Canada and the United States. A US report on the Triad exports to North America and

Europe of 2007 estimated annual profits from narcotics at $200 billion and human trafficking at $3.5 billion.

The roots of the Triads are found in secret societies that date back to 1000 BC when monks led peasant bands to fend off raids by despotic warlords. Over the centuries, these gangs became power brokers within the Chinese dynasties and played a part in deposing the Last Emperor in 1911. The 'Black Societies' thrived in the warlord era of the Twenties, Thirties and Forties, particularly in the trading city of Shanghai, where the Green Gang had 100,000 members. When Japan invaded, they fought with the Republican forces of Chiang Kai-shek to defend their province. However, when the Communists of Mao Tse Tung came to power in 1949, a tough crackdown on the gangs forced many to emigrate to America and Europe, as well as to the Portuguese gambling enclave of Macao and, of course, to Hong Kong. There the English term 'Triad' became used to describe the triangular symbols on the banners of one of the clans, the Heaven and Earth Society.

Triads flourished in the colony, partly due to the corruption of the British police force there through the Sixties and Seventies. When a clean-out finally came, one officer, when questioned about the number of his colleagues who were taking bribes, said: 'Well, the force was 8,000 or 9,000 strong and I definitely knew of two people who weren't. One was religious and the other was just crazy.'

The Triads are still strong in Hong Kong, with a tighter band of 100,000 members controlling an empire worth billions of pounds. The city's largest and most powerful Triad family, Sun Yee On, with 40,000 members, has massive influence over local businessmen and party officials. Its mysterious, unnamed 'Dragon Head' (Triad equivalent of

'Godfather') is officially listed as one of the 50 most powerful people in Asia. The Triads are also strong in the island gambling haven of Macao. On the eve of the Portuguese colony's handover to China in 1999, a bloody power struggle raged over the illegal betting trade. Its scale can be gauged by the 2010 trial of a casino manager who admitted laundering $450 million through Hong Kong bank accounts.

The blatant manner in which the Triads operate can be judged by the activities of two 'Dragon Heads', one based in Hong Kong and the other in Macao, and both at the height of their powers at the time of the colonies' handover to China. Cheung 'Big Spender' Tze-Keung, Hong Kong's most notorious gangster of the Nineties, once described his Macao opposite number Wan 'Broken Tooth' Huok-koi as 'a genius – he thinks I'm a genius, and I think he's a genius.' The two men played baccarat together and 'Broken Tooth' once lost more than US$1 million, saying: 'I was really mad. But I put the cards in my pocket and went home to bed. That way, I didn't have to kill him or do anything to him, because I wasn't really the loser.'

'Big Spender' Tze-Keung was a small-time crook running gambling dens until he and his gang hijacked an armoured truck carrying $20 million in 1991. He was caught and sentenced to 18 years but got out after three on a technicality. He held such a grudge against the police for his experience in jail that he rammed a bulldozer into a prison guardhouse and firebombed the house of Hong Kong's Secretary of Security. After hitting the big time, he travelled the world playing at major casinos, reputedly once winning $2 million in a single night in the Philippines.

In the 1990s, Tze-Keung was implicated in the kidnapping

of two of Hong Kong's richest tycoons – Walter Kwok, one of the world's richest property developers, and Victor Li, son of the billionaire Li Ka-shing – who were held for ransom of $US 210 million. Although Kwok himself refused to discuss the abduction, *Newsweek* magazine reported that his family paid a ransom of $US 80 million. The other abductee, Li, was reportedly kept in a refrigerator with air holes drilled in it. A ransom of $US 125 million ($1 billion Hong Kong dollars) was paid to free him.

One Hong Kong police official told *Newsweek*: 'Big Spender's goal was to hold people in such a state of terror that all he had to do was threaten them over the phone and they'd pay him big money.' An intensive police operation finally cracked his gang and 30 members were arrested. Their boss was captured in mainland China.

In December 1998, he and several accomplices were found guilty of kidnapping and smuggling explosives. They were executed within hours of being sentenced to death. Hong Kong does not have the death penalty, and it was the first time that a Hong Kong resident had been executed under Chinese law. Later, another 32 gang members were rounded up and a cache of weapons, explosives, along with millions of dollars in cash and luxury cars were seized.

Tze-Keung's opposite number in Macao, Wan 'Broken Tooth' Huok-koi, was also at the height of his powers when caged in 1998. As leader of the 14K Triad, an estimated 10,000 members regarded 'Broken Tooth' as their boss and referred to him as 'Big Brother'. He had made most of his money by controlling the VIP suites for high-rollers at Macao's casinos. He was also an inveterate gambler himself.

'Broken Tooth' so gloried in his infamy that he financed a

gangster film about his life, titled *Casino*, and promoted it with a Hollywood-style publicity campaign. He was arrested in May 1998 after a bomb destroyed a car belonging to Macao's chief of police and he was given a 15-year prison sentence. Several of his top lieutenants were also jailed.

With the liberalisation of the communist state in recent years, the Triads have re-exported their criminal enterprises back into mainland China and handle most drugs sales, money laundering, extortion, prostitution, gambling and contract murder in Shanghai, Tianjin, Shenyang and Guangzhou. 'Gang-related crime has become a threat to social stability and to the economy,' the Public Security Bureau reported. 'Murder, rape, robbery, kidnapping, assault ... they dare to do anything.'

The number of those involved in organised crime on the mainland has risen from around 100,000 in the mid-Eighties to between 1.5 and 2 million today. The 120 million-strong floating population of migrant workers make ready recruits.

An indication of Triad presence is the increasing number of bound bodies pulled from the Yellow River and other Chinese waterways. One of Henan Province's worst gangs roamed the countryside unchecked for 13 months, robbing farmhouses and killing 76 people. Seven members of the gang, including its leader who personally cut the throat of 40 victims, were captured and executed in 1999.

Some Triad families have close relations with the police – and are even organised by them. In 2007 ten members of a police-run gang in Inner Mongolia were jailed for robbery, rape, gambling and bribery. But the Triads have spread much further afield, from Australia to Canada, and have added to their traditional money-making through drug trafficking, loan sharking, prostitution, smuggling, gun-running, and extortion by adding high-tech crime such as credit card fraud and computer software piracy.

One of the cruellest of the fast-expanding Triad trades is the export of humans. It is perhaps the least welcome aspect of China's extraordinary trade boom with the Western world. The group name for the many gangs who smuggle people abroad is 'Snakeheads'. For anything up to £50,000 they will transfer their human cargo to wealthier countries, principally in North America, Europe, Australia, Japan and Taiwan.

Snakeheads, mainly based in China's Fujian region, hide their living cargo in trucks and on ships. Subtler means include the use of false passports and visas, bribing of officials, fake business delegations and tour groups. But the object of people trafficking is not always to provide their customers with a better life abroad. Young women are often kidnapped to become labourers, mistresses or prostitutes.

One of the most ruthless people smugglers was a slightly built, 5ft tall woman from the Fujian region named Jing Ping Chen – but known to police across Europe as 'Sister Ping'. Before her arrest in 2003, she was believed to have smuggled more than 200,000 men and women into the EU and her organisation was linked to the deaths of 58 Chinese, whose bodies were found in an air-tight truck entering Britain through Dover Docks in 2000.

According to the National Criminal Intelligence Service, organised immigration crime is one of the fastest-growing areas of the underworld. At least 600,000 people enter the EU illegally each year and around 80 per cent are brought in by Snakehead gangs. The smuggling industry is as lucrative as the drug trade – across Europe the business is worth £8 billion – but for those who are caught the penalties are far lower.

According to Britain's National Criminal Intelligence Service, 'the top Snakeheads control the facilitation process from end to end. They have contacts in China, the UK and at every stop along the route'.

'Sister Ping' was seized by Dutch police and brought before a Rotterdam court who heard that she had earned at least €15 million from her criminal activities. She was sentenced to three years in jail and fined €10,000 for offences related to human trafficking, with the judge declaring that she was 'the leader of a structured group focused on smuggling human beings'.

Despite Ping's conviction, the trade in human cargo shows no signs of slowing down. But worse is the trafficking of children. A 2011 report by China's Public Security Ministry said that police had rescued 'tens of thousands' of abducted children and women. It highlighted one raid against a gang trafficking Chinese women to African nations for prostitution. In 2012 Chinese police broke up major child trafficking gangs across 15 regions and provinces, including Hebei, Shandong, Henan, Sichuan and Yunnan, arresting 802 smugglers and freeing 181 children.

Child-trafficking has become a serious problem in China because of the country's one-child policy and lax adoption laws. A traditional preference for male heirs in China has created a thriving market for baby boys – and, equally tragically, a surfeit of unwanted baby girls.

The Snakeheads who trade in human misery are closely allied to the Triads. The violent enforcer for 'Sister Ping' in Holland was her boyfriend, who happened to be head of the local 14K Triad. But despite the violence revealed in the 'Sister Ping' court case, the trend nowadays is otherwise. As with the Mafia in America, a new generation of Dragon Heads are adopting a discreet policy of conducting their criminal operations behind the scenes. They have done well out of China's free-wheeling cowboy capitalism but criminologists can only guess at the scale of their multi-billion operation, for the Triads are now a secret society who really do keep their secrets.

Wherever their tentacles spread, the rules of secrecy are maintained by elaborate initiation ceremonies that can last six days and can involve ritual dances, blood-letting and Taoist and Buddhist prayers. The Hung clan, for instance, welcomes new members with a 200-year-old initiation oath that goes, in part: 'I shall not disclose the secrets of the Hung family, not even to my parents, brothers or wife. I shall never disclose the secrets for money. I shall die by a swarm of swords if I do so.'

CHAPTER 19

OLYMPIAN TASK FOR SHANTY TOWN GANGBUSTERS

They were momentous decisions that sent a nation into a frenzy of excitement. On 30 October 2007, Brazil won its bid to host the World Cup in 2014. Two years later, on 2 October 2009, the country's bid for the XXXI Olympiad was also a success. But among the massive challenges that the two awards created was one that the host nation did not shout about … how, in a few short years, could it repair its reputation as one of the most criminalised countries in the world?

For every 100,000 citizens, Brazil suffers 24 homicides, with countless muggings, kidnappings, robberies and endemic gang violence. So to save the nation's reputation in advance of the two great sporting events, a major clean-up was ordered not only of the thousands of crime-ridden favelas, or shanty towns – almost 1,000 of which blight Rio de Janeiro alone – but the other criminal elements that have given Brazil this bad reputation.

Today almost three million Brazilians live in these favelas, so it was no straightforward task for the police in their campaign to regain control from the gangs that have long stalked the overcrowded townships. In preparation for the forthcoming sporting events, the government established more than 25 'pacification units', as favela-based police operations are called. Under the pacification programme, elite police units enter violent slums and evict the heavily armed drug gangs that have held sway for decades. Once security is established, officers trained in community policing move in and set up permanent outposts in the slums, mostly near tourist destinations or in areas seen as geographically key to World Cup and Olympic venues. The next step was for city officials to bring in basic services that many of the shanty towns had never received, such as sewage, legal electricity and rubbish collection.

Rocinha, the largest favela in Brazil, was pacified by the authorities in November 2011. This sprawling shanty town in the hills of Rio de Janeiro straddles a main highway that connects the main Olympic venues to wealthier neighbour-hoods, including the famous towns of Copacabana and Ipanema. Rocinha was established in the 1930s when landless rural workers began occupying the area, which was once a coffee plantation. They found low-paying jobs but no housing, so they set up makeshift settlements. With a further influx of economic migrants fleeing poverty in the north-east of Brazil during the Fifties, the count at the last census in 2010 showed a population of 70,000. Like all of Rio's favelas, Rocinha has suffered from decades of neglect. In the absence of state intervention, gang leaders moved in. During the Eighties it became home to former left-wing politico-criminal gangs that seized control of the entire community, enforcing their rule with an iron fist and enriching themselves through the drug trade, the area becoming the city's leading cocaine distribution point.

Rocinha's oldest gang is the Comando Vermelho or CV (Portuguese for 'Red Command') founded in 1979. Its original members came from Candido Mendes prison on the island of Ilha Grande. They were a collection of ordinary convicts and left-wing political prisoners who were members of the Falange Vermelha (Red Phalanx) that had fought Brazil's military dictatorship. Although most of the original leaders are dead, it is still a force to be reckoned with. The Comando Vermelho's main rivals are the Terceiro Comando, a criminal organisation founded in 1990, and the Terceiro Comando Puro that split from the Terceiro Comando in 2002.

But Rocinha's largest gang is the Amigos dos Amigos (Friends of Friends) which, before the recent police intervention, enjoyed unchallenged control of the shanty town. ADA was formed in 1998 by a senior gangster in Comando Vermelho, who had been expelled for organising the murder of another member. Two of the ADA's most notorious leaders were neutralised by police – one killed, one jailed. Erismar Rodrigues Moreira, also known as 'Bem-Ti-Vi', was shot dead in 2005, ending his command over a militia that he armed with gold-plated weapons. The second ADA leader to be removed was Rio's most wanted criminal, Antonio Francisco Bonfim Lopes.

A notorious drugs baron, Lopes, who was known simply as 'Nem', had been one of Bem-Ti-Vi's bodyguards. When his boss was killed, he grabbed his chance to move up the pecking order. He eliminated the gang's obvious successor and took control of the Rio slums with an army of 200 rifle-toting soldiers. The sale of some 200 kilos of Bolivian cocaine a month brought Nem an annual fortune of around £35 million. Rivals and informants were eliminated, their bullet-riddled corpses burned in improvised crematoria in the rainforest around the slum. Running his business from a luxurious three-storey mansion in Laboriaux, a neighbourhood at the crest of Rocinha, he earned a reputation for his ecstasy-fuelled raves at which a number of Brazilian celebrities put in appearances. When police began a concerted crackdown on his empire, Nem went undercover. He used steroids and plastic surgery to alter his appearance and in 2010 even tried to fake his own death, paying a doctor to sign a bogus certificate stating that he had died of kidney failure.

'Nem' was finally arrested in 2011 after being found hiding in the boot of a car when it was stopped at a roadblock. His four-strong entourage told police they were diplomats from the Democratic Republic of Congo and tried to invoke diplomatic immunity before offering a hefty bribe. 'Why is the car boot shaking?' asked a suspicious cop before Lopes was found curled up inside.

'The gangs are being dismantled,' said Rio state police chief Alberto Pinheiro Neto announcing Nem's capture. As his squads handed out pre-paid mobile phones to residents to encourage collaboration, he added: 'This is a good moment for law-abiding citizens who want to see their children living in peace to pass information on where criminals, guns and drugs are hidden.'

So, after half a century of shocking neglect, Rocinha and other 'pacified' slums are benefiting from new development and investment. Although the drug trafficking gangs still have a toe-hold on the favelas, the Brazilian military police call the shots. It is a mixed blessing for the residents who once complained about the total absence of any government authority; they now decry police corruption and abuse, and there is a cynicism about an initiative that sometimes seems more driven by real estate speculation than a concern for residents. But most, including even some in the drug gangs, agree that the makeover is worth trying. Rocinha has now become a destination to which the fashionable and the well-to-do drive to in their bulletproof cars for a taste of the nightlife and kind of parties that the Amigos dos Amigos once used to host.

Before the 'clean up' that now sees the shanty towns permanently patrolled by police armed with machine-guns keeping watch in front of squad cars with flashing lights, Brazil had deserved its reputation for violence. In 2003 a record 51,043 murders took place. However, during the late 2000s the crime rate has been on a firmly downward trend. In 2008 Rio de Janeiro registered the lowest homicide rate in 18 years, while São Paulo now records 'only' about ten homicides per 100,000 population – down from 35.7 in 1999.

The worst outbreak of violence in Brazilian history began in São Paulo on the night of 12 May 2006. It was an escalation of a war between the state authorities and the city's largest criminal faction, Primeiro Comando da Capital (First Command of the Capital). Street rioting began after 700 jailed members of the PCC were transferred to tougher prisons. Extraordinarily, the PCC had for years been run with seeming impunity from within the São Paulo state penitentiary system by means of cell-phones, female visitors, lawyers and corrupt officials. The authorities had hoped that by moving the leadership to higher-security facilities, ties would be severed to gang members on the outside. But using their smuggled phones, the PCC inmates managed to coordinate violent protests that left dozens dead, both inside and outside the jails.

In unprecedented scenes throughout Brazil's capital city, heavily armed gangs hijacked and torched more than 60 buses, Molotov cocktails were thrown into banks and police stations came under attack from Mobs wielding machine-guns, machetes and home-made bombs. A police officer was shot in the head while he dined at home with his wife. Prisons saw some of the worst violence: mutinies broke out in 71 of the 105 jails in the state, with uprisings spreading to a further 70 jails including those in the neighbouring states of Parana and Mato Grosso do Sul. More than 120 hostages were taken. Meanwhile, street violence spread to the interior and to towns along the coast, including Guaruja, Santos and Cubatao.

By the third day of rioting, the authorities ordered schools to be closed, transport halted, shopping centres and office buildings shut down. When the situation was finally brought under control, the casualty list read like the aftermath of a military battle: military police 23 dead and 22 wounded, state civil police seven dead and six wounded, municipal guards three dead and eight wounded, prison guards eight dead and one wounded, prisoners 17 dead, civilians four dead 16 wounded, suspected criminals 79 dead.

The casualty list added up to 141 dead and 53 wounded – proving beyond doubt the power of a single gang, the PCC, to disrupt an entire nation. One of the prisoners transferred and placed in solitary confinement in the Presidente Venceslau penitentiary was Marcos 'Marcola' Willians Herbas Camacho, the leader of the PCC and the man who allegedly ordered the attacks. Marcola, who began his career as a pickpocket at the age of nine, became known as 'Playboy' because of his lavish lifestyle but was confined to jail in 1999. In 2006 Camacho testified before a congressional committee, admitting that he was the leader of the PCC but saying that his own life was now 'worthless' since his successor had already been chosen. He told the committee that the PCC was organised 'like a web made up of a comprehensible organised hierarchy' that stretched across the state and was still successfully run from behind prison walls.

In a separate interview at the time, Camacho revealed the key to the gang's strength, saying: 'You are the ones who are afraid to die; I am not. Here in prison you cannot come and kill me, but I can arrange for you to be killed out there. We are a new species.'

Primeiro Comando da Capital was founded in 1993 with the purported goal of fighting oppression inside the São Paulo prison system and avenging the 'murder' of prisoners during the so-called Carandiru Massacre of October 1992 when São Paulo State Military Police quelled an uprising at the Carandiru Penitentiary, killing 111 inmates. The massive 2006 riots were not the first spate of violence attributed to the PCC. In 2001 the gang enacted a multi-prison rebellion and in 2003 murdered an unpopular judge.

It seems that the PCC are the gang that the authorities cannot quell. The soaring number of attacks on police is usually blamed on PCC members. At least 95 police officers were killed in São Paulo in 2012 compared to 47 the previous year. In early 2013 rioting again erupted, this time in Santa Catarina, south of São Paulo, a normally tranquil state famed for its tourist resorts. Between 30 January and 5 February, there were 54 violent attacks, including numerous assaults on police stations, the burning of buses, trucks and cars. The attacks were clearly coordinated from within prisons and, according to the state's public security department, were prompted by the transfer of inmates from a jail in the state capital, Florianopolis, to another some 180 kilometres south in the city of Criciuma. The prison switch followed the indictment of nine people, including four prison gang leaders accused of conspiring to gun down a prison guard outside her home in October 2012. Local media revealed another reason for the violence – a video filmed at another prison showed guards abusing inmates. In one scene, prisoners were forced to kneel naked while guards attacked them with pepper spray and rubber bullets.

According to a police intelligence report by the National Public Security Secretariat, the gang has seen a surge in membership, with a presence in 21 of Brazil's 27 states. Strongest expansion is in the São Paulo region, where 135 of the 152 prisons are said to be effectively under PCC control. Consequently, the gang's resources have also soared, the report putting its annual income from drug trafficking alone at $32 million. The main trade is in cocaine from neighbouring Bolivia and Paraguay.

The PCC is now so strong that its leaders believe they can negotiate at government level to achieve political objectives. Their success in forcing Brazil's leaders to make concessions to end the 2006 riots has encouraged their ambitions. This has also boosted recruitment. New members swear a 16-point manifesto advocating social and political change in Brazil. They then routinely pay dues of anything between $25 and $225 a month, which are supposedly used to support the families and pay legal fees of their imprisoned comrades.

And these prisons are full. In 2010, there were 473,600 people incarcerated in Brazilian jails, with drug-linked crime responsible for 85,000 of the total. Prison conditions generally are harsh and unsanitary. There is severe overcrowding, with six to eight prisoners often crammed into a cell meant for three. The alleged ill treatment by staff, plus prisoner-on-prisoner violence, makes membership of a gang virtually necessary for survival. A 2003 Amnesty International report accused the Brazilian prison authorities of brutality, saying: 'Torture and ill treatment continues to be widespread and systematic in police stations, prisons and juvenile detention centers. In some cases, police reportedly used torture as a method of extortion'.

Outside the prisons, police corruption remains a problem particularly in Rio. Dozens of police officers have been arrested on suspicion of working for drug traffickers and selling guns, while a senior officer was suspected of ordering the murder of a judge who investigated police corruption. The army has also been tainted with accusations of illegality when called in to support the police. In 2008 units were deployed to Rio's Providencia area, where three locals were held by a band of 11 soldiers 'for disrespecting authority'. The men, aged 17, 19 and 24, were taken to a neighbouring shanty town controlled by a rival drug gang. Their bullet-ridden bodies were later found on a rubbish tip. The deaths brought hundreds of Providencia residents onto the streets, burning buses and throwing missiles at army patrols.

Another headache for the Brazilian authorities in encouraging visitors to the country is the nation's highly publicised spate of kidnappings, particularly plaguing São Paulo. Recent figures revealed that one person was kidnapped in the city every two days.

The most infamous abduction was that of Marina da Silva Souza, mother of Brazilian football's brightest young hope, Robson de Souza, better known as Robinho. After seizing her in November 2004, the kidnappers first demanded that Robinho stop playing football – seen as a psychological ploy to show that they were in control. They next sent him a videotape of his mother, in which the kidnappers could be seen cutting off her hair. 'I don't know what sort of people do these things,' said Robinho. 'They are people with evil in their hearts.' After 41 days in captivity, his mother was finally freed after the soccer star paid a ransom equivalent to £43,000. This encouraged the kidnap gangs: five other footballers' mothers were kidnapped during the next five months.

The kidnap gangs are so well organised that a special anti-abduction task force, the Divisao Anti-Sequestro, operates in São Paulo. Since its formation in 2002, when about 30 victims were being held at any one time, it has had some success. Recently, however, the gangs have tended to change their tactics. The new style of abduction is known as 'express kidnapping'. In 2012 there were more than 250 of these lightning seizures in greater São Paulo. Victims are generally grabbed in shopping malls, grocery stores or car parks, and then held only long enough for them to empty their bank accounts via ATMs.

The other worrying growth in organised crime is far away from the crowded cities. Piracy in the Brazilian Amazon made international headlines in 2001 following the murder of Sir Peter Blake, a world-famous sailor and environmentalist who was shot by a gang known as the 'Water Rats' while on a research expedition to the region.

The 53-year-old New Zealander had returned from dinner

with his crew in Macapa, a remote city on the northern bank of the Amazon delta, when a gang of eight men arrived at his boat by rubber dinghy. Blake reached for his gun and shot one of them before the robbers opened fire. He himself died from gunshot wounds and two members of the crew were injured.

Local boatmen say attacks are now common in Pará, a sprawling, sparsely policed region that has led to the formation of an anti-piracy task force. Eight boats and 50 officers are deployed but Pará's security minister admitted that tackling river crime in such a vast region – the 'largest hydrographic basin in the world' – was not easy.

The gangs' modus operandi is typical of the attack in June 2011 on a passenger vessel by gunmen who approached in small motorboats, firing into the air. Once aboard, the men threatened to execute some of the 140 passengers, including children. All survived but one passenger said: 'They had pistols, revolvers – lots of weapons. They said they would kill us. They put guns to the children's heads and even said they would cut the fingers off those who didn't hand over their rings. It was two hours of terror.'

During the same year, a sailor was killed when two boatloads of pirates raided his vessel as it transported fruit to Belém. Two other sailors were shot by pirates in the neighbouring state of Amazonas. Police blamed a gang known as the 'Black River Pirates'. Larger ships carrying 300 passengers have also been targeted.

Another ongoing gang problem that Brazil is tackling with urgency is human trafficking – both for prostitution and for forced labour. According to the United Nations Office on Drugs and Crime, sex trafficking of women occurs in every Brazilian state. Women, often from the state of Goiás, are found in forced prostitution abroad, principally in Portugal, Italy, Spain, the Netherlands, Switzerland, France, Germany, the United Kingdom, the United States and Japan. The trade is linked to foreign organised criminal networks, particularly from Russia and Spain. Brazilian women and children are also subjected to forced prostitution in neighbouring countries such as Argentina, Venezuela and Paraguay.

Human trafficking for forced labour has been a problem in Brazil since the late Sixties when farming began expanding into Amazonia, the contemporary slogan being that this was 'a land without men for men without land'. While the land-grabbers got rich, however, the poor farm workers lured there by the traffickers found it a land without hope. It is estimated that there are now 25,000 to 40,000 people working in conditions of slave labour in the agricultural sector. Thousands of slavery cases are reported annually to the authorities, usually associated with plantations growing sugar cane and African palm. Both are used for production of ethanol, billed as an environmentally friendly alternative to petrol. On sugar plantations, the cutters harvest much of the crop by hand using machetes.

A 2007 raid on an estate in Pará that produced 13 million gallons of ethanol a year uncovered more than 1,000 indentured labourers working 14-hour days. The authorities described the three-day raid as 'Brazil's biggest attack to date on debt slavery'. The practice involves luring poor labourers to remote locations, where they rack up increasing debts to the plantation owners, who charge exorbitant prices for food and the horrendous accommodation.

There is a saying: 'Sadly in Brazil, everything that's bad becomes a fashion'. The nation's gangsters have long tended to prove this true. Brazil's formidable organised crime networks have been on the warpath and have increasingly targeted symbols of the state. In the year following the transfer of the Olympic mantle to Brazil at the end of the London Games in July 2012, more than 100 police officers were killed, at least 40 of them clearly victims of summary executions.

Frustration exploded onto the streets again during spring and early summer of 2013. As well as Rio de Janeiro and Brasilia, more than 80 cities saw an estimated one million Brazilians clash with police in violent demonstrations against what was seen as governmental corruption. Increases in taxes and public transport fares, plus neglect of local services, incited rioters who blamed the financial crunch on the need to pay not only for the World Cup but for the Olympics, too – the nation's pride in these global events being soured by the suspicion that the beneficiaries were more likely to be big business, bent administrators and the burgeoning web of organised crime than the average Brazilian struggling to make ends meet.

The challenge of hosting the 2014 FIFA World Cup and 2016 Olympics gave governmental and law enforcement agencies the determination to tame the country's gangster culture. But an appraisal of the task ahead came from Jose Junior, the head of AfroReggae, a favela-based cultural organisation in Rio that works closely with the government to remove youths from gang life. He said: 'If this doesn't work, if the country doesn't manage to change by 2016, I think it will take another 50 years to solve these problems.'

CHAPTER 20

THE MOBSTERS WHO MAKE MILLIONS OUT OF THE 'SLUMDOG' KIDS

India's racketeers are specialists in the vilest of trades, child slavery. It's a shameful scandal, as portrayed in the movie *Slumdog Millionaire*, but the reality is far, far worse. As many as 200,000 children a year fall into the hands of slave traders. Many are sold by their poverty-stricken parents for as little as £11. Others are reported missing and are never seen by their families again, kidnapped by gangs who sell them on to their employers. In recently released statistics that shame the booming super-state, there are estimated to be 10 million child slaves working in India's factories and backstreet sweatshops.

Thousands of illegal placement agencies flourish in cities like Delhi where there is a high demand for youngsters. 'Employers are specifically looking for children because they are cheaper, complain less and can be exploited,' says the Indian human rights agency Shakti Vahini. 'Some parents might be willing to lose their children to the agencies in the hope that they'll live a better life in the city and send back money but instead what the children go through in the cities is nothing less than hell.'

India is under increasing pressure to make a start on stamping out the trade in youngsters. In June 2012 the US State Department labelled India as a child-trafficking hub and urged the country to bring its laws into line with UN conventions. The country's labour minister has promised a new law banning child labour, but that will not happen swiftly, according to Gursharan Kaur, wife of Indian prime minister Manmohan Singh, who warned: 'It is the poor who send their children to work due to their low earnings. If their own families do not understand the child's rights, who will?'

It is not only youngsters who fall victims to these racketeers, however. In the stream of migration from countryside to city, many women are also being trafficked for bonded labour, forced marriages and sexual exploitation. A previous US State Department report spelled it out: 'India is a source, a destination and a transit country for men, women, and children trafficked for the purposes of forced labour and commercial sexual exploitation. Internal forced labour may constitute India's largest trafficking problem; men, women, and children in debt bondage are forced to work in industries such as brick kilns, rice mills, agriculture, and embroidery factories. Some estimate this problem affects tens of millions of Indians. Those from India's most disadvantaged social economic strata are particularly vulnerable to forced or bonded labour and sex trafficking. Women and girls are trafficked within the country for the purposes of commercial sexual exploitation and forced marriage. Children are also subjected to forced labour as factory workers, domestic servants, beggars, and agricultural workers'.

Child-snatching is one of the many illegal roles of specialised gangs dealing in kidnapping, smuggling and the contract killings of rival businessmen. They offer their services openly around Mumbai's busy JJ Hospital Junction. These gangs, making millionaires out of their 'Slumdog' victims, are thought to have more than 10,000 heavies as full members.

A 'refinement' by Indian gangsters – already mired in drugs, extortion, gambling and prostitution – is 'apartment theft'. Because of the extreme housing shortage, tenants are leaned on to move out of rent-controlled buildings so that they can be replaced with higher-paying occupants. Other areas targeted by Indian mobsters are the building industry, plantations and horticulture.

Bollywood is not untouched. Half the money ploughed into India's massive film industry is said to have come from crime. Stars of the screen have traditionally been quite open about their criminal connections – often the only way of ensuring their next roles. And some of Mumbai's crime 'dons' are as famous as the superstars themselves. One of the most infamous, Dawood Ibrahim, head of the crime Syndicate 'D-Company' which is heavily into the movie business, has had films loosely based on his activities, with titles like *Black Friday* and *Shootout at Lokhandwala*.

Ibrahim, born in 1955, began his career of crime in Mumbai working for the Karim Lala gang in the 1980s, exploiting sweatshop labour in the fast-expanding textiles industry. He then switched his headquarters to Dubai, where he formed his D-Company, initially dealing in the ship-breaking industry, which swiftly became a conduit for smuggling arms, explosives and contraband into India. He set up real estate and betting businesses and was believed to control much of the 'hawala' system – the commonly used unofficial way of transferring money without raising the attention of official agencies.

In March 1993, 13 bombs exploded across Mumbai, killing 257 people and injuring 800. The first blast was beneath the Stock Exchange, followed by others over a three-hour period across several districts of India's financial capital. The powerful explosives had been packed into cars and scooters, under a manhole cover and in a hotel room. Some brokers and investors were trampled to death in the stampede. Leaders of the city's notorious 'Tiger Memon' crime family were subsequently found guilty of what was widely seen as an act of Islamist terrorism. Among them was Sanjay Dutt, a Bollywood star accused of buying and supplying weapons. The prosecution claimed that the prime motive for the attacks was revenge for the loss of homes and property during previous anti-Muslim riots. And it was claimed that the main organiser and financier of the operation was Dawood Ibrahim – by then on the run and labelled India's 'Most Wanted'.

The gangster-turned-terrorist is believed to have forged links with al-Qaeda and to have also provided the logistics for a further murderous attack on the city. In November 2008 Islamist terrorists were responsible for 12 coordinated shootings and bombings across Mumbai, killing 174 people. The only terrorist who was captured alive confessed that Ibrahim's organisation had provided arms and explosives to the Pakistani-based militants who carried out the attacks. In 2011 Ibrahim, now living in Pakistan, was placed at Number Three on the Forbes list of 'World's Top Ten Most Dreaded Criminals'.

Long before Dawood Ibrahim rose to infamy via Bollywood, organised crime was rife in Indian cities. The earliest example of what is now considered the 'Indian Mafia' can be traced back to the 1860s when what was known as the Thanevale Gang, based in Mumbai, were responsible for over 80 per cent of all opium and heroin trafficking. Narcotics are still the Number One illicit trade in India, which has the dubious distinction of being the world's largest legal grower of opium. Quite apart from the criminal diversion of the home-grown product, the country has become a major transit point for heroin entering from the major Asian opium growing areas, the Golden Triangle and the Golden Crescent, on its way to Europe.

There are some ruthless men in the Indian underworld but some of the women are just as tough. Quite a few of them have made a mark in the world of crime, according to authors Hussain Zaidi and Jane Borges in their 2011 book, *Mafia Queens of Mumbai*. 'Women in the Mumbai underworld are dangerous, strong-willed and unlike their male counterparts, more focused and determined,' says Borges. One of them, Ashraf Khan, became a gang leader of some influence after her husband was killed – some reports say in a police shoot-out, others by Dawood Ibrahim's men. After his death, Ashraf transformed herself from happy housewife to cold and calculating killer. Calling herself 'Sapna Didi', she seduced another Mumbai gangster, Hussain Ustara, who tutored her in the use of weaponry, from a Mauser pistol to an AK47 assault rifle – and even her feet, for he taught her kick-boxing too.

The couple then muscled in on Ibrahim's businesses, causing him severe losses. Once they almost got killed while looting one of Dawood's drug consignments smuggled across the border with Nepal. Ashraf and Hussain were hijacking a batch of donkeys laden with contraband when Dawood's men surrounded them. She kicked one of the animals and escaped in the ensuing mêlée. Ashraf and Hussain realised that they would never be safe as long as Dawood was alive, so plotted to kill him very publicly while he watched a one-day international cricket match at Sharjah. Dawood got wind of the plot – probably through an informer within Ashraf's gang, says author Zaidi – and four hitmen burst into her home in South Mumbai. She died of 24 stab wounds. Hussain was also eliminated, while on a visit to one of his mistresses near Agripada in 1998.

The book *Mafia Queens of Mumbai* created a publishing sensation because it revealed that so many of India's crime 'kings' over the last couple of decades have actually been 'queens'. The authors identified a woman, as yet unconvicted of any crime, as being head of a massive prostitution racket in Mumbai's smart Malabar Hill district. The clients tended to be politicians or rich businessmen and their sons – who would be secretly filmed and then blackmailed. The book also identified Mumbai's 'wealthiest drugs baroness'. She ran the trade with her daughter, both of whom have been cleared 12 times on charges of heroin dealing. An oddity of her gang is that she employs eunuchs as bodyguards.

The veteran female who wielded most power over the city, however, is named by Hussain Zaidi as Jenabai Chavalwali. During India's prohibition days in 1939 she amassed enormous wealth as a bootlegger. She was the elder sister of notorious gangster Haji Mastan and became aunt to the young Dawood Ibrahim. So trusted was Jenabai that she was able to forge a landmark peace pact which brought together the Ibrahim and Mastan gangs with their sworn underworld enemies, the Pathan gangsters led by Karim Lala. Together they formed a force that, she declared, 'even the government will stand no chance against.'

One of India's most wanted criminals was Archana Sharma, girlfriend of gang leader Om Prakash, also known as 'Babloo'

Srivastava. She is still on the 'wanted' list because no one knows whether she is dead or alive.

Hailing from Lucknow, the university-educated Archana moved to Dubai in 1993 and opened a fashion store. There she met 'Babloo' Srivastava and together they travelled the world – until Interpol caught up with him in Singapore and he was extradited and jailed. Archana followed him back to India and had a brief stint as a Bollywood actress – appearing in a movie titled *Gangster* – before devoting herself to a full-time career of crime, organising violent extortion rackets for her jailed boyfriend.

In 1997 she was arrested by Delhi police in a murder case but jumped bail. The following year she turned up in India's seventh largest city, Pune, where she organised the abduction of a businessman, whose body was found hacked to shreds in his abandoned car. She had employed a team to follow the victim for 34 days before striking. Sharma resurfaced briefly in Kolkata in December 1998, where her kidnap target was a wealthy hotel owner. This time a police tip-off foiled the plot. She has not been seen since, and there were reports that she had been killed in Nepal for cheating a drugs cartel. But the Indian press still regularly asked the question: Is the 'Lady Don' dead?

Sharma's principal rival in Pune was Arun 'Daddy' Gawli, whose murderous rule began when he personally disposed of the owner of a garment company in the early Eighties. His gang went on to run a systematic extortion racket and contract killing operation in Pune. Gawli was a protégé of gangster Rama Naik, who was working for Dawood Ibrahim. (That name again. All recent criminality in India seems to be linked to Ibrahim, though perhaps only by repute. Even Archana Sharma was reported to have been granted his protection when she went on the run.)

The triumvirate of Pune gang bosses fell out over a property deal in 1987. Naik was murdered and his partner Gawli blamed Dawood. Thus began a deadly rivalry between the two men, which extended to Mumbai, where 'Daddy' Gawli was, by the Nineties, probably the only gangster strong enough to oppose Dawood. In 1993 he even ordered the murder of Dawood's brother-in-law, Ibrahim Parkar.

Gawli's downfall came when he tried to muscle his way into the political power base, back in Pune. A long-standing contract killing had been offered by local property developers on a leading member of the Shiv Sena party, Kamlakar Jamsandekar. In March 2007 four hitmen entered the politician's house and shot him dead at point-blank range in front of his daughter. The following May, Gawli and 11 members of his gang were arrested. Big 'Daddy' avoided execution but, after a long-delayed trial, in August 2012 he was given a life sentence.

Historically, Indian police have always acted with supreme force against the nation's hardened criminal gangs. But the men in khaki have in recent years been mired in allegations of corruption, mafia links and human rights violations. In 2000 Prime Minister Atal Biharee Vajpayee pushed through a massive modernisation programme that improved police stations, weaponry, transport, computerisation, as well as police pay and housing. This infusion of funds from the centre has made a substantial difference to the enforcement of law and order in many states. But as a Mumbai newspaper commentator recently said: 'The task of changing medieval cops into modern ones won't be achieved in a decade.'

CHAPTER 21

THE CRUSHING OF COLOMBIA'S WARRING DRUG CARTELS

The heart of the worldwide cocaine industry has, since the 1970s, been the once-lawless South American country of Colombia. It is still home to some of the most violent yet sophisticated drug trafficking organisations in the world. Their enormous multi-national cocaine empire provides enough capital to buy ships, planes and even a submarine to smuggle large quantities of cocaine to the United States.

The Colombian drugs industry started modestly. In the mid-Seventies marijuana smugglers began exporting small quantities of cocaine to the US hidden in suitcases. At that point, cocaine could be processed for $1,000 per kilo in jungle labs and sold on the streets for between $50,000 and $100,000. A violent thief named Pablo Escobar had grander plans and masterminded the criminal enterprise that became known as the Medellín Cartel, hiring pilots to fly light planes directly into the

US. The vast profits allowed the cartel to reinvest in high-tech laboratories, swifter boats, larger airplanes and even an island in the Caribbean, where they could refuel. Astonishingly, the Colombian National Police discovered that traffickers had hired engineers from Russia to supply and refit a former military submarine as a sure way of crossing the Caribbean to the American mainland undetected.

Southern Florida, and Miami in particular, became the main import centre for South American narcotics. Distribution networks were highly sophisticated, using electronic homing devices to keep track of shipments while monitors tapped into the radio frequencies of federal and state law enforcement agencies. Much of Miami's economic boom came from the drug trade as legitimate businesses, mainly in construction, were bought to disguise operations. The so-called 'Cocaine Cowboy Wars' between rival gangs inspired the 1983 film *Scarface*, starring Al Pacino.

When, under pressure from the US, the Colombian government tried to sweep the town of Medellín clean of drugs, the megalomaniac Escobar declared war on the authorities. His renegade army was responsible for the murder of hundreds of government officials, police, prosecutors, judges, journalists and innocent bystanders. By the early Nineties the cartel had split into factions and many of its leaders were caught and jailed. Pablo Escobar was hunted down and killed after a long series of jungle battles.

The drugs industry switched to the west Colombian city of Cali, controlled by Escobar's main rivals, the Rodriguez Orejuala brothers, who had started out as kidnappers, once demanding a £500,000 ransom. This sum launched their drugs empire – but instead of killing politicians and police, they bribed them. The Cali Cartel funded politicians, hired top international lawyers and invested their drugs profits in legitimate businesses. But in 1995 their leaders were also hauled into jail – though with relatively soft sentences allowing them to continue running their empire from behind bars.

In the late Nineties, after the Cali and Medellín Cartels had fragmented, a third major group came to prominence. The Norte del Valle Cartel, based in the southwest of the country, became the most powerful organisation in the Colombian drugs trade.

According to a US government investigation, in the 15 years from 1990, the Norte del Valle cartel exported more than 500 metric tons of cocaine worth in excess of $10 billion from Colombia to Mexico and ultimately to the United States for resale. The cartel paid a right-wing paramilitary group to protect its members, its laboratories and its drug routes. The 2004 US investigation revealed how the cartel bribed and corrupted Colombian police and legislators to foil raids on its supply chains. Through wiretaps, gang members were able to listen in to communications between Colombian and American law enforcement agencies. So powerful was the cartel that it even bribed politicians to delay the extradition of Colombian narcotics traffickers to the US.

The Norte del Valle Cartel was run by the Montoya Sanchez family, whose leader Diego was on the FBI's list of the world's 'Ten Most Wanted Fugitives'. In September 2007 an elite Colombian force mounted a strike on a gang hideout, a ranch in the forested Valle del Cauca and captured Diego Montoya Sanchez, hiding in a creek-bed. He was extradited from Colombia to Miami a year later, the fourth Montoya family member to end up in American custody. All were subsequently convicted of conspiring to import cocaine and two of them convicted of 'obstruction of justice by murder', the sentences handed down in October 2009 ranging from 19 to 45 years.

The FBI celebrated that 'a brutal chapter in the history of drug trafficking has come to an end' thanks to unprecedented cooperation between the US and the Colombian government. Acting US Attorney Jeffrey H. Sloman claimed: 'This milestone prosecution effectively dismantled the violent and prolific Norte Valle Cartel. Nonetheless, we in law enforcement understand full well that today's victory is not the end of the war on drugs. We remain poised and committed to continue to fight the flow of illegal narcotics into our communities.'

A 'milestone' or just a stepping stone? It did not take long for another gang to take up where the Norte del Valle Cartel left off. Based in Colombia's eastern plains, the El Dorado Cartel, also known as 'The Junta', was run by Luis 'Don Lucho' Caicedo and Daniel 'El Loco' (The Madman) Barrera. According to 2010 US indictments, Caicedo and Barrera had overseen hundreds of tons of cocaine exports every month, with an average sale of $11 million in cocaine per shipment. Over the years, the ill-gotten proceeds added up to hundreds of millions of dollars, possibly even billions. To ensure that their drugs could be produced without interference and make it out of the country securely, the cartel paid protection money to the United Self-Defence Forces of Colombia, a notorious right-wing paramilitary group.

It seemed that the cartel unravelled in 2010 after Caicedo was arrested in Argentina and quickly extradited to Florida. In exchange for a reduced ten-year sentence, he reportedly revealed the identities of 246 associates in the cocaine business. It is suspected that one of those he snitched on was his partner, 'El Loco' Barrera, who was arrested in Venezuela in September 2012 as the result of a complex four-nation endeavour. The operation that swooped on him while chatting on a payphone involved everything from wiretaps to a broad coalition of Venezuelan police, Colombian intelligence officials, the British MI6, and agents from the CIA and the US Drug Enforcement Administration.

Barrera was a legend in the cocaine business, noted for torture and murder of those who crossed him. Marking him as Colombia's 'Public Enemy Number One', President Juan Manuel Santos said: 'He dedicated 20 years to doing bad things to Colombia and the world – all types of crime and perverse alliances with paramilitaries.' While on the run, Barrera had undergone plastic surgery and burnt his fingertips. The reward offered for his capture by the US was $5 million – the same as for Osama Bin Laden. Colombia added $2.7 million to that. President Santos, who called him 'the last of the great kingpins', heralded his arrest as a major victory in the drugs war.

Barrera's arrest was the third detention of a Colombian drug baron over the course of a year of successful international cooperation. In June 2011, Venezuelan authorities captured the head of the Los Rajostros Cartel, Diego Perez Henao. His gang, a major exporter of cocaine to the US via Mexico, is said to have controlled half the members of the paramilitary criminal organisations involved in drug trafficking in Colombia. The cartel's previous leader, Javier Antonio Calle Serna, surrendered to US authorities on the island of Aruba in May 2012. He was charged with the 2008 murder of Wilber Varela, a Colombian drugs baron whose smuggling routes he supposedly took over.

The destruction of the Medellín, Cali, Norte del Valle and El Dorado Cartels means that the drugs industry in Colombia is now fragmented, with different gangs along the manufacturing and supply chain making it more difficult to stamp out the trade. Also, worryingly, with cocaine use in the United States dropping, the gangs are increasingly heading shipments towards Europe and Asia.

The US Drugs Enforcement Agency and the Colombian National Police believe there are more than 300 active drug smuggling organisations in Colombia today. Cocaine is shipped to every industrialised nation in the world and profits remain incredibly high. And the trade is spreading. Colombian crooks' profits from cocaine have encouraged gangsters to open laboratories in other countries, including Honduras, Guatemala, El Salvador, Jamaica, Dominican Republic, Trinidad and Tobago and, of course, Mexico.

General Oscar Naranjo, the retired commander of the Colombian national police who became security adviser to the new Mexican government, has claimed that cartels such as the most recently busted Caicedo-Barrera organisation ended up working as no more than suppliers to Mexican Syndicates. If that is the case, then it's also a sign of how far the Colombian cartels have fallen and been supplanted by the larger and more dangerous Mexican cartels, with the Colombian gangs playing only a supporting role.

If the ultimate control of the international drugs industry is gradually switching away from Colombia to Mexico (as will be seen in the next chapter), the change of power base will be of no comfort to the hard-pressed US agencies who have had so much success in smashing the South American cartels. The problem still lies on their own doorstep.

One final case history reflects the lawlessness and almost casual slayings that have marked the near-half century of Colombia's drugs trade with the United States. It's the saga of Griselda Blanco, the most ruthless female gangster of recent years, who was shot dead by two motorcycle assassins as she was out shopping in the city of Medellín in 2012.

It was a suitably dramatic ending for the 69-year-old cocaine trafficker, who was an insatiable fan of the movie *The Godfather*. Blanco was known as 'La Madrina', Spanish for 'Godmother', and even named her youngest son Michael Corleone after the main character in the film trilogy. Her other nicknames were the 'Cocaine Queen' and the 'Black Widow'. 'We don't know why they killed her,' said the local police chief, 'but the first hypothesis would be revenge or a settling of accounts.'

Blanco had certainly gained enough enemies in her murderous lifetime. Born in a shanty town in the Colombian coastal city of Cartagena in 1943, she began her criminal career as a 12-year-old pickpocket and prostitute, eventually commanding a billion-dollar empire that exported 1,500 kilograms of cocaine per month by boat and plane. She established many of the smuggling routes used by the Medellín Cartel and solidified her place in Colombian criminal legend as the mentor to drugs king Pablo Escobar.

Blanco had a reputation for ruthlessness, ordering the killing of dozens of rivals to get to the top of the drug smuggling business in the Seventies and Eighties. Prosecutors believe she was responsible for at least 40 murders, though some police put the number closer to 250. Her nickname 'Black Widow' arose from the claim that she had killed a couple of her husbands. It was also said that she slit the throats of some of her lovers after she had slept with them.

The title 'Cocaine Queen' came after she launched her drug operations in Florida in the Seventies. She eliminated other drugs gangs by having machine-gun assassins spray bullets indiscriminately at her rivals and their families. One infamous attack took place at a Miami mall in 1979, when screaming shoppers ran for their lives as two hitmen riddled a store with bullets, leaving two dead and two wounded shop workers. Blanco ordered the killing of a Colombian drug dealer in the busy concourse of Miami Airport. Because he was nicknamed 'The Pig', she ordered that he be carved up with a bayonet. One less violent legacy of her reign as drugs Godmother was that she is said to have revolutionised smuggling by developing her own line of underwear with secret compartments for drugs.

Griselda Blanco's fall from power began when a Colombian drugs Syndicate put a $4 million price on her head, forcing her into hiding. Back in Colombia, three of her four sons were murdered. Only Michael Corleone survived. Blanco was seized by police in California and in 1985 was jailed for cocaine trafficking. Three years later she was further sentenced to 20 years for three murders – the 1982 contract killings of two drug dealers and a toddler. The two-year-old died when bullets meant for his father hit the boy instead. Blanco was deported back to Colombia in 2004, where she earned warped fame through the film documentary *Cocaine Cowboys* and its sequel, *Hustlin' With The Godmother*.

The podgy 69-year-old was gunned down on 3 September 2012 as she left her local butcher's shop. Her assassins escaped by motorbike and Blanco died on her way to hospital. A former Florida homicide detective who had helped put her behind bars commented: 'It's surprising to all of us that she had not been killed sooner. When you hurt so many people like she did, it's only a matter of time before they find you and try to even the score.'

CHAPTER 22

THE COST OF A SIX-YEAR WAR ON DRUGS... 'EXTRAORDINARY VIOLENCE'

Shamed by its inability to control the violent crime lords who terrorised the country with seeming impunity, the Mexican government in December 2006 declared full-scale war on its drug gangs. The result was that Mexico became a battleground. The official death toll since President Felipe Calderón launched his military offensive against the cartels soared to more than 70,000 police, traffickers and civilians. The true figure is believed to be even higher.

The violence is horrific but is now an everyday event. Over a three-year span ending in January 2013, more than 20 sitting mayors were killed by cartels and many other politicians were murdered or simply disappeared. One such victim whose assassination made worldwide headlines was a politician who had been hailed as a heroine for standing up to the cartels. Dr Maria Santos Gorrostieta, 36-year-old ex-mayor of Tiquicheo, west of Mexico City, survived two assassination attempts in 2009, firstly when gunmen raked her car with bullets, killing her first husband, and secondly when she was again ambushed and suffered even more serious injuries. In a famous act of defiance, Dr Gorrostieta posed for pictures showing the extent of her wounds and subsequently ran for the Mexican Congress, although she failed to win a seat. In November 2012 the mother of three and her second husband were abducted. Her body was found at a roadside near San Juan Tararameo three weeks later. She had been killed by a blow to the head. But she had also been stabbed, her arms and legs bound and her waist and chest covered in burns, indicating that she had been tortured. Her husband remained missing.

Massacres of civilians, beheadings and mass graves have also become increasingly common. For instance, on one Sunday in September 2012 as Mexicans celebrated their Independence Day, the dismembered corpses of 17 men were found dumped beside a highway in Jalisco, a part of central Mexico disputed by drug cartels. The bodies were naked, mutilated and stacked with chains around their necks. Only a week earlier, a shoot-out between local police and an armed convoy left two people dead and two injured in the same municipality. And in May of that year, police found 18 human heads and remains packed into two abandoned cars along a Jalisco highway. Even those figures pale into insignificance when compared with the 74 dead migrants found near the town of San Fernando in August 2010. Mexico's crime groups regularly leave behind such grisly remains as they battle for control of trafficking routes and markets.

In this chaotically administered, crime-ridden country, no one can be certain about the true value and cost of the narcotics trade. Analysts have estimated that wholesale earnings from illicit drug sales range from £10 billion to £30 billion a year. And the government figure for the cost in lives of its six-year war on the trade was put at 72,000. In 2013, however, a civil rights group said this was a 'wild under-estimate of the slaughter'. Propuesta Cívica (Civic Proposal) published the grim statistic that an additional 20,851 victims had simply disappeared. This possible death toll put Mexico far ahead of other Latin American nations ravaged by organised crime. In Colombia, where drug barons have torn the country apart for decades, it is estimated that 50,000 people have gone missing, but this figure is over the past 40 years.

The Propuesta Cívica report listed 138 soldiers, 1,300 police officers and 58 journalists who were known to have been assassinated by cartel hitmen. Tragically, it also included missing women and children – many of whom were believed still to be alive, kidnapped by the cartels from remote villages and put to use as sex slaves. The group's director Pilar Talavera said: 'We published our results so the public, and the world, can begin to understand the scale of violence. We also want to pressure the authorities to disclose official information on the disappeared. What the relatives need most is to learn what may have happened to their loved ones.'

The civil rights report sent those desperate to learn the fate of loved ones onto the streets carrying placards with photos of the missing. But it also triggered a wider wave of anger in Mexico, where President Enrique Peña Nieto, who assumed office in December 2012, promised 'greater transparency' than his predecessor Felipe Calderón, who declared war on the six cartels battling for control of trafficking routes into the US.

Although Mexican drug trafficking organisations have existed for decades, they have become more powerful since the demise of Colombia's Medellín and Cali cartels in the 1990s and the more recent fragmentation of the Norte del Valle and El Dorado cartels. Their influence further grew as the US stepped up anti-narcotics operations in the Caribbean and Florida.

The ties between Mexican and Colombian gangs were forged by a bent policeman. The birth of all Mexican drug cartels is traced to former Mexican Judicial Federal Police agent Miguel Angel Felix Gallardo, known as 'the Godfather', who founded the Guadalajara Cartel in 1980 and controlled all the smuggling corridors across the Mexico-USA border throughout that decade. He started by exporting marijuana and opium into the US and was the first Mexican drug chief to organise an international alliance with the South American cartels in the 1980s.

For decades, drug trafficking organisations used Mexico's entrenched political system to create what the US Council on Foreign Relations in a 2011 report described as 'a system-wide network of corruption that ensured distribution rights, market access, and even official government protection for drug traffickers in exchange for lucrative bribes'. However, it was not until the late Eighties that Mexican gangs rose to their current prominence, in the wake of the successful dismantling of Colombia's drug cartels. As the Colombian route was disrupted, Mexican gangs shifted from being mere couriers for Colombia to wholesalers. Thus, with the Colombians losing their monopoly position, the Mexican cartels quickly came to dominate the trade, controlling 90 per cent of all the drugs that cross the border into the United States.

By the time Calderón took office in 2006 with a pledge to eradicate trafficking organisations, drug violence was already on the rise. In fairness to the ex-president, his six-year campaign did break up most of the cartels. He deployed more than 50,000 troops and federal police against them and many of the main gang leaders were either arrested or killed. The Calderón administration argued that the violence proved that this aggressive strategy was forcing gangs to split and take on one another – though often in increasingly brutal and gruesome fashion. The principal cartels were the Sinaloa, Beltran Leyva, Arellano Felix, Carillo Fuentes, La Familia, The Gulf Cartel (also known as New Federation) and Los Zetas.

At the start of Calderón's crackdown, violence was concentrated in Mexico's northern border regions, especially Chihuahua, as well as Pacific states like Sinaloa, Michoacán and Guerrero. Ciudad Juárez, across the border from El Paso, Texas, was the most violent city, blighted by a gang-related death toll of more than 3,000 in 2010. Violence has dropped markedly since. However, Guerrero, home to the resort of Acapulco, as well as Sinaloa and Nuevo León remains among some of the most violent regions. One of the focal points for violence since 2010 has been Mexico's third-largest city, Monterrey.

In a 2012 report by the US security firm Stratfor, experts argued that the proliferation of cartels had by then been reduced to two main players: the Sinaloa and the Los Zetas, with the latter being the biggest cartel in terms of geographic presence. The US government has described Los Zetas as 'the most technologically advanced, sophisticated, and dangerous cartel operating in Mexico'.

The Los Zetas Cartel originated in the Mexican Army, when several commandos joined forces to form a drug trafficking organisation under brothers Osiel and Antonio Cárdenas Guillén. Los Zetas is based in the industrial hub of Monterrey, once touted as Latin America's safest city but now plagued by gang-related violence as rivals battle for control of drug distribution and other rackets. In May 2012 horrified citizens awoke to find nine bodies, four of them women, hanging from an overpass leading to a main highway in Nuevo Laredo. Hours later, police found 14 human heads inside coolers outside the city hall along with a threatening note. Shortly afterwards, a Zetas killer, described as Mexico's deadliest female assasin, was arrested in Monterrey. Maria Jimenez, a 26-year-old widow nicknamed 'La Tosca', confessed to 20 killings and several other violent crimes. She had personally gunned down rival drug traffickers and a police officer.

The arrest of 'La Tosca' failed to stem the violence, however. A week later, 18 people were found decapitated and dismembered near Mexico's second largest city, Guadalajara. Within days, a further 49 bodies, decapitated and mutilated, were found dumped on a roadside near Monterrey. The victims, six of them women, had their heads, feet, and hands cut off to make identification difficult. Police suspected the dead were members of the opposition Gulf Cartel but were certain that the perpetrators were Zetas gangsters.

There were a few immediate victories in Mexico's federal police war against Los Zetas. In late May 2012 Daniel Jesus Elizondo Ramírez, nicknamed 'El Loco', was arrested in Monterrey after throwing a hand grenade at pursuing cops and was charged with the dumping of the 49 decapitated bodies. A month later, another Zetas member, Gregorio Villanueva Salas, known as the 'Piracy Czar' because of his control of the pirated music industry, was also charged with several grenade attacks. The pair admitted they were acting on orders from their leader, Miguel Angel Trevino Morales, but it would be another year before this cartel kingpin was caged.

The ultra-brutal Morales regularly ordered beheadings, hanging and massacres of rivals. His trademark was the use of ice picks to pin warning signs on the chests of his victims' bodies but his favoured technique was the 'guiso', or stew, in which enemies would be placed in 55-gallon oil drums and cooked alive. Among crimes for which the 40-year-old Zetas leader was wanted was the murder of more than 260 migrants who were dumped in mass graves after being kidnapped in two separate incidents in 2010 and 2011. They are believed to have refused to work for him as drugs mules. Morales was seized on a dirt road outside Nuevo Laredo while heading for the US border in a pick-up laden with eight guns and $2million in cash. His arrest, along with his bodyguard and his accountant, was a much needed boost to President Nieto, under criticism for failing to take a tough enough stance against the cartels.

The Sinaloa Cartel, based on the Pacific coast, is no less violent than the Zetas. They operate in Mexico's 'Golden Triangle', covering the states of Sinaloa, Durango and Chihuahua. Through mergers with other gangs, by the mid-1990s, the Sinaloa Syndicate was believed to have reached the size of Colombia's Medellín Cartel during its prime. In 2008 the cartel split into a number of warring factions, which became a major cause of the epidemic of drug violence Mexico has since suffered. Murders by the cartel often involve beheadings or bodies dissolved in vats of alkali and are sometimes filmed and posted on the Internet as a warning to rival gangs.

In 2008, 12 decapitated bodies were found piled up outside the Yucatán state capital of Merida. The same year, nine headless men were found in the Guerrero state capital of Chilpancingo. In 2011 the bodies of 15 men, all but one of them headless, were found on a street outside a shopping centre in the resort city of Acapulco. Handwritten signs were left on the corpses signed by 'El Chapo's People' – a reference to Sinaloa leader Joaquín 'El Chapo' Guzmán. His cartel is thought to have killed the men for trying to intrude on the gang's turf. The executions were particularly gory even for Acapulco – a city where 27 people had been killed on the streets over the previous weekend alone. Those victims included two police officers cut down on a main road in front of tourists and locals, six people who were shot dead and stuffed in a taxi, their hands and feet bound, and four others elsewhere in the city.

The most sickening Sinaloa act of violence occurred in September 2011 when the cartel put a 'warning' video on the Web showing the execution of two of their own members – beheaded with a chainsaw while still alive. Both men, a drug runner and his uncle who had somehow upset the cartel leadership, were seated shirtless against a wall as they answered questions posed to them by their executioners. The older man, who mentions 'El Chapo', says resignedly: 'Think next time you decide to "give the finger" [to cheat], think about it very carefully, because it's not easy being here, and you never return back. With these people you don't play around.'

'El Chapo' himself has been on the run since 2001 when he escaped from a Mexican prison in a laundry truck. There has been a $7 million bounty on his head ever since. Joaquin Guzmán, whose fortune was estimated by *Forbes* magazine at more than $1 billion, was named by the US Treasury Department in 2012 as the 'world's most powerful drugs trafficker'. Authorities said his cartel has recently been expanding its drug business abroad, building international operations in Central and South America and the Pacific. In 2013 Guzmán formally received the title of Chicago's 'Public Enemy Number One' because of his cartel's control of narcotics supply to the city – the first time the Chicago Crime Commission had used the infamous label since Al Capone in the 1920s. Shortly afterwards, there was speculation that the kingpin had been killed in a jungle shootout with a rival gang in Guatemala's Petén province, near the border with Mexico.

So, after six years of ex-President Calderón's military onslaught against the cartels and the subsequent more measured approach of his successor President Nieto, who is winning the Mexican drugs war? A gloomy verdict on Calderón's campaign came from the US Department of Justice which reported that Mexico remained a major supplier of heroin to the American market, and the largest foreign supplier of methamphetamine and marijuana. Mexican production of all three of these drugs had increased since 2006, as had the amount of drugs seized at the US-Mexican border. While assessments vary as to how much of the marijuana originates in Mexico, a 2010 report estimated it at anywhere from 40 to 67 per cent. An estimated 95 per cent of cocaine travels through Mexico into North America, up from 77 per cent a decade earlier. Overall, the US State Department found that its nation's drug users send between $19 billion and $29 billion into the coffers of Mexican drug cartels.

There were other depressing side-effects of Calderón's strategy. From 2006 to 2012, the President sent more than 50,000 soldiers onto Mexico's streets, invested billions of dollars on equipment and training, attempted to reform the police and judicial systems, and strengthened Mexico's partnership with the United States. But the Council on Foreign

Relations reported that a legacy of 'political manipulation of law enforcement and judicial branches, which limited professionalisation and enabled widespread corruption' had left the government with 'only weak tools to counter increasingly aggressive crime networks'.

One of the main problems was local policing – or the lack of it. The drug cartels, with their massive resources, had repeatedly infiltrated the ranks of underpaid cops, from lowly traffic officers to the very top. The Calderón administration attempted to counter police corruption by dramatically increasing the role of the military in the fight against drug cartels. Not only were tens of thousands of military personnel deployed to supplement, and in many cases replace, local police forces, they were also recruited to lead civilian law enforcement agencies. Mexico's judicial system, with its autocratic judges and lack of transparency, was also highly susceptible to corruption. The US Congressional Research Service noted that even when public officials were arrested for working with a cartel, they were rarely convicted.

Calderón's militarisation strategy also resulted in accusations of serious human rights abuses. A 2011 report by Human Rights Watch found that 'rather than strengthening public security in Mexico, Calderón's war has exacerbated a climate of violence, lawlessness, and fear in many parts of the country'. The report, which looked at five states, documented more than 175 cases of torture, 39 disappearances, and 24 'extrajudicial' killings. The Mexican administration countered these accusations by heralding the successes of its offensive against the cartels. Through bilateral cooperation with the United States, it boasted, the government had killed or captured 25 of the country's top 37 most wanted drug kingpins.

A year before the change of presidential leadership, a report by the US National Drug Intelligence Center forecast: 'Major Mexican-based trans-national criminal organisations will continue to dominate wholesale drug trafficking in the US for the foreseeable future and will further solidify their positions through collaboration with US gangs'. Nieto's main election promise in 2012 was to switch the focus of the drugs war from tackling the gangs and hunting drug barons to reducing the crime and violence that affect the lives of ordinary citizens. He announced a national gendarmerie, initially 10,000 strong, to take over from the troops on the ground and focus on law enforcement. The federal police force would also be boosted.

Analysts differ on how to address Mexico's growing internal strife but an increasing number reluctantly agree that the US war on drugs is a failure and necessitates a new approach. As President Nieto changed his internal strategy, gradual moves were being made at state level in the US towards legalisation and decriminalisation of marijuana, one of the primary substances involved in the drugs war, raising new questions about overall policy. Regardless of the various proposals, most observers are less than optimistic. An academic who is one of America's leading experts on Mexican organised crime, David Shirk of the University of San Diego, said: 'It is ultimately the great shame of the last decade that we've made all this effort, we've lost all of these lives, and at the end of the day we've made no real substantive progress in reducing the availability of drugs – and the cost is extraordinary violence.'

CHAPTER 23

HORRIFIC HUMAN SACRIFICES OF THE VOODOO KILLERS

The spookiest drugs gang of all time were sickeningly brutal but also unbelievably brave … because they believed they could defy death! They used voodoo to 'protect' themselves, to wield power over others and to satiate their bloodlust.

The group were led by handsome Adolfo de Jesus Constanzo, born in Miami of Cuban extraction, who in the early Eighties moved to Mexico to offer his gang's backing to local drugs lords. But the 'services' they provided were more vile than even the warring narcotics cartels were accustomed to. For Constanzo and his drug-crazed followers were adherents of the black magic arts of Palo Mayombe, a violent African cult who believe the spirits of the dead can be harnessed if the gods are regularly appeased with living human sacrifices.

Born on 1 November 1962, in Miami Beach to a 15-year-old mother, Constanzo grew up in Florida and Puerto Rico.

His mother followed the Santeria, or Saint's Path, a quasi-Christian religion brought to the New World by African slaves hundreds of years ago and adapted to fit in with the ways of their Catholic masters. Palo Mayombe is the dark sister of the Santeria. If the Santeria, which involves sacrifice of animals, could be likened to 'white' magic, Palo Mayombe is definitely 'black'. The religion accepts no afterlife, so an adherent is free to do whatever he wants here on earth; the spirits of the dead exist in a kind of limbo, forced to wander the material plane. Newly-dead spirits can be harnessed by a Palo Mayombe priest, if regularly fed with fresh blood.

The religion centres round a nganga – a cauldron kept constantly filled with blood, a goat's head, a roasted turtle and, most importantly, a human skull – preferably that of a person who has died a violent and painful death. Non-believers, especially Christians, are considered to be animals and natural victims. The more painful and horrific their death, the more potent the spell that the high priest can cast.

Constanzo, though never rich as a child, lived fairly well. His mother married a prosperous small businessman, who took the family to Puerto Rico. When his stepfather died in 1973, his mother re-married and moved back to Florida. This marriage was not a success, however, and ended in acrimonious divorce. At just 12 years of age, Adolfo found himself the head of the family. To support them, he began shoplifting and trading in drugs. Through his teens, he earned a police record for theft and for a while the Miami drugs squad had him under observation.

At about this time, he realised he was bisexual. He was later to sire two children, but during his teens, before he could slake his lust elsewhere, his principal sexual satisfaction came through frequenting gay bars. It could be that things got too hot for the slim, dark and handsome youth with piercing eyes, or simply that he saw his main chance south of the border. At any rate, at the age of 21, Constanzo headed off to Mexico City, the smog-bound, sprawling urban mass where grinding poverty held hands with undreamed-of opulence. It was to the wealthier quarter that he gravitated.

Rich, bored businessmen and their wives were turned on by this youth and his exciting occult religion. Telling fortunes with apparently uncanny accuracy earned him his own small fortune. His fame as a sorcerer spread and he soon became the darling of the wealthy and the powerful. But it was the often superstitious leaders of narcotics cartels who fêted him the most. At a time when the richest market for illegal drugs, the United States, was cracking down hardest on the trade, credulous drugs family godfathers turned to him for advice and magical protection. Incredibly, Constanzo was able to demand up to $50,000 a time for spells to protect the smugglers.

It was subsequently discovered that much of his 'divination' came through corrupt Mexican police and customs officials. Florentino Ventura, the head of Mexican Interpol, was later to shoot his wife before turning the gun on himself when investigations got too close. However, the source of Constanzo's knowledge mattered not at all to the drug barons. His word quickly became law. And all the while, to ensure that his protective spells came true, dismembered and decapitated corpses were regularly found floating in rivers and lakes outside Mexico City.

By now, Constanzo was calling himself the 'padrino' (godfather) of his own Palo Mayombe group, selling his services to the highest bidders, who for a while happened to be the close family of drugs overlord Guillermo Calzada. The ambitious Constanzo suggested to Calzada that because his magic was the source of the family's success, he deserved half the proceeds. Calzada perhaps understandably refused and Constanzo left in a rage. A few days later he called to express regret for his demands and offered, as a sign of remorse, to perform a special ceremony that would give extra protection to the whole cartel.

On 30 April 1987, Calzada, his wife, his mother, his partner, his secretary, his maid and his bodyguard met Constanzo in an abandoned factory. All seven reappeared a few days later when their bodies were dragged from a river. They had been dreadfully mutilated before being killed. Their extremities – their fingers and toes and, in the case of the men, their genitals – had been sliced off. Significantly, their heads were missing. These had gone to feed the padrino's nganga.

Constanzo was now hooked on his own mumbo-jumbo, believing ever more implicitly in his voodoo powers. Flush with cash through drug dealing and extortion, he moved his gang of savage killers to Matamoros, near the Texan border, where the narcotics cartels were even richer. There, in his remote Santa Elena ranch, he enjoyed a strange ménage-à-trois with his American ex-girlfriend, Sara Aldrete, and his two homosexual lovers, Orea Ochoa and Martin Quintera, who were treated as servants by their boss.

As he had done in Mexico City, Constanzo, with Aldrete's help on this occasion, inveigled his way into the family of another drugs overlord, Elio Hernandez. Again he presented the Palo Mayombe rituals as the key to the family's prosperity – and, sure enough, his business picked up. The Hernandez gang was now totally under the spell of the Constanzo's voodoo group, and by 1988 the area round Matamoros was thick with dismembered corpses. Between May that year and March 1989, Constanzo tortured and ritually sacrificed at least 13 people. The victims were usually rival drug dealers but sometimes included strangers picked up at random.

On one occasion, the victim was a police undercover agent who had infiltrated the gang but had been discovered, possibly through a tip-off from one of the police officers on Constanzo's payroll. On another occasion, Hernandez himself was ordered to supply the coup de grâce to a struggling young victim at the bubbling nganga. Only after slicing off the youth's head did he recognise the green and white striped football shirt he was wearing. He had killed his own cousin.

Constanzo's normal method of sacrifice was to have the victim brutally beaten, then dragged into a shed containing the sacred cauldron. Here he would cut off the nose, ears, fingers, toes and genitals of the hapless wretch and partially flay him. Then the others would be ordered out while Constanzo sodomised him. Only then would there be a merciful release through death.

It was essential to the success of the ceremony that there should be as much pain as possible and the victim should die screaming. The spirit had to be confused and terrified as it left the body, making it easier to subjugate. And it was this particular evil that was to bring about Constanzo's downfall. In March 1989, the chosen victim was a small-time Mexican drugs dealer unknown to the gang. Every torture was applied to him, but the tough little man would not cry out, even when his upper body was skinned. He endured every torture, even castration, but died silently.

Constanzo declared the ceremony a failure and sent his men

out to kidnap a softer touch. He was easy to find. A group of students were celebrating the end of term at their university by crossing the border for a night of cheap alcohol, perhaps a woman or two and possibly a session of pot smoking or cocaine snorting. When one became separated from his colleagues, he was pushed into the back of a truck and driven to the Santa Elena ranch.

His name was Mark Kilroy, a 21-year-old medical student, and he must have screamed sufficiently to satisfy Constanzo before his brains were tipped into the nganga, for the padrino declared the ceremony a great success. The gang was now unstoppable. With an American spirit as well as any number of Mexican spirits to protect them, they believed themselves not only safe but invisible to the law. This time, however, the cultists had over-reached themselves. Kilroy's parents, aided by the boy's uncle, a US Customs official, fought for a thorough investigation by the lax Mexican authorities. The manhunt that ensued across both sides of the border had a swift result.

Mexican police set up a roadblock near Matamoros. One of the Hernandez brothers, Serafin, was at the wheel of a truck when he approached it – and, having been told by his leader that he was invisible, drove straight through it! The cops scrambled into their cars and followed at a discreet distance as Hernandez led them directly to Constanzo's ranch. There they found some evidence of drug trading – but no sign of Constanzo himself. Hernandez was arrested and taken to local police headquarters, where he was subjected to a 'Mexican interrogation'. With the help of a little soda laced with Tabasco squirted up his nostrils, an agonising, though undetectable torture, he broke and revealed the horrors of the hellish ranch. Returning to the ranch, he pointed out a number of shallow graves around the nganga shed. He also began to name names.

Detectives rounded up several of the cultists who, puzzled by the lack of promised protection, were forced to do the dirty work of digging up the bodies. One of the first they unearthed was that of the American student, Mark Kilroy. The grave was marked by a short length of wire sticking out of the ground. Subsequent examination revealed that the wire had been threaded the length of the boy's spine. Once the body had decomposed sufficiently, it had been Constanzo's intention to pull out the backbone and add it to the stomach-churning mix in his nganga.

Constanzo, along with his favoured inner circle, fled to Mexico City, where they laid low in an apartment in a poor part of town – Constanzo foolishly leaving his luxury limousine in the street nearby. On 6 May 1989, two beat cops spotted it and strolled over to investigate, thinking it might have been stolen. When Constanzo saw them, he assumed the game was up and opened fire from the apartment. An armed siege ensued.

Inside the apartment, panic reigned. As Constanzo's gunmen were exchanging fire with police, the padrino himself was stuffing armfuls of cash into a fire. As Sara Aldrete cowered with Orea Ochoa under a bed, Constanzo and a hitman nicknamed El Dubi emptied their guns into the street. At other windows, more cultists were spraying the police with bullets. When they were almost out of ammunition, Constanzo suddenly became calm again. He called together El Dubi and his current lover, bodyguard Martin Rodriguez, whom he led into a walk-in wardrobe. Then he ordered El Dubi to shoot them both. When the gunman simply stared aghast, Constanzo slapped him across the face and ordered: 'Do it or I'll make things tough for you in Hell. Don't worry, I'll be back.'

Those were his last words. He and his lover died in a hail of lead. The rest were taken alive. In all, 14 cultists were given lengthy jail terms on charges from multiple murder to drug running. There being no death penalty in Mexico, the maximum sentence that could be handed down was 50 years for aggravated homicide. Oddest among the accused was Sara Aldrete, the all-American ex-college student from Brownsville, Texas, who had thrown away a glittering future as an athlete to join the cult. At her trial and in subsequent interviews, she proclaimed her innocence and complained bitterly about the treatment she said she had endured at the hands of the police. 'I could not leave the gang,' she explained in her defence, 'because they threatened to use witchcraft on my family.' She was sentenced to 62 years without possibility of parole.

The detailed confessions of the other cultists allowed police to close the files on a number of mystery killings. There had been 15 human sacrifices at the Matamoros ranch, two at another ranch nearby and several in Mexico City. Added to these were the slayings of rival gang members and those of Constanzo's own followers who had been killed to maintain discipline. In Matamoros, the police had the nganga and the shed in which it was housed exorcised by a white witch and a priest. Then they doused the building with petrol and burned it to the ground. Constanzo's body was claimed by his mother and taken back to Miami, where he was cremated.

CHAPTER 24

'DEVIL'S CHILDREN' – DRIVEN TO KILL BY A MESSIANIC MADMAN

'**C**harles Manson is the greatest advertisement for the death penalty.' So said Stephen Kay, the long-serving principal prosecutor in California's most infamous gang massacre. Few who were involved in the case would disagree. For Manson was not only the epitome of sheer evil himself, the messianic madman also had the power to transform others from fresh-faced innocents into blood-lusting murderers.

How this scruffy, unprepossessing fantasist managed to mesmerise his gang of followers to commit sickening acts of brutality is an unsolved mystery. Forty years after the 1969 killing spree by his 'Devil's Children' sect, former Los Angeles District Attorney Kay was still warning: 'He can cast a spell and that's how he got other people to do his killing. He had such evil control – and he still has it today.'

Manson himself had long recognised the danger he posed to

the public. Early in his criminal career, he had pleaded with the authorities to be allowed to remain locked up in jail. If only they had granted his wish. For within two years, he had gathered together a cult of impressionable devotees who were willing to kill at his command.

Manson was born illegitimately in 1934 to 16-year-old prostitute Kathleen Maddox in Cincinnati, Ohio, on 12 November 1934, his birth name being recorded as 'No Name Maddox'. The identity of his father is unknown and his surname derives from one of his mother's lovers at the time. Manson lived in foster homes but, still in his early teens, he became a juvenile delinquent who spent much time in detention centres. Inexorably, his escalating criminality led to harsher penalties. At the age of 16, he was sentenced to two years at the National Training School for Boys in Washington DC and was not freed until his eighteenth birthday.

In his teens, Manson showed violent sexual tendencies, usually directed towards other men. During one such period at a detention centre, he grabbed a boy from behind and held a razor blade to his throat as he carried out a violent rape. Eventually, with his file marked 'Dangerous' and 'Not to be trusted', he was transferred to the Federal Reformatory in Virginia.

Soon after his release on parole in 1954, he married Rosalie Jean Willis, a 17-year-old waitress. Despite his previous homosexuality, Rosalie was pregnant when the two travelled to California in a stolen car. Convicted of the theft, Manson was sentenced to three years at the Terminal Island jail in San Pedro. Faithful Rosalie visited him often, sometimes taking along Charles Manson Junior, but then suddenly stopped her visits. Manson discovered she had fallen for someone else and, although paroled in 1958, he was never to see Rosalie or his son again. In between jail sentences, Manson married again and sired another son: a second Charles Manson Junior. That marriage did not last either.

By the time he was 32, Manson had spent most of his life in prison. So institutionalised was he that, when yet another parole came up, he asked to remain within the four walls he knew as home. He did not feel easy being released into a society that he felt had dealt him a bad hand. But the authorities refused his plea to be a voluntary inmate and in 1967 the criminal menace was once more back on the road, this time heading for San Francisco, centre of the hippy flower-power cult. With a guitar on his back, the drug-taking drifter and aspiring musician mixed with other drop-outs and discovered that he could exercise a strange magnetism over them.

'He surrounded himself with young and impressionable hangers-on,' recalled Manson expert Vincent Bugliori, the former prosecutor who would eventually try the evil killer. 'The kids were literally at his feet, so he started up what he called his "family". Manson at that point became a maestro, orchestrating what everyone else did. He had this phenomenal ability to gain control over other people and get them to do terrible things.'

This strange mix of misfits – runaway youngsters, homeless bikers and small-time criminals – moved south, settling in run-down Spahn Ranch, a former Wild West movie set outside Los Angeles. Further vulnerable youths were lured into the gang with the promise of free sex and drugs. Among them were impressionable girls who so adored Manson that they willingly gave up stable, middle-class lives to be with him.

One such devotee was 20-year-old Linda Kasabian who, in July 1969, was introduced to the 'family' by Manson follower

Catherine Share, known as 'Gypsy'. Kasabian, who moved to the ranch with her daughter, won the trust of the group when she volunteered to steal $5,000 in cash from her estranged husband. She was then presented to the leader of the commune. 'Meeting Charles for the first time was very exciting,' she later recalled. 'There was a magnetism about him – charisma, charm, power. I felt really safe and protected. We were like his children.'

By the summer of 1969, Manson had gathered a hard core of 25 devotees with more than 60 other 'associates'. In his drug-befuddled state, he became obsessed with The Beatles' *White Album*, which he believed was directed at him. 'In every single song on the album, he felt that they were singing about us,' Catherine 'Gypsy' Share later recalled. 'He thought that The Beatles were talking about what he had been expounding for years – a forthcoming racial cataclysm.'

Manson ordered his followers to prepare for an imminent race war that he dubbed 'Helter Skelter', his ultimate mission named after the title of a track on *The White Album*. He told them that the songs contained hidden messages that had meaning only for him. Songs such as 'Revolution 9' were especially prophetic for the 'family': they believed it all led to another battle of Armageddon, Manson's term for a planned race war in which American Blacks would reign supreme over the Whites. Only Manson and those who chose to stay with him would be spared the mass racial slaughter. Chosen Blacks, spouted Manson, would become part of the 'family', numbering no less than 144,000. They would become his 'Chosen People'. He had taken the term from The Bible, referring to the 12 Tribes of Israel, each numbering 12,000. Together, he said, they would take over the world. And The Beatles, Manson proclaimed, would be his 'spokesmen'. Manson told his disciples that nothing could be achieved unless he had utterly devoted followers, who alone could change the world. They would strike out at the white Establishment; they would kill.

A parallel mission of Manson at the time was to achieve his ambition of becoming a star by using a tenuous connection with a member of the Beach Boys group, Dennis Wilson. The dream was shattered, however, when Wilson's associate, record producer Terry Melcher, son of film star Doris Day, failed to offer him a contract. This brought together two lines of thought in the mind of the deranged Manson. He decided to launch an attack on Melcher's Los Angeles home.

According to Vincent Bugliori, the house came to symbolise the entertainment establishment that had rejected him. 'Manson wanted to start Helter Skelter by murdering white people and framing the black man for it,' said Bugliori. With mounting paranoia, he began arming his followers. 'It wasn't peace and love anymore,' recalled Catherine Share, 'it was almost like an army.'

Helter Skelter got underway on a hot August night in 1969 when Manson allotted his murderous mission to Linda Kasabian and three other followers: Susan Atkins, Patricia Krenwinkel and Charles Watson. He ordered them to drive to Melcher's home, in an isolated area between Beverly Hills and the San Fernando Valley, and launch a vicious attack on the occupants. Manson had not adequately researched his 'war' strategy, however. Melcher was no longer at the bungalow-style property, which was being rented by film director Roman Polanski and his pregnant wife Sharon Tate, who had recently returned there to have her baby after working in London. Polanski was still in Europe directing his latest film.

Unaware of this, Atkins, Krenwinkel, Kasabian and Watson entered the grounds of 10050 Cielo Drive, Benedict Canyon, shortly before dawn on 9 August, to begin a horrific slaughter. Sharon Tate and a group of friends were partying at the mansion when the self-styled 'Angels of Death' stealthily made their way towards the house. Linda Kasabian acted as lookout while the other three, wielding knives and uttering frenzied war cries, set upon the partygoers. Within a couple of hours, they had completed their grisly task and, in an explosion of mind-numbing violence, five innocent people had been butchered.

No one will ever know the extent of the terror and suffering the victims endured before the gang smeared the mansion walls with bizarre messages in the victims' blood. The scene police later encountered showed evidence of unbelievable brutality. The body of Steven Parent, the 18-year-old guest of the house's caretaker, was discovered slumped in his car in the driveway. Parent had encountered the raiders as he drove from the house. They had flagged him down and then shot him four times.

Their next find was the body of Abigail Folger, heiress to a coffee fortune, lying on the lawn. She had been cut to pieces as she tried to flee. Inside the house – which had the word 'Pigs' scrawled in blood on the door – they found the body of Hollywood hair stylist Jay Sebring. He had been stabbed, and then finished off with a gunshot. Polish film director Voytek Frykowski had been battered with a club by Watson, while repeating the mantra: 'I am the Devil come to do the Devil's work'. Frykowski had then been finished off by Atkins, who stabbed him six times with a knife.

The most sickening sight was the pathetic body of Sharon Tate. The 26-year-old actress had begged to be spared for the sake of the child she was carrying, due in just a month's time.

Her pleas for mercy had been greeted with derision and she suffered 16 stab wounds, killing both her and her unborn baby boy. A nylon rope was knotted around her neck and slung over a ceiling beam and the other end tied around the hooded head of Sebring.

Despite the gory proof that there was no limit to the powers he wielded over his followers, Manson was displeased with the night's events at the Tate residence. He felt he had not achieved his aim to spark a race war. There was more bloody work to be done, and this time he wanted to be in on the action himself.

The night after the slaughter, the four Tate murderers were again summoned, along with Steve Grogan and Leslie Van Houten, a former college queen and youngest member of the cult. Linda Kasabian was dispatched to murder an actor friend of hers – a plan that she thwarted by knocking on the wrong door. The others cruised the better neighbourhoods of Los Angeles in search of potential victims before settling on the home of Leno and Rosemary LaBianca, who owned a small chain of supermarkets. Manson burst into the couple's Waverly Drive mansion, tied them up and left them to the mercy of three of his cult slaves: Watson, Krenwinkel and Van Houten.

A sword, knives and forks were used in the barbaric slaying. Police found a fork protruding from Leno LaBianca's body, with the word 'War' carved into his stomach. He had been stabbed 26 times and symbolically hanged, with a bloodstained pillowcase used as a hood. A cord around his throat was attached to a heavy lamp and his hands were tied behind his back with a leather thong. Rosemary's nightdress had been pushed over her head and her back and buttocks were covered in stab wounds. She too was hooded by a pillowcase and had been hanged by a wire attached to a lamp. The word 'war' had been cut into her abdomen. On the walls, written in blood, were the words 'Death to the Pigs' and 'Rise'. The killers had misspelt 'Healter Skelter' on the fridge door.

Los Angeles police did not initially connect the two raids, and it was only the arrest of Susan Atkins in another investigation that brought the cult members to justice. She was picked up in connection with the slaying of musician and drug dealer Gary Hinman at his Topanga Canyon home ten days before the mass murders. He had been tortured to death and his blood used to scrawl the words 'Political Piggy' on a wall. Police were also investigating the disappearance of another man, Donald 'Shorty' Shea, a part-time movie stuntman who had mysteriously vanished from Spahn Ranch.

In custody, Susan Atkins was still 'high' on the experience of the headline-making, but still unaccounted for, butchery on Cielo Drive. She bragged about her role, sickening cellmates with her claims of drinking Sharon Tate's blood. 'I was there,' she boasted. 'We did it! It felt so good the first time I stabbed her. When she screamed at me, it did something to me, sent a rush through me, and I stabbed her again. I just kept stabbing her until she stopped screaming. It was like a sexual release, especially when you see the blood. It's better than a climax.'

In December 1969, the 'family' were rounded up and the incredible story of messianic Manson and his so-called 'witchlets' was flashed around the world. Charles Manson, the short, scraggy ex-con who had spent more than half his life behind bars, was charged with nine murders: the Tate and LaBianca massacres and two other slayings. But he was suspected of orchestrating as many as 25 other killings from his desert ranch. Suddenly Manson became the most talked-about criminal in the annals of Californian law enforcement.

At his sensational trial, Manson cut a terrifying figure as he spoke of his weird band of disciples. He said: 'These children who come at you with knives, they are your children. I didn't teach them. You did. I just tried to help them stand up. You eat meat and you kill things that are better than you are, and then you say how bad and even killers your children are. You made your children what they are. I am only what lives inside each and every one of you.'

On 29 March 1971, guilty verdicts were returned on all counts against the Manson gang. Looking at the jury who had convicted her, Susan Atkins warned them to lock their doors and to watch their children. The hearing had taken 38 weeks and was then the longest criminal trial in American history. It cost $1.25 million and 31,176 pages of transcript were taken. Sentencing them, Judge Charles Older said: 'It is my considered judgment that not only is the death penalty appropriate but it is almost compelled by the circumstances.' The sentences were commuted to life imprisonment in 1972 when California's death penalty was banned by the courts as being 'cruel and unusual punishment'.

Leslie Van Houten succeeded in gaining two retrials because her lawyer, Robert Hughes, had disappeared during her initial trial. His remains were later found in the mountains, and members of the Manson cult were suspected of his murder. Van Houten failed to win her freedom and was again sentenced to life imprisonment.

The years that rolled by following the court cases failed to dull public fascination with the abhorrent slayings, particularly the sadistic butchery of pregnant Sharon Tate. It became clear that Manson's gang had been ordered to kill completely different victims and that Sharon and her friends had simply been in the wrong place at the wrong time. The fact that record company boss Terry Melcher had once sneered at Manson's attempts to get a recording contract with him appeared to have sealed the fate of a group of totally unconnected people. There was also media speculation that the murdered Voytek Frykowski and Jay Sebring were known drug dealers and that Manson had wanted to take over their business.

The unanswered question remained, however, as to how one deranged man could mesmerise seemingly 'normal' young people to the extent that they could enact mindless massacres. Linda Kasabian, who, fearing for her own and her daughter's lives, escaped Manson's clutches and testified against him in court, winning herself immunity from prosecutors, once said: 'I can never accept that I was not punished for my part in this tragedy.' And in an attempt to explain how a mother could temporarily turn murderess, she recalled the night she was acting as lookout while her friends brutally murdered Sharon Tate and four others. 'I felt like I was dead,' she said. 'There was no emotion, no feeling. It just didn't register.'

The horrific story of the Manson gang's vile crime has resurfaced at regular intervals. In 1994 a 'Free Susan Atkins Campaign' was launched, her supporters proclaiming that the one-time church choir singer was now rehabilitated. However, after hearing evidence from Sharon Tate's sister, Patti, her appeal was refused and Atkins died of cancer behind bars in 2009. Patti, who was only 11 years old when Sharon was murdered, said: 'Every year up until her death, my mother would attend parole hearings of the murderers and she had to come face to face with them. That used to make her mad because one of these people knew Sharon and they were totally indifferent to what they had done. They just destroyed their blood-soaked clothes, washed their hands with a neighbour's watering can and walked down the street to kill more people.'

One Manson 'family' member was released, however. Steve Grogan had been in prison since being convicted with Manson and another follower, Bruce Davis, of the murders of musician Gary Hinman and of Donald Shea around the time of the Tate massacre. Grogan was freed in 1985 after leading police to Shea's body. Bruce Davis was still fighting for his release in 2013 after spending 40 years behind bars protesting that he had only been a bystander at the two slayings. When Manson prosecutor Stephen Kay heard of the parole application, he warned of the dangers of allowing a member of the cult back on the streets, saying: 'Would you want to wake up and find Bruce Davis next door? I think not.'

There is, of course, no chance of Manson ever being released. The crazed killer admits he would strike again if he was ever given his freedom. He ranted: 'I was pretty upset for a long time. I was really mad at a lot of people. I'm still willing to get out and kill a whole bunch of people. That's one reason I'm not too fast on getting out. Because if I got out, I'd feel obliged to get even.'

In 1987 Manson was controversially allowed to give a television interview from jail. Dressed in prison uniform of blue smock shirt and trousers, he was then still easily identifiable, his hair and beard still black, wild and long, his ravings disturbing: 'I can do anything I like to you people because that is what you did to me,' he said. 'Maybe I should have killed four or five hundred people that I might have felt better; then I would have felt I had offered society something.'

In June 2011 prison authorities issued a new photograph of Manson. It could have been the image of any old lag: a 76-year-old grey-haired and bearded grandfather whose greater part of life had been spent in jail. But there was one distinguishing mark on the staring face that recalled the reality of whose cold, eerie eyes were staring out of the picture. The swastika was still clearly seen on his forehead – the chilling reminder of a gang leader whose 'family' were responsible for one of America's most horrific acts of slaughter.

CHAPTER 25

SUPER-CROOKS WHO CARVED UP AN ENTIRE COUNTRY

As Communism came to an end in the Soviet Union, freedom-loving citizens rejoiced – but so too did a sinister breed of super-crooks. And as the old regime dissolved, summit meetings took place across the nation to carve up big business in the newly promised free-market economy. It was then that the Russian Mafiya was born and is now among the world's largest and most powerful criminal groupings. Never has organised crime become such a pervasive force so swiftly, and seldom has the violence been as extreme as in Russia.

When the Soviet Union imploded at the end of the 1980s, the resulting vacuum allowed the Mobs to quickly seize immense power. With the old state structure discredited and the government unable to enforce the law, the grasping gangsters grabbed easy pickings from money laundering, racketeering, extortion, arms smuggling, art theft, cyber-crime, human trafficking, prostitution, drug trafficking, arson, fraud, counterfeiting and simple larceny.

However, the biggest prizes were gained out of those businesses in the muddled process of changing from collectives to private ownership. The Mafiya penetrated almost every sector of the economy, from banking to energy to mining to heavy industry. Their net has now stretched worldwide. Of the estimated 6,000 separate Mafiya groups, more than 200 are said to have a global reach, having expanded to 50 countries and with a membership of up to 300,000. Combined they are labelled Russkaya Mafiya but singularly they are known as 'Bratva' (brotherhood), 'Bragada' (brigade) or 'Vorovskoy mir' (world of thieves).

Despite the Mafiya's massive growth, the Russian authorities appear to be in denial. In December 2009 the head of the Russian National Central Bureau of Interpol, Timur Lakhonin, asserted: 'Certainly, there is crime involving our former compatriots abroad – but there is no data suggesting that an organised structure of criminal groups comprising former Russians exists abroad.' A more realistic appraisal was given in response by prominent French criminologist Alain Bauer, who described the Mafiya as 'one of the best structured criminal organisations in Europe, with a quasi-military operation'.

So how did they become so powerful? The seeds of the present-day Russian Mafiya were sown in the gulags – the remote, brutal prison camps where dictator Joseph Stalin, attempting to wipe out the so-called 'world of thieves', had deported those he had not executed. They became a prison elite and, when after Stalin's death 8 million inmates were released from the gulags, they returned to the cities of Soviet state as the toughest warlords in the underworld.

Criminal activity flourished, a black market boomed and corruption began to spread throughout the government. When in the 1980s Mikhail Gorbachev loosened restrictions on private business, the Soviet Union was already beginning to collapse. More gangs emerged, exploiting the unstable governments of the former Republics, and at its highest point even controlling as much as two-thirds of the Russian economy.

One of the West's leading experts on the Mafiya is Mark Galeotti, a professor at New York University, who specialises in Russian criminal organisations. In his books on the subject, Dr Galeotti lists five types of Mafiya grouping. At the lower end of the chain are gangsters dealing in traditional criminal enterprises such as prostitution, protection and robbery. The second category is that of specialists like money-launderers. Higher up the ladder are the white-collar criminals, whom the Professor describes as pseudo-businessmen, often forming conglomerates controlling an array of seemingly legitimate businesses. At the top of the Russkaya Mafiya hierarchy are the deal-makers and commissioners of crime, the equivalent of the Sicilian Mafia's 'Cupola' or the US Mafia's 'Commission'.

Operating in parallel with this hierarchical structure are the corrupt sections of the police and the military. The latter sell high-quality protection and weapons. It has been alleged that members of the army's 16th Spestnaz Brigade have moonlighted as hitmen for the Mafiya. An entire working submarine was once sold to a Colombian drugs cartel. Corruption within the police is also endemic. In 1994 about 500 rogue police officers were arrested on corruption charges when it was discovered that Moscow's Tenth District precinct were operating a vice ring, using police cars to take prostitutes to clients who rang the police station with their orders!

Nationally, the largest gang in Russia is reckoned to be the Solntsevskaya, named after the Moscow suburb of Solntsevo. With about 5,000 members, it specialises in drugs, gun running and extortion. An American hotelier, Paul Tatum, complained to police in 1995 that Solntsevskaya heavies had threatened his life. He was shot dead the following year. The Solntsevskaya has overtaken the country's former major player, the Dolgoprudnenskaya, which rose to prominence in Moscow's Dolgoprudny suburb in the late eighties and quickly spread nationwide. Its main field of operations is prostitution and sleazy clubland. Smaller players are the Orekhovskaya gang, founded by former KGB agents, and Moscow's Ostankino and Lubertsy clans. St Petersburg is dominated by the Tambov Syndicate.

Oddly, in the same way that the US Mafia is dominated by Sicilians and Neapolitans, so the Russian Mafiya has Chechens and Georgians playing a disproportionately large role. The biggest Chechen crime gang is the Obshina, whose riches have come from kidnapping and bank robbery but who have also elbowed their way into the lucrative East European cigarette smuggling racket. Most of these gangs' members identify themselves by a complex system of tattoos that can give detailed information about the wearer and their gang allegiances.

Thanks to these thuggish foot soldiers, extortion has become a way of life in Russia. Few victims dare speak out but one Canadian entrepreneur, Doug Steele, told journalists how owning a Moscow nightclub had cost him $1 million in pay-offs not only to Mafyia bullies but to police and city officials. He spoke out after foiling a kidnap attempt, saying: 'You have to grease the palm or you won't be in business. If it was not for the Mafyia there would not be an economy. They are a major driving force behind what goes on here.' The Russian government appears to agree. In a leaked report, the security services estimated that criminal organisations control, either directly or indirectly, 60 per cent of state companies, 40 per cent of private business and 80 per cent of banks. Which might explain why, in a five-year period, almost 100 Russian bankers were murdered.

A former manager of Moscow's Prombank revealed how blatantly the local crime lords try to extort money from the banking system. He said: 'They no longer come and ask for fixed sums of money. They demand something that allows them to gain control of your entire business. I told them I would not cooperate.' The Mafyia do not normally take 'no' for an answer; the manager subsequently survived a grenade attack.

Any institution with access to large amounts of money can expect a visit from the Mafyia. Even the Afghan Veterans' Association, which has a welfare role similar to the British Legion, has been used to launder dirty money. Its head was murdered in 1994. After it split into two groups, the chief of one branch survived an assassination attempt the following year. In 1996 the leader of the other faction, his wife and 11 others were killed when a bomb exploded in a cemetery during a funeral.

Russia sees around 10,000 fatal shootings a year, more than 500 of which are contract killings. One of the most sensational was the murder of one of the country's most powerful Mob bosses, shot dead by a sniper in broad daylight in central Moscow in January 2013. Aslan 'Grandpa' Usoyan, a Kurdish 75-year-old, had survived at least two previous attempts on his life. Usoyan, who had built a vast crime empire stretching across the former Soviet Union, had been at war with rival Mafyia gangs, particularly in Sochi, home to highly lucrative construction projects as the resort prepared to host the 2014 Winter Olympics.

In Soviet times, the KGB would have kept a lid on such turf wars but its successor, the FSB (Russian Federal Security Service) is under-funded and demoralised. The national police have an elite Berkut (Eagle) force and conduct much-publicised commando-style raids, yet appear to catch only lesser gangsters. Professor Mark Galeotti commented: 'We are going to see more blood on the streets. The Russian underworld is a much more volatile place than it was five years ago, particularly because of the influx of Afghan heroin and the opportunities created by the Sochi Winter Olympics.'

A US diplomatic cable released by WikiLeaks in 2010 described Russia as 'a virtual mafia state'. But it has long since ceased to limit its activities to its own borders. Louis Freeh, former director of the FBI, said that in the mid-1990s the Mafiya was the organisation that posed the greatest threat to US national security.

The ease with which Russian mobsters operate abroad was highlighted when Vyacheslav Ivankov, one of the country's most brutal criminals, arrived in the United States in 1992, having just served a prison sentence of ten years. He was allowed in on a business visa, claiming that he wanted to set himself up in the film industry. But it was said that Mafiya compatriots had sent him to the US because he was killing too many people back in his homeland. Within a year, from his Brooklyn headquarters, he had built up an international operation that included narcotics, money laundering and prostitution and had made ties with the American Mafia and Colombian drug cartels. Ivankov was arrested by the FBI in 1995 and charged with the extortion of about £2 million. In

2004 he was deported back to Moscow, where five years later he was shot dead by a mystery assassin.

Another visiting Russian, Ludwig 'Tarzan' Fainberg, was arrested in Miami in 1997 and charged with global arms dealing while acting as an intermediary between a Colombian cocaine cartel and the corrupt Russian military. Extraordinarily, Fainberg had helped the cartel get six Russian military helicopters in 1993 and the following year had arranged the purchase of a Soviet-era submarine for cocaine smuggling to the US. But federal agents had been keeping watch on the Russian and the cartel's agent, Cuban-born Juan Almeida. When arrested and threatened with life imprisonment, Fainberg testified against Almeida in exchange for a shorter sentence of 33 months.

Elsewhere, the Russians have been unwelcome guests in crime 'hotspots' around the globe. In 2010 a EU report complained that the French Riviera and Spanish Costas were being blighted by Russian organised crime, the latter branded as a virtual 'Mafiya state'. In Israel, the large influx of Russian Jews has caused the formation of new Mafiya branches and a resultant crime wave that has caused calls for strengthened police action by the Israeli government.

The Mafiya operate in Britain, sometimes with dramatically bloody results but more often in a softly-softly fashion. 'It exists but it's invisible,' was how one security expert described it in 2012. London is the chosen home for many rich Russians seeking a haven from their homeland, where they have little faith in the rule of law. They feel safer in the capital they have affectionately dubbed 'Londongrad'. According to Andrei Soldatov, a leading crime author, the Mafiya is well established, with clandestine Syndicates heavily involved in money laundering in the City of London. They are also engaged in electronic fraud, commercial espionage and trafficking in people and drugs. Sadly, warns Soldatov, Britain has been ill-prepared for the threat from these Russian gangsters.

A leaden hint at the growth of a new hidden underworld encroaching on London came in March 2012 with an attempted hit on a former Russian banker. A lone gunman shot German Gorbuntsov, 45, five times with a pistol as he entered an apartment block in the Canary Wharf financial district. Gorbuntsov, who used to own four banks, had been days away from giving evidence to an investigation into the assassination attempt on a former business associate. Left for dead, his life was saved by medics, who treated him at an unnamed hospital guarded round the clock by a Metropolitan Police team.

Another expatriate who fled west was flamboyant Georgian billionaire Badri Patarkatsishvili, who arrived in Britain in 2008. He was one of the oligarchs who made a fortune from the privatisation of state-owned industries during the presidency of Boris Yeltsin but fell from favour when Vladimir Putin succeeded him. Patarkatsishvili was found dead at his Surrey mansion from a suspected heart attack in 2008 at the age of 52. He had earlier claimed that a four-man hit squad had been sent to London 'to do something against me'.

Patarkatsishvili was behind many of Russia's most successful privatised companies, including the oil group Sibneft, of which he was a founding partner along with Boris Berezovsky, another exiled oligarch. Berezovsky had fled to Britain in 2006 after surviving assassination attempts in Moscow, including a bomb blast that decapitated his chauffeur. He told a journalist: 'I do not feel safe – here have been three attempts to kill me here in London. There are elements who want rid of me.' In March 2013 the 67-year-old tycoon was found dead in the bathroom of his Berkshire mansion. He was said to have hanged himself but at his inquest, which opened and was adjourned four months later, police told the Berkshire coroner they were unable to 'completely eliminate' the possibility that he had been murdered.

Yet another Russian expatriate who died in suspicious circumstances was Alexander Perepilichny, whose body was found close to his Surrey mansion in 2012. The 44-year-old had been helping Swiss prosecutors in a money-laundering case involving Russian officials and had also provided evidence over the 2009 death in custody of Sergei Magnitsky, a lawyer who had exposed corruption in government circles.

Perepilichny had fled to Britain three years earlier with his young wife and children after falling out with members of a criminal network thought to include corrupt members of the Russian police, tax office, judiciary and government. At the time of his death, he was providing information to William Browder, once a big investor in Russia, who fell foul of the same gang. The financier fled to Britain under threats from the criminals, who aimed to hijack his Hermitage Fund investment firm and milk it of $230 million. Browder's lawyer, 44-year-old Sergei Magnitsky, bravely remained in Russia when his client fled the country. Thrown into prison and held for a year without charge, he was repeatedly tortured to make him withdraw his testimony against the gang, which included members of the Interior Ministry's own police force. Finally, his jailers beat him to death in November 2009.

'Sergei had been held hostage – and they killed their hostage,' said Bill Browder, who in July 2013 was convicted in his absence of tax fraud and sentenced to nine years in a prison colony. At the same Moscow 'show trial', Sergei Magnitsky was also posthumously convicted of fraud – bizarrely one of the very crimes he claimed to have uncovered among the higher echelon of Interior Ministry officials.

'The verdict will go down in history as one of the most shameful moments for Russia since the days of Joseph Stalin,' said Browder, who warned that Russia had turned into a 'criminal state'. He added: 'The Mafiya and the Russian government security services are now one and the same. Any place where there are lots of Russians will attract the security services to carry out their dirty business outside of Russia.'

The murder of Alexander Litvinenko in 2006 was the most high-profile example of this collaboration. A former officer of the KGB and its successor the FSB, he fled from court prosecution in Russia and was granted political asylum in the United Kingdom. According to his wife and father, he subsequently worked for MI6 and MI5. In 2006 Litvinenko, then aged 43, met former KGB agents for tea in a London hotel. He suddenly fell ill and died within three weeks from poisoning by radioactive polonium-210. From his deathbed, he accused Kremlin-led assassins.

Murders such as those of Litvinenko in London and Magnitsky in Moscow caused an international outcry that led to a campaign, fiercely opposed by President Putin, to ban 60 officials accused of complicity from entering the European Union and the United States. Browder believes it is justified. He said: 'Imagine Russian criminals with all their powers and connections. Then imagine they also have access to the police and all the powers of the state to carry out their criminal enterprises – that's how powerful these people are. It is becoming increasingly obvious that the entire government apparatus in Russia is not there to provide leadership and services for the population. It functions only for top officials to steal as much money as they can.'

CHAPTER 26

EUROPE IN CRISIS?
NO, IT'S A BOOM TIME
FOR CRIME!

Business has been booming in Europe, even through its years of desperate financial crises, but it is not the kind of trade that's welcome – for when times are hard, crime is king. The boom in organised Mob rackets was already underway as borders came down with the European Union's new Eastern members, the consequent increase in legitimate imports being matched by a flood of illegal drugs, counterfeit luxury good, fake euros and traffic in humans. A report from the EU's law enforcement and criminal intelligence agency Europol revealed that while the global economy suffered its roughest ride from 2008 onwards, organised crime actually profited from the downturn. The report pointed out that cash-strapped consumers tended to choose counterfeit products. The jobless were prey to gangmasters and pimps; the dispossessed turned to drugs. And relaxed customs controls and low-cost airlines made the trafficking of goods and humans easier.

It is clear from the Europol's analysis that, just as the once-independent nations of Europe can no longer be studied in isolation when it comes to legitimate trade, so the illegal trade of the region's major crime gangs must be seen as a transnational problem for the forces of law and order. This chapter will attempt to define some of the present flashpoints and the fears for the future as gang culture spreads across the continent. Europol's so-called Organised Crime Threat Assessment breaks up Europe's gangs into various 'hubs'.

The North-West Hub, with Holland and neighbouring Belgium at its core, is described as 'the most important geographical crime centre'. Gangs from these countries, plus Britain and Ireland, are operating there in competition with Eastern European groups, as well as gangs originating from Turkey, Pakistan, China, Vietnam, Colombia and Africa. In many cases, says Europol, such gangs are comprised of the children of first-generation immigrants now living in the EU. The North-West Hub also has strong links with the Middle East, specially Dubai, a key financial centre and logistics base for gangsters. There, they make contacts, deals, launder money and coordinate shipments.

The Southern Hub is dominated by Italian organised crime groups, using the port of Naples for cocaine and cannabis trafficking, along with illegal immigration, euro forgery and fake goods. According to Europol's files: 'Both Camorra (Naples) and Apulian (Puglia) crime groups have established extensive links with Chinese groups to distribute counterfeit products such as software, CDs, movies and luxury goods'. More dangerous is the explosion in synthetic drugs, such as amphetamines and methamphetamine, and fake pharmaceutical products made in China, Hong Kong, India, Thailand and Turkey.

The North-East Hub is the home of Baltic and Russian gangs, with the twin crime centres of Lithuania and St Petersburg. The 'open door' to smuggling of drugs and humans into Europe is Kaliningrad, a tiny territory of Russia that sits in the middle of EU territory. Dubbed 'the Corridor of Crime', Kaliningrad is best known for AIDS epidemics, drug plagues, pollution, bleak tower blocks – and 20,000 crimes a year among a population of 400,000.

The South-East Hub uses the gangster-ridden Balkan states as a corridor from the Black Sea and Romania to the Mediterranean ports in Slovenia, Croatia and Montenegro. The Balkan regions suffer from 'the presence of pre-established transnational organised crime networks,' says Europol, adding: 'Smuggling via the Balkans has proved to be a low-risk route into the EU.'

This region provides the ultimate proof that crime recognises no national boundaries. For instance, Romania is the easternmost country within the EU. More than 1,500 miles to the west is the United Kingdom. In 2013 alarming statistics were revealed about Britain's prison population – showing an increase of almost 40 per cent in little over a year in the number of Romanian criminals in British jails, from 454 to 624. As the total of UK-born inmates fell, the ranks of Eastern European prisoners soared amid a crime wave by migrants exploiting EU freedom of movement rules. The figures raised fears about the impact on Britain with the looming 2014 removal of border controls on crime-ridden Romania and neighbouring Bulgaria.

A warning that Britain's problems were about to multiply came in even more alarming reports from Germany, where the influx of Romanian and Bulgarian immigrants has already caused a crime wave. There has been a six-fold increase in migration since the two countries joined the EU in 2007. The Association of German Cities warned of 'social unrest' and spoke of 'peace being extremely endangered'. One crime hotspot is the north-western city of Duisburg, where newcomers, crammed into crumbling apartments and without work to feed their families, have formed lawless gangs. Duisburg's mayor, Soeren Link, sparked nationwide soul-searching when he announced in 2013 that his city could no longer cope and that the cost to the town of dealing with the problem was around £15 million a year. His warning was supported by a report from the city's police blaming Romanian family gangs for an explosion in crime, particularly pick-pocketing, prostitution and muggings. As an example of the fear gripping German citizens, Mayor Link said one 65-year-old woman had bought a 200,000-volt stun gun for her protection.

Being the richest country in Europe, Germany has long attracted economic migrants, who have formed their own communities and spawned their own gangs, initially for protection but ultimately for their own self-serving ends. In fact, Germany has turned not only into a multi-cultural society but a multi-criminal one. And there's a pattern to this criminality – the Turks traditionally run the drugs trade, the Poles and Romanians dominate the car-theft sector, the Italians organise money laundering and the Yugoslavs specialise in vice. Hans-Ludwig Zachert, former head of the Bundeskriminalamt (BKA), Germany's federal police agency, has described the foreign gangs rather sweepingly, as 'Public Enemy Number One'.

Turks are the largest ethnic minority in Germany, with an

estimated three million living there. During the 1980s and 90s, and particularly after reunification, cities were blighted by racist violence targeting the newcomers. The Kreuzberg district of Berlin was the scene of turf wars between skinheads and neo-Nazis and the most feared Turkish gang, the '36 Boys', named after the old postal code of their area. One neo-Nazi gang, dubbed the 'Zwickau Cell' after the hometown of its leading members, were blamed for a nationwide spree of racially motivated murders. The group was thought responsible for the deaths of eight Turkish and one Greek immigrant between 2000 and 2006, as well as a German policewoman in 2007.

Another infamous murder spree was caused by feuding between Italian Mafia factions. The Calabria-based 'Ndrangheta were responsible for seven murders in Duisburg in 2007. A gun attack left six victims, one aged only 16, dead in two cars outside a restaurant where they had been celebrating an eighteenth birthday. Since then, there have been more than 25 prosecution cases against Italian organised crime Syndicates operating in Germany. The Italian Mafia, who focus mainly on the drug trade and money laundering, are particularly strong in Bavaria. The state's police chiefs have urged greater resources and international cooperation to clamp down on the creeping threat posed by the cash-rich Italian Mafia.

One aspect of Germany's crime wave has caused cops to kick-start a war on the nation's violent biker gangs. The motorised thugs had been fighting an escalating battle against police – and each other – with increasing numbers ending up behind bars. After a 2012 report by federal prosecutors revealed that one in every ten crimes was linked to a motorcycle gang, urgent laws were passed to stem the menace. Some chapters of biker thugs have been outlawed, making it illegal even to show their club 'colours'. Others have had their assets confiscated.

The first German chapter of the Hells Angels was founded in the 1970s in Hamburg around the infamous red-light districts of St Pauli and Sternschanze. But, as in North America, Australia and elsewhere, the growing gangs of German Hells Angels became locked in a bloody war over territory with the rival gangs of 'Bandidos'. Berlin and Frankfurt have been the centres of most biker crime, with many outbreaks of violence in the capital, where Hells Angels chapters claim to be defending the city against Bandidos trying to muscle in. The turf war sees gang fights and murders on the streets. In 2009 a Berlin Bandidos leader was stabbed and shot to death in the eastern Hohenschönhausen district. Two months later in Duisburg's red-light district, a Bandidos was executed with a single bullet to the head. A shocking case that same year involved associates of the Flensburg Hells Angels, who were accused of having extorted €380,000 from a businessman – who felt under so much pressure that he went berserk, stabbed his wife and seven-year-old daughter to death and set fire to his home.

In early 2010 a Bandidos was stabbed in Kiel shortly after shots had been fired at the house of the local Hells Angels leader. Soon afterwards in Bonn, a Hells Angels shot dead a police officer of the SEK (Spezialeinsatzkommando) during a house search. The gunman was acquitted of murder charges by claiming he acted in self-defence because of previous Bandidos murder threats. In May 2010 the warring gangs declared an armistice but investigators doubted their commitment. They were right. The Bandidos lured in hundreds of new young recruits, mainly from immigrant families in former East

Germany, and poured back on to the streets. But the Hell's Angels went on the defensive and violence again erupted, particularly in the east, Berlin and the northern state of Schleswig-Holstein. The attacks have since escalated from knife assaults to shootings to bombings. As feuding spread to Cologne in 2012, provincial authorities followed Frankfurt's action in shutting down the local chapter of the Hells Angels, confiscating all its property and banning public display of its regalia. The North Rhine-Westphalian home secretary said: 'Hells Angels intentionally ignore the basic values of our society. They close themselves off, set up their own rules and practice vigilante justice.'

Race plays a significant part in the gang wars. In a mass defection, 76 members of the Berlin Bandidos switched gangs to join their previously sworn enemies, the Hells Angels – seen as a 'nationalistic' revolt against their Turkish immigrant leadership. The Hells Angels issued what amounted to a declaration of war, vowing: 'No other gang will be tolerated in Berlin.' But in May 2012 police raided the city's chapter and ordered it disbanded. That failed to stem the violence. Within days, gang leader André Sommer was shot in the street and left in a coma. Two Bandidos bosses were shot in revenge.

Later that year, police retaliated in force, sending 1,000 officers in mass raids across northern Germany. They were relying on information from a Hells Angels supergrass whom they arrested for blackmail, pimping and human trafficking. He told prosecutors of torture sessions and executions. As a result, police in Kiel began digging up a warehouse in a vain search for a body said to be buried in the concrete foundations.

Two-wheeled gangsterism is peculiarly virulent in Germany but the problem is fast spreading across the rest of Europe –

partly due to overseas biker gangs arriving on the Continent to fight for control of drugs, weapons and human trafficking. In January 2013 Europol reported that the arrival of notorious gangs, including Comancheros and Rebels from Australia, Rock Machine from Canada and Mongols and Vagos from the US has exacerbated tensions with established clubs. Europol said the number of biker gang chapters across the continent had increased dramatically to more than 700, with the greatest growth in north-east and south-east Europe. It warned of a repeat of the Nordic biker wars of the 1990s that left at least 11 dead and dozens injured during a three-year battle between Hells Angels and Bandidos in Scandinavia that involved the use of car bombs and machine guns.

Just as biker violence is often an 'imported' problem across northern Europe, so gang rivalry in the south is also split along racial lines. In Spain, home-grown gangs regularly clash with rivals of Latin American origin, particularly in the poorer Madrid suburbs. The overall number of immigrants soared from 1.8 per cent of the Spanish population to more than 10 per cent in the two decades from 1990, the largest groups being Ecuadorians and Colombians. The result is that Hispanic street gangs in the capital have tripled their membership, say police, who accuse them of being behind violent street attacks, kidnappings and killings. The largest and most powerful groups, the Latin Kings and Latin Queens, claim to control certain suburban streets that they have renamed 'Inca Land' or 'Aztec Kingdom'. They identify themselves by ancient mystical symbols, such as the five-point crown, but wear modern rap-style clothes and gold bead necklaces.

The Latin Kings were originally formed by immigrants to the United States and introduced into Spain only in 2000.

Their founder, young Ecuadorian Eric Javier Vara Velastegui, known as 'King Wolverine', retained control of his gang from prison after being sentenced to 40 years by a Madrid court for rape, violent assault and kidnapping. The Latin Kings' big rivals are the Netas, founded in the prisons of Puerto Rico, and the Dominican Don't Play, from the Dominican Republic. Recently a new and violent group has emerged in Catalonia. Known as the Mara Salvatrucha ('Salvadorian Gang'), it was formed by Central American migrants to Los Angeles in the Eighties. Worryingly for the Spanish, its ominous motto is: 'Rape, Control, Kill'.

Out of the Spanish cities and onto the highways, two other types of gang are more mobile menaces. Bikers are a growing problem, according to the national Policia, who in 2009 raided Hells Angels MC chapters in Barcelona, Valencia and Malaga, where members were charged with drugs and weapons trafficking and extortion. A search of 30 properties yielded military-style weapons and ammunition, bulletproof vests, a kilo of cocaine, neo-Nazi literature and €200,000 in cash. The other problem out on the Autopistas is blatant highway robbery. Crime gangs target hire cars and foreign vehicles, tricking their victims with loud noises, apparent accidents, supposed vehicle problems or pleas for help before stealing bags and valuables. A hotspot for the gangs is the AP7 highway running south down the Mediterranean coast from the French border. GB-registered cars are regularly targeted and the British Embassy in Madrid warned: 'Motorists may be driving along the motorway and not notice there's a car close up behind. Someone in the other car throws a stone, creating a loud bang. The British drivers pull over to see what has happened and the gang causes a distraction to steal from them or simply mug them. It's a growing problem.'

By contrast, crossing the border into Portugal might seem like the introduction to a peaceable paradise. In 2012 the annual index published by the Institute for Economics and Peace ranked Portugal the sixteenth most peaceable nation in the world. That is not to say it is devoid of crime; the country has always been prone to street offences like purse-snatching and pick-pocketing. But in common with other European countries, the atmosphere altered with the influx of new waves of migrants. Street gangs, particularly in greater Lisbon and Porto, became a source of deep discontent from the Nineties when immigrants arrived from diverse locations around the globe – in particular, the Ukraine, Moldova, Romania, Brazil and former Portuguese territories in Africa. The gangs have been blamed for damaging commuter lines, petrol stations and violent attacks in nightclubs.

Ethnic gangs have caused even greater social upheavals in France where, just like Spain, pan-European crime has become an 'imported' problem. Since the summer of 2011 the French government has been working with Romanian authorities to repatriate 15,000 Roma travellers living in makeshift camps and squalid squats. They are deemed responsible for a tenth of all crime in France – half of which, said Interior Minister Claude Guéant, is down to children. 'It is a cruel, unacceptable situation,' he said. 'These children are exploited by mafia bosses who draw them into delinquency and slavery. That cannot be allowed to continue.' This sort of petty crime is particularly prevalent in busy public areas like the Gare du Nord in Paris. There, teams of young beggars and pickpockets work the concourse, while their Fagin-like masters lurk nearby. Many of these youngsters have been arrested several times but the authorities are powerless to act. A clampdown in 2012 saw hundreds of new expulsion orders issued to the Roma travellers, and begging was banned on the Champs-Élysées and the more popular tourist spots of Paris.

A study by France's Public Security Department (DCSP) in 2011 showed that the number of street gangs nationwide had inexplicably doubled since 2008. Almost 500 separate gangs were identified, mainly with memberships of no more than 20, who defend their territory aggressively. With no identity-related insignia, they tend to target schools, shopping malls and street corners, where they deal in drugs and commit petty theft. In a single year, 1,096 gang members were arrested, 438 of whom were minors. Among the most violent gangs are Tamil groups such as the Red Boys, the Viluthus and the Sathanai. In Paris, a 26-year-old Sri-Lankan was found after a gang fight with his head split in two and his hands cut off with an axe or a sabre. But the ethnic gangs are not all male. With names like the Tokyo Girls, Bana Danger and Momi Fiuu, ghetto gangs of black girls aged as young as 14 terrorise parts of Paris and cities as far away as Nice on the Riviera.

A disturbing link between the two cities emerged in a court case that ended in May 2013 with a seven-year jail sentence for a modern-day Fagin who masterminded the biggest child pick-pocketing gang seen in France, with 500 young girls threatened with beatings and even rape unless they each stole €300 a day. Bosnian gypsy Fehim Hamidovic, aged 60, was accused of running a Dickensian gang of Roma girls as young as 12 who were forced to steal cash and valuables from tourists or face cigarette burns or even more brutal abuse. At the time the ring was dismantled in 2010, police estimated it was responsible for 75 per cent of all thefts in Paris's Metro system. Two girls, aged just 11 and 14, testified that they were responsible for transferring the entire Paris group's earnings to Nice. If the takings were less than €60,000 a week, then they would be 'detained and beaten'.

Crime of a more organised nature has long plagued Nice and its neighbours, where the glittering Mediterranean coast traditionally offers rich pickings for Riviera rogues. From cat burglars to Corsican drug czars, from The Pink Panther to The French Connection, crime in the region from Marseilles to Monaco has often been falsely glamorised. The sprawling, multi-cultural melting pot that is Marseille is often portrayed as the crime capital of France, and gambling, prostitution and drugs have long funded the fearsome families running the city.

Oddly, before World War Two the smuggling of cheese from Italy was also lucrative. The mobsters who dominated the underworld in those days were mainly Corsican – Paul Carbone and his local sidekick François Spirito, both of whom collaborated with the Nazis. After the war their businesses fell to a new chief gangster, the Corsican Antoine Guerini, and his brothers. They developed what became known as The French Connection, with Marseille the centre for the export of drugs to the US.

Chicago-style gang warfare arrived there in the 1970s when police estimated that more than £70 million a year was being raked in from drugs, casino rackets, prostitution and extortion. In 1970 alone, more than 100 people died in a wave of shootings that began with the jailing of 70-year-old crime czar 'Mimi' Guerini for his part in a gangland murder.

The spate of killings was stepped up in 1977 after the shooting of ex-jockey Jacques 'Tomcat' Imbert, who owed his nickname to his reputation for having nine lives. Imbert, who ran a nightclub in the small Riviera resort of Cassis, was shot

23 times by three hitmen from a rival gang. He survived, though he lost an eye and was permanently crippled. A month after Imbert's shooting, one of his three attackers was executed at a cemetery while visiting his son's grave. Next day the second man was killed in the street. The third man was murdered a few weeks later, shot as his car stopped at traffic lights.

The battle for power on the Riviera erupted into bloody violence again in 1978 when nine people were gunned down in a Marseille bar, riddled with 91 bullets. Five of the victims had police records but the other four were thought to be innocent customers, shot to keep them quiet. Police, who were working closely with the FBI, said they believed the killings were 'Mafia-linked'.

Despite the mix of drugs, gambling and prostitution that has dominated the Marseille Mob scene, Jacques 'Tomcat' Imbert was still at large in the city after four decades, having avoided any serious convictions and serving only short prison terms. Describing himself as 'retired', he told a reporter in late 2012: 'The cops always came to ask me about the jobs I didn't do. For the ones I did do, I never saw anyone.' A legend on the streets of Marseille, he said he felt secure enough not to need bodyguards and to be able to drink in bars with his back to the door. As he pointed out, who'd want to kill a man who had come back from the dead?

Meanwhile, France's second city is still battling waves of murderous warfare. Local Marseille politicians even asked for the army to be sent in to tackle the gangs, who nowadays go equipped with Kalashnikovs and other combat weapons. A police spokesman in 2012 described the situation as 'terrifying and inhuman because the violence has no limits'.

This may be a digression, but when dealing with the French

propensity to glamorise the shadier side of life, it is an opportunity to be reminded briefly of the career of the most notorious Gallic gangster of them all. He was the dashing Jacques Mesrine who, after an early round of bank robberies in Canada, returned to his homeland with the boast that he would become 'the world's most famous crook'.

In 1973 Mesrine and his gang committed a dozen armed robberies, netting millions. When captured that year, he escaped from a court in Compiègne with a gun that an accomplice had hidden in a lavatory – and using the judge as a human shield. Mesrine nurtured the image of a dashing and gallant vagabond, telling a girl bank clerk who had pressed the alarm button: 'Don't worry, I like to work to music.' In court again in 1977, he and a gang member escaped by squirting soapy water into the eyes of their guard, donning his uniform and fleeing over a wall. In 1978 he robbed the flat of a judge who had previously sentenced him to 20 years' jail. When police came running up the stairs, he fooled them by shouting, 'Quick, Mesrine's in there', and sped past them into the night. On 2 November 1979, police watched as Mesrine, then aged 42, walked with his girlfriend from his swanky Paris apartment to his BMW. Once in the car, the cops took no chances. Twenty-one bullets shattered his windscreen. Mesrine died instantly – though his legend lives on.

It would be neat to end this chapter on the dark but disparate threads of European lawlessness with this story of a dashing anti-hero. Sadly, the reality of modern-day Continental criminality is depressingly lacking in glamour. The clearest indication of how times have changed in the realms of European gangsterism is not on the smart streets of western capital cities but on the tacky avenues of Buzescu, Romania, lined with tasteless palaces. Buzescu, a town about 50 miles south of the capital Bucharest, has only 5,000 inhabitants but 30 registered scrap metal dealers. It is a hub from which copper, bronze and lead are transported around the world. This is where the proceeds end up from the theft across Europe of metal worth millions – from rail lines, telecom networks, power stations, churches and even war memorials. In Buzescu, the Roma community is among the country's wealthiest, its gang leaders building huge gaudy mansions, with turrets, pillars and gold-painted roof tiles. Horses and carts rumble by outside but on the driveways stand BMWs, Porsches and Mercedes.

Across the other side of Europe, in the theft-ravaged Belgian city of Charleroi, magistrate Philippe Dujardin lamented in 2013: 'In Romania whole neighbourhoods are built with money from the National Belgian Railway Company. The people who live there are leaders of a veritable mafia.' And in Britain, where metal theft is thought to cost £1 billion a year, copper continues to be ripped from railways, endangering thousands of travellers, and plaques with the names of the fallen vanish overnight from war memorials.

CHAPTER 27

THE ROOTS OF EVIL...
AND WHY THERE
IS NEVER 'A
HAPPY ENDING'

Sicilian Mafia leader Salvatore 'Toto' Riina was the man who ordered the most infamous 'hit' in Italian criminal history. On 23 May 1992 a half-ton bomb was placed in a drainage pipe under a motorway between Palermo and its international airport. Riina's men hid in a building above the road and waited. Just before 6pm a convoy of six cars approached. As they passed an old fridge, left at the side of the road as a marker, Mafioso soldier Giovanni Brusca pressed a switch. A vast explosion ripped upwards through the tarmac, catapulting the first car into the air until it landed 70 metres away, among olive trees. The second car, despite being reinforced and bullet-proofed, had its engine blown away and the rest of the car plunged into the crater made by the bomb. The third car was damaged but intact. Killed in the lead car were three bodyguards: Rocco Dicillo, Antonio Montinaro and Vito

Schifani. They had been guarding the principal occupant of the second car, Giovanni Falcone, who died alongside his wife Francesca. The explosion had been so powerful that it registered on local earthquake monitors.

The death of Giovanni Falcone shocked the nation. Most adult Italians remember where they were when they heard the news. Several public figures declared themselves ashamed to be Italian. For Falcone was the country's bravest, most determined law enforcer. The Sicilian Mafia's nemesis, his death not only demonstrated the organisation's continued power, it also finally destroyed the myth that had lingered in southern Italy that the ancient secret society was run, as the clichéd claim went, by 'men of honour'.

The Mafia's romanticised roots are as shadowy as its rotten modern-day operations. Even the derivation of the name itself is unknown. It may come from a Sicilian dialect term for bravado or possibly from an Arabic word, *mehia*, which means boastful. All that is certain about the Mafia's origins is that it was formed in the thirteenth century as a patriotic underground movement to resist Sicily's unwelcome rulers, the French. And on Easter Monday 1282, these freedom fighters led a bloody massacre of the foreign invaders as the bells of the capital, Palermo, rang for vespers.

Over the centuries this secret brotherhood flourished, dedicated to protecting the local populace from the despotic rulers of the island. Similar societies were subsequently founded on the mainland – the four principal crime organisations now being the Sicilian Mafia, or Cosa Nostra as they also call themselves, the Camorra in Naples, the Sacra Corona Unita in Apulia, and the 'Ndrangheta in Calabria. Almost inevitably, all abused their autocratic powers to exploit and subjugate their people rather than protect them. But the real boom years followed the Allied armies' invasion of Sicily as a stepping stone to the Italian mainland in World War Two. Sicilian families in particular took advantage of the transatlantic drugs trade. Now its evil influence is worldwide – despite attempts by brave politicians, judges and policemen to stamp them out in their home territory.

Most famous, even heroic, among these was Giovanni Falcone. Born in a poor district of Palermo in 1939, Falcone recalled growing up horrified by the violence in his hometown. He became a lawyer and, at just 27, a prosecutor specialising in fraud cases. A senior magistrate, Rocco Chinnici, took him under his wing and had him investigate Sicilian construction companies and local politicians who had demanded kickbacks for granting licences. Falcone was offered bribes and subjected to threats but ignored both and obtained several convictions. One of his successes was the 1984 conviction of the Christian Democrat mayor of Palermo, Vito Ciancimino, the first Italian politician formally to be found guilty of membership of the Mafia. Falcone also helped gather evidence of transatlantic connections by the local Inzerillo and Spatola clans to the Gambino mobsters in America. The exposure of the global scale of Mafia activities was one of his principal achievements. Thanks to this evidence, Sicily's chief magistrate, Gaetano Costa, signed 80 arrest warrants – but also signed his own instant death sentence. Costa was killed in August 1980, the third local prosecutor to be murdered in a decade.

As the Mafia's international operations grew, so too did the ruthlessness of its methods. Also assassinated was Palermo police chief Boris Guiliano, who had been on the verge of a major breakthrough in his investigations. It marked the beginning of a new era of violence. Falcone became a member of a select anti-Mafia pool of judges and prosecutors formed by his mentor Rocco Chinnici. In joining the group, he knew he would be a target but said the threat of death was 'not more important to me than the button of my jacket – I'm a real Sicilian!' In 1982 Carlo Alberto Dalla Chiesa, the Carabinieri general who had smashed apart Italy's terrorist Red Brigades, was sent to Sicily to coordinate the central government's anti-Mafia policy. Only 100 days after taking office as prefect of Palermo, he was machine-gunned to death in the street. When Judge Chinnici was also killed – blown up by a car bomb in 1983 – Falcone became effective head of the anti-Mafia pool and the authorities in Rome gave him beefed-up powers to take revenge for the murders.

His new role made Falcone a prisoner in his home town. For most of the next decade, he worked in a bomb-proof bunker underneath Palermo's law courts, his desk dominated by electronic devices and video screens showing the approaches to his office. His home was similarly protected and whenever he ventured out, he was escorted by a convoy of armoured police cars. But through the Eighties, he managed to recruit a brave and brilliant team of prosecutors – and it was their work which eventually led to the most dramatic victory against the island's gangsters. Falcone, along with fellow magistrate Paolo Borsellino, drew up 8,000 pages of indictments for some of the most serious professional criminals known to the world, among them leaders of the Corleone clan and Michele Greco, alleged Boss of Bosses, known as 'the Pope'.

In what was known as the 'Mafia Maxi-Trial', held in a fortified courthouse through 1986–87, hundreds of convictions, mostly for murder or drug trafficking, were made possible by informers. The most important of these so-called *pentiti* was Tommaso Buscetta, a jailed member of the island's Porta Nuevo family, who was later put under a witness protection programme in America. Buscetta refused to confide in anyone other than Falcone, and when persuaded to spill the beans, he warned Falcone: 'This will make you famous – and bring your death.' In his evidence, Buscetta revealed the existence and workings of the Sicilian Mafia Commisssion, enabling Falcone to argue that Cosa Nostra was a unified hierarchical structure whose leaders could be held responsible for crimes committed on their behalf. The trial culminated in the conviction of 342 Mafiosi, sent down for a total of 2,665 years, including 19 life sentences. Sadly for Falcone, a series of appeal court acquittals based on the validity of 'supergrass' evidence meant that most of them were later freed. Undaunted, Falcone explained to a journalist: 'Each investigation reveals a little more of the map of the Mafia. But it is a Hydra, with many more heads to replace the old you manage to cut off. You can never say you have won.'

After his successes in the Maxi Trial, the seriousness of Tommaso Buscetta's warnings became clear. Despite the care he took with his safety, in 1989 as he relaxed outside his beach house, a security guard noticed an abandoned sports bag at the water's edge. It contained 58 sticks of plastic explosives, primed to explode if picked up. After the incident, he told a friend: 'My life is mapped out. It is my destiny to take a bullet by the Mafia some day. The only thing I don't know is when.'

In 1991 the tireless gangbuster left Sicily to take up a job in Rome's Ministry of Justice but was under no illusion about the continuing threat to his life. He described the Mafia as 'a panther with an elephantine memory'. The Mafia had already retaliated violently against others they saw as having harmed them. In 1988 they murdered Palermo appeal judge Alberto Giacomelli and his son, allegedly on the orders of 'Toto' Riina. In 1991 another prosecutor, Rosario Livatino, was killed, the same year as a politician and an anti-Mafia businessman were murdered.

Falcone's own horrific murder in May 1992 was followed by a day of mourning ordered by the government in Rome. Thousands gathered at Palermo's Basilica of San Domenico for the funeral, which was broadcast live nationally, all regular television programmes having been suspended. Meanwhile, Salvatore Riina reportedly threw a party, toasting Falcone's death with champagne.

Only two months after Falcone's death, the Mafia caught up with his closest friend and colleague, Paolo Borsellino, and dealt with him in the same brutal fashion. A similar car bomb was detonated as Borsellino drove to his mother's home in Palermo, killing not only the valiant law enforcer but five policemen. In his last video interview, given just two days before his friend's murder, Borsellino had spoken about the possible link between Cosa Nostra and rich Italian businessmen such as future Prime Minister Silvio Berlusconi. The interview has since received little coverage on Italian television, much of which is owned by Berlusconi, who also controlled the state channel during his mandates as prime minister.

The deaths of Falcone and Borsellino caused widespread revulsion against the Mafia and led to a major crackdown by the authorities, resulting in the swift capture of Riina and many of his Corleone family associates. Riina was sentenced to life imprisonment for sanctioning the murders of Borsellino and Falcone, as well as dozens of other slayings. Riina's hitman Giovanni Busca, who personally detonated the bomb that killed Falcone, was also jailed and later became an informant. He revealed how easy it had been to live a normal life in Sicily despite being on the Carabinieri's 'Most Wanted' list. Riina, for instance, had enjoyed his 30 years as a 'fugitive' living openly at home in Palermo, visiting his local hospital for treatments and registering all four of his children under their real names.

Following the arrests and a further government crackdown against the Sicilian Mafia, a campaign of terrorism erupted on the mainland. This appeared to have been the result of a secret summit of the remaining bosses to formulate a shock campaign aimed at scaring the Italian government into a retreat. It resulted in a series of bomb attacks in 1993 in Rome, Florence and Milan that left ten people dead and 93 injured, as well as damaging centres of cultural heritage such as Florence's Uffizi Gallery.

Only when control of Cosa Nostra fell to a new Godfather, Bernardo Provenzano, in 1995 did the violence ease, with a softly-softly policy known as 'pax mafiosi'. Provenzano himself was arrested in 2006. The vacuum after the caging of 'Toto' Riina and Provenzano was taken up by Matteo Messina Denaro, a young bespectacled multiple murderer with a reported weakness for sports cars, designer watches and sharp suits. Born in Sicily's Trapani province in 1962, Denaro, nicknamed 'Diabolik' after an Italian cartoon character, was said to be running a resurgent Cosa Nostra empire. Now known as the Don of Dons, he is believed to have personally executed at least 50 people and ordered the deaths of scores more.

Denaro cemented his blood thirsty reputation during the 1993 bombings – he chillingly boasted: 'I filled a cemetery all by myself' – and has been on the run ever since. He is one of the world's Top Ten most wanted criminals and yet, incredibly, all that the police have to go on is a black and white photograph taken more than 20 years ago. Giacomo Di Girolamo, author of *The Invisible*, a book on the mobster, says: 'Denaro is a modern Mafia boss, the opposite of the traditional image of the Godfather. He has numerous lovers and a child out of marriage. He knows which businesses to get involved in, and this is primarily drugs.' His estimated £2.5 billion worth has been steadily built up through lucrative deals with Colombian drug barons and masterminding the import of heroin and cocaine into Europe. It is believed that if there was an attempt to revive the Cupola, a kind of consultative committee of regional bosses that met from time to time to resolve internal disputes and forge long-term strategy, it would see Messina Denaro as unrivalled chairman of the board.

It was the fear of this precise threat – the revival of the Cupola – that in December 2008 saw sweeping raids by more than 1,200 Carabinieri officers stretching from Sicily to Tuscany. They arrested 94 people, many of them veteran Mafiosi including Salvatore Lombardo, the 87-year-old boss of the town of Montelepre, in Palermo province. Investigators say those seized had been trying to re-establish the authority of the Cupola to solidify the Mafia's power structure after a leadership void caused by the high-profile arrests of dons like Provenzano. Leading anti-Mob magistrate Pietro Grasso said operations over recent years had Cosa Nostra 'on its knees'. This latest round up, Grasso said, 'keeps it from getting up.' Few observers were that confident.

It is true that most of Italy's organised crime network has been ordering up fewer hits, the number of which peaked in 1982 when there were more than 700 murders in Palermo and surrounding towns alone. This face of the organisation may appear less violent but it's no less sinister, according to Giuseppe Cipriani, who became mayor of the fabled Mafia stronghold, Corleone, in the wake of the assassination of the two magistrates. 'The Mafia changed strategy, that's all,' he said. 'They just sat down and decided it at the table. It doesn't mean they might not start bringing back the bombs.'

In recent years it has become difficult to judge the power of the original Sicilian Mafia, whose influence was global but many of whose leaders are now in prison or in hiding. But where a crime vacuum opens up, there are always crooks to see a new business opportunity – and many of the cleverest to take advantage of this situation have been from rival Mafia organisations on the mainland. The weakened Cosa Nostra has had to yield most of the illegal drug trade to their rivals the 'Ndrangheta from neighbouring Calabria – now the country's biggest crime organisation (as reported in the next chapter) and estimated to control the import of 80 per cent of all cocaine sold on the streets of Europe. But business boomed at home too …

The modern mobsters have kept the Italian police busy in very different ways from the old days. They now find themselves investigating fraudulent businesses – including tailoring for top Milan fashion houses, pirating of DVDs and handbags, fishing of endangered bluefin tuna, brewing genetically-modified beer and 'green initiative' recycling. Even Italian food icons like olive oil and Parma ham have not remained sacrosanct. Coldiretti, the Italian farmers' union, reported in 2008 that the Sicilian Mafia was adding flavouring to colza oil, often used to lubricate machinery, before relabelling it as olive oil. Fake Parma hams and other beef products falsely branded as 'gourmet Chianina breed' are confiscated in industrial quantities by Italian police. All four of Italy's biggest gangs – the 'Ndrangheta, the Sacra Corona Unita, the Camorra and the Cosa Nostra – invested huge stakes in this new and lucrative business. Pirated handbags and DVDs accounted for £5 billion of Mafia income and the food industry netted the underworld £5.2 billion, according to Tano Grasso, head of Italy's anti-racketeering commission. Perhaps unsurprising then that the Mafia is estimated to be the biggest business in Italy, with organised crime netting bosses the equivalent of approximately 7 per cent of the country's gross domestic product.

Italy's famous fashion industry is rife with fraudulent Mafia investment. Roberto Saviano, an investigative journalist and anti-Mafia campaigner, disclosed how leading fashion houses regularly outsource orders to sweatshop tailors controlled by the Camorra. Mob tailors will win legitimate contracts and be supplied with the necessary raw materials – while others are allowed to flood the market with counterfeit clothes.

In Naples, the gang bosses line their pockets by illegally fishing for endangered bluefin tuna. But the Camorra, who supposedly 'managed' 2,500 illegal bakeries, have not had it all their own way: a group of Neapolitan shopkeepers organised an unprecedented rebellion against the racketeers in 2011, with local bakeries as well as butchers and grocers summoning up the courage to try to loosen the Camorra's stranglehold on the city. 'We decided we couldn't go on,' explained spokesman Salvatore Russo, a grocer in the city centre. 'They would demand money and those who didn't pay were shot in the legs, or beaten up, or stolen from. We've marked out our position, we've dug a moat, but it's going to take a lot more to win the war.'

That's what Roberto Saviano discovered after writing a book about the Camorra. In it, he revealed that the ruthless Casalesi clan made hundreds of millions of euros each year by illegally dumping waste, much of it toxic, in addition to extortion rackets, drug trafficking, smuggling of illegal migrants and arms dealing. The journalist, whose exposé *Gomorrah* and the successful movie it spawned made him a household name, had to flee his home when he learned that the organisation's dons had ordered his death. Saviano fought back by hauling them into the dock and in 2012, six years after he was forced into hiding, he appeared in a high-security Naples courtroom to look his enemies in the eye. He confronted Camorra bosses Francesco Bidognetti and Antonio Iovine via video link so that he could sue them and two of their lawyers for threats and defamation. The gang leaders were already behind bars, along with other members of the Camorra's Casalesi clan, after being rounded up for a string of offences. The last of the fugitives, Michele Zagaria, was found in an underground bunker beneath his home north of Naples in 2011. All were sentenced to life in solitary confinement in prisons hundreds of miles from Naples.

With so many of the old-style Mafia leaders in jail or on the run, a new phenomenon has been observed – the rise of the female gangster. As *Time* magazine reported: 'Today's Mafia is transforming itself, and two new character types are emerging: the college graduate in a tailored suit who wields nothing sharper than his felt-tip pen, and the "Signora Boss" who has stepped from the proverbial kitchen to the front lines of Italy's organised crime network. More women are moving into positions of real power, often filling in for their husbands and brothers who are in prison or on the run.' For instance, Ninetta Bagarella, wife of jailed Corleone boss 'Toto' Riina, who directed Cosa Nostra for a decade, is thought to be the brains that complemented her husband's brutality. 'These women's roles go well beyond raising a family,' said Corleone's Mayor Cipriani. 'Women in the Mafia not only have acquired authorisation, they are now the ones who do the authorising.'

Across on the mainland, a 30-year feud between rival families of the Camorra crime Syndicate led to an explosion of female violence in 2002. After exchanging slaps and threats at the local beauty parlour in a Naples suburb, several female relatives from the Graziano family cornered a carload of women from the Cava clan and opened fire with automatic weapons. Three of the Cava women were killed and two were seriously wounded. After toasting their success with male relatives, the Graziano women were taken into custody by local police, whose wiretaps had captured details of the feud.

It is to be hoped that such senseless blood-letting is a thing of the past. These days the mobster's prime focus is on butter, not guns. And to make the profits multiply, top bosses have turned to that prototype man in the tailored suit. He is the true motor for the New Mafia, toting a business or economics degree – but still having a 'family' connection. An Italian governmental financial report of December 2012 described the Mafia as 'the country's richest firm' with a turnover of more than £116 billion a year. Giovanni Colussi, a Rome-based expert on organised crime, best summed up thus: 'The

Mafia adapts, it can even change its core business, but it always remains the Mafia. It can't become another thing.'

One would not wish to end this chapter – one that has recorded so many murders and misery – on a flippant note. However, a newspaper story that is at first glance inconsequential nevertheless reveals the power that Mafia leaders still hold over the beleaguered citizens of southern Italy. In February 2013 a local don was arrested after trying to force an entire community to vote for his daughter on a TV talent show. Domenico Ferrara – his nickname in Neapolitan dialect is *O' Muccuso* (the Snotty One) and *Zi' Mimmi* (Uncle Mimmi) – handed out mobile phones so locals could cast multiple votes for 13-year-old Vania. Significantly, he made sure the phones were returned so he could check his orders had been carried out. But the votes of the terrified community of Villarica, Naples, were only enough to propel Vania to second place in the final of the show, *I'll Leave You With A Song*. Details of the fix emerged as police arrested Ferrara and eight of his clan on suspicion of drug trafficking. A raid on his house uncovered 320 mobile phones. Police chief Captain Francesco Piroddi said: 'The Ferrara clan exercised complete control over the district of Villaricca. This number of phones cannot be explained away.'

In 2010 another Italian talent show, *Songs and Hopes*, had been condemned after a contestant, the daughter of another Camorra boss, dedicated to her father the song 'You Are the Best Daddy In The World and I Wouldn't Change You For Anything'. At the end of the live broadcast, the girl was seen embracing her father, Gaetano Marino, who was sitting in the front row. It was a touching moment for the proud papa … who returned to his home in the resort of Terracina to be gunned down in a classic gangland hit.

That's the way it goes. When dealing with the centuries-old saga of the Italian Mafia, there is and never will be a happy ending.

CHAPTER 28

'NDRANGHETA – TENTACLES OF THE 'NEW' MAFIA MONSTERS

The best way of describing the newest and toughest secret criminal society to emerge from the back streets of Italy is to quote local anti-mafia magistrate Roberto Di Palma, who said: 'The 'Ndrangheta is like an octopus, and wherever there is money, you will find its tentacles.' It is a prescient warning because all the evidence suggests that, while the Sicilian Mafia, like the US Mafia, has been fading into the shadows, the little-known 'Ndrangheta (pronounced 'en-drang-ay-ta') have been taking over as Italy's Public Enemy Number One and must now be acknowledged as having become a criminal empire with global clout. With its public bloodbaths, assassinations, brutal feuds and insidious corruption, the Calabria-based 'Ndrangheta is said to be bigger, more deep-rooted and more influential than even the Sicilian-originated Mafia itself.

So how did an organisation that is less well known than the

Cosa Nostra or the Naples-based Camorra become so powerful? The history of the 'Ndrangheta , whose name derives from an ancient Greek word for 'defiance and valour', can be traced back to the 1860s when a group of Sicilians were banished from the island by the Italian government. They settled across the Strait of Messina in the mainland region of Calabria and formed small criminal groups specialising in kidnapping and political corruption. At the time, they were still referred to as the Mafia or Camorra and sometimes the Picciotteria or Onorata Società (honoured society). In the folk culture surrounding 'Ndrangheta in Calabria, references are often found to the glamorous mediaeval Spanish secret society Garduña, though there is no historical evidence to substantiate a link between the two organisations. The first time the word 'Ndrangheta was mentioned before a wider audience was by the Calabrian writer Corrado Alvaro in the *Corriere della Sera* newspaper in September 1955.

Until 1975 the 'Ndrangheta restricted their Italian operations to Calabria, mainly involving themselves in extortion and blackmail. Within that region, the society grew to become a loose confederation of about 100 groups, called Cosche (or families), each of which claims sovereignty over a territory, usually a town or village. These Cosche are connected family groups based on blood relationships and marriages. There are approximately 100 such families, with a core membership of between 4,000 and 7,000 – although with the spread of the society throughout Italy and beyond, the membership is likely to have topped 10,000. For instance, the 'Ndrangheta are now strong in the industrial north of Italy, in and around Turin and Milan.

A 'Ndrangheta crime family is called a locale (place) which

may have branches, called 'Adrian, in neighbouring towns or city districts. 'Each 'Ndrina is autonomous on its territory and no formal authority stands above the 'Ndrina boss,' according to Italy's Antimafia Commission. Thus the 'Ndrina leader in control of a small town or a neighbourhood has dictatorial power, which is passed on through the generations. Sons are not just expected, but in most cases required, to follow their fathers into the family business, receiving from birth the title of Giovane d'onore (young man of honour).

Like similar secret societies, the 'Ndrangheta initiates its members with rituals that vary from clan to clan and are designed to bind them to silence for life. Even when the Italian government in 1999 legislated to make it easier to turn State's evidence and become so-called pentiti (penitents) the 'Ndrangheta code of silence remained almost entirely intact, with only a handful of low to medium ranking mobsters turning state witness. The exception came in July 2013 when a police deal with informer Giuseppe Giampa, a mobster in the town of Lamezia Terme, led to 65 arrests, including doctors, lawyers and prison officers. Assets worth €200 million were seized from five businessmen. According to the Italian news agency Ansa, Giampa was suspected of ordering about 20 murders in a mob war for control of the town between 2005 and 2011. Until this breakthrough, the 1999 amnesty, which had wrought havoc within the ranks of Costa Nostra, had failed to make significant inroads among the seemingly impervious ranks of the Calabrian mobsters. Their brutal, old-fashioned code of conduct has made combating the new breed of Mafioso extremely difficult.

The explanation for the 'Ndrangheta's impenetrable nature is partly adherence to its peasant roots. Although the city of

Reggio Calabria is the provincial capital, the society's membership is concentrated in poor villages such as Platì, Locri, Africo, Altomonte and San Luca. The latter village is considered to be the society's stronghold – 'Ndrangheta's answer to Corleone, the Sicilian village made famous by the *Godfather* movies. San Luca is home to one of its most powerful clans, made up of the allied families of Strangio-Nirta and Pelle-Vottari-Romeo.

If the tentacles of the 'Ndrangheta now stretch across Calabria and the world, San Luca is where the head is. A winding maze of sloping alleyways, the village feels outwardly normal. Then one might notice the ever-watchful 'sentinelle', youths astride mopeds or motorcycles who act as look-outs. There are also the scattered, bullet-ridden garbage bins that locals use for target practice. Then, on passing the local cemetery, a visitor may spot the growing number of newer plaques, the memorials to recent murderous feuds – boosted by a new generation of 'Ndrangheta 'foot soldiers', who were invested at a lavish ceremony hosted by local clan bosses.

Out into the countryside and down a cactus-flanked mountain path one comes to the Shrine of our Lady of Polsi. This has long been the place of pilgrimage for 'Ndrangheta, with bosses from outside Calabria, travelling from as far afield as Canada and Australia, regularly attending meetings. At least since the 1950s, the chiefs of the 'Ndrangheta locali have met regularly here during the September Feast. These annual meetings, known as the 'crimine', have traditionally served as a forum to discuss future strategies and settle disputes among the locali. Each year, a new crimine boss is elected to host the meeting and mediate over the activities of all 'Ndrangheta groups. This capo crimine has limited authority, it appears, because he dare not interfere in clan feuds and is unable to control the level of inter-family violence.

In this regard, the 'Ndrangheta resembles the Sicilian Mafia as it once was. It is murderously confrontational. Disputes between even minor village-based clans can lead to public bloodbaths. On a larger scale, the so-called Second 'Ndrangheta War of 1985–91 between the Condello-Imerti-Serraino-Rosmini clans and the Destefano-Tegano-Libri-Latella clans cost more than 700 lives. Which makes it all the more extraordinary that so little is known about 'Ndrangheta in the world outside Calabria. Until recently, its highest profile activities were four decades ago when the prevailing faction began to kidnap rich people from northern Italy for large ransoms. The grandson of the richest man on earth became one of their victims.

John Paul Getty III, a tall, freckle-faced youth of 16, was kidnapped in the Piazza Farnese in Rome on 10 July 1973. When a ransom note arrived, his family suspected the drama was a ploy by the rebellious teenager, who had joked about staging his own kidnapping to extract money from his frugal grandfather, oil tycoon John Paul Getty. A second ransom note demanding $17 million arrived belatedly, because of an Italian postal strike. But matters then got serious.

The boy's father, John Paul Getty II, asked Getty Senior for the money – but he refused, arguing that to give in to the criminals would encourage the kidnapping of his other 14 grandchildren. This refusal condemned the boy to be chained to a stake, blindfolded for five months. Eventually the gang cut off their hostage's right ear as evidence of their willingness to kill him. In November 1973 an envelope containing the ear and a lock of hair was delivered to a newspaper with a threat of further mutilation unless a reduced sum of $3.2 million was paid. The message that accompanied the delivery read: 'This is Paul's ear. If we don't get some money within ten days, then the other ear will arrive. In other words, he will arrive in little bits'.

The notoriously frugal Getty Sr. now agreed to contribute to the ransom, although only $2.2 million because that was the maximum sum that was tax deductible. He offered to loan the rest to his son but only at an agreed rate of interest. Still anxious to reduce his outgoings, Getty Sr. then negotiated a deal direct with the kidnappers and got his grandson back for about $2.9 million. The teenager was found alive in southern Italy shortly afterwards, in December 1973.

Initially, the world's media described the kidnappers as local small-time crooks. Indeed, when nine of them were arrested, one was found to be a carpenter, another a hospital orderly, another a minor ex-convict. But the identity of a fourth, an olive-oil dealer from Calabria, gave a clue to the real villains – for the rest were high-ranking members of the 'Ndrangheta, including the flamboyant Saverio 'Saro' Mammoliti (whose story is such a sensational saga of 'Ndrangheta showmanship that it will be told at length later in this chapter). Only two of the accused were convicted and sent to prison; the others, including the 'Ndrangheta bosses, were acquitted for lack of evidence. Most of the money was never recovered. It is believed to have been invested in construction machinery and trucks, which helped win all the transportation contracts for the Calabrian container port of Gioia Tauro.

This is significant because although the 'Ndrangheta began in the dirt-poor villages of Calabria, its leaders have become adept at the world of high finance. Back in 2007, its business volume was estimated at almost €44 billion a year, almost 3 per cent of Italy's GDP, according to the European Institute of Political, Economic and Social Studies. This turnover was generated largely by drug trafficking but also from ostensibly legal businesses such as construction, restaurants and supermarkets.

Today, drugs remain its most profitable activity, with an estimated 62 per cent of the total turnover. But although murders and bombings tend to make the headlines, the 'Ndrangheta are also engaged in counterfeiting, gambling, fraud, theft, labour racketeering, weapons smuggling, loan-sharking, alien smuggling and kidnapping. They have a growing grip on Italy's financial and economic nerve centres, controlling banks, restaurants, shopping centres, construction companies, betting shops, luxury boutiques, supermarkets, night-clubs, discotheques and gaming arcades throughout Milan and Lombardy, according to Laura Barbaini, the Milan prosecutor leading an investigation into the Calabrian Mafia.

According to a report by the Italian DIA (Department of the Police of Italy against organised crime) and Guardia di Finanza (Financial Police and Customs Police): 'The 'Ndrangheta is now one of the most powerful criminal organisations in the world.' The report says its drugs monopoly means that 80 per cent of Europe's cocaine passes through 'Ndrangheta handlers in the Calabrian port of Gioia Tauro. According to Alberto Cisterna, prosecutor in Reggio Calabria: 'The 'Ndrangheta's drug smuggling techniques are endlessly inventive and ingenious.'

A former chairman of the parliamentary Antimafia Commission, Francesco Forgione estimated that only a third of the 'Ndrangheta's illicit profits are ploughed back into crime, and two thirds are invested in 'legitimate' businesses. The logical next step, he said, may be for the 'Ndrangheta to dominate the politicians themselves. And he complained that law enforcement to control the spread of the crooked Calabrians is hampered by a lack of both human and financial resources.

The 'Ndrangheta has become 'as adept at money laundering and online transactions as it once was with sawn-off shotguns and extortion rackets in the wilds of Calabria,' says Mario Venditti, an anti-Mafia prosecutor in Milan. One of the best examples of fraud is with EU money. Brussels has been willing to hand over vast sums to Calabria and other Mafia-plagued regions of Italy over the years, despite the very real risk of taxpayers' cash ending up in criminal hands.

Since 2007, the EU has authorised some €3 billion to Calabria alone, ostensibly to develop one of Italy's most backward and isolated areas. Yet hefty slices of that cash have gone to the 'gangsters in business suits', who are thought to have taken 'pizzo', or illicit tax, on the building of everything from roads to wind farms. According to a 2008 report by the Antimafia Commission, the vast container port of Gioia Tauro received €40 million in EU development grants in the 1990s – helping it to become one of the major importers of drugs into Europe, with direct links to Colombian and Mexican cartels.

The extent of its grip on public life has now been laid bare in Reggio Calabria, where, according to a local joke, the weather is the only thing that cannot be bribed. In an unprecedented move, the Italian interior ministry in 2012 suspended all 30 city councillors amid fears of 'Mafia contagion' and dispatched three commissioners from Rome to take over. It followed the arrest of three councillors and the boss of a local garbage company who was suspected of colluding with 'Ndrangheta bosses to inflate the cost of public works contracts. Dozens of Calabrian town councils were already under similar 'direct rule' but this was first time it had happened to an entire provincial administration.

The Calabrian Mafiosi, says Giacomo Amadori, an investigative reporter, have 'swapped rough rural clothes and flat caps for slick city suits'. But they retain the 'blood ties' that originally knitted the clans together in Calabria. To foil investigators and phone taps, they use impenetrable dialect, and even a whistled code used by shepherds in the Aspromonte Mountains around their Reggio Calabria stronghold.

Security concerns have now led to the creation by the 'Ndrangheta of a secret society within the secret society. The membership of the so-called 'La Santa' is known only to fellow members. Contrary to 'Ndrangheta traditions, these 'santisti' are allowed to establish close connections with state representatives and even affiliate them with the Santa. Italian investigators believe these connections are often established through Freemasonry – which 'santisti' are permitted to join, thereby breaking another rule of the traditional code.

By such means, and with the probability of corrupt political protection, the 'Ndrangheta is now so invisible that it has spread around the world unnoticed. 'Ndrina are operating in Germany, Belgium, the Netherlands, France, Eastern Europe, Australia, Canada and the United States. An exasperated Florida district attorney complained that, of all organised criminal groups, the 'Ndrangheta has proved the most difficult to understand, let alone penetrate. It is, he said, 'invisible, like the dark side of the moon.'

In June 2012 an Italian prosecutor felt it necessary to warn Australia about the standing of 'Ndrangheta in that country due to the murder of an Australian detective by saying: 'The

'Ndrangheta is the organisation that runs the international cocaine market. It doesn't do its business in Calabria but around the world. It has infiltrated all economic sectors and it controls voting and political candidates at a national and international level. I urge the Australians not to underestimate this organisation. Otherwise it will be too late.'

It was certainly too late for Detective-Sergeant Geoffrey Bowen. On 22 March 1994, the day before the start of a court case against a 'Ndrangheta leader named Dominic Perre, Bowen was brutally murdered by a parcel bomb that had reached his Adelaide National Crime Authority (NCA) office without being detected.

Bowen was a senior detective with the NCA who was exclusively involved with Operation Cerberus; the investigation into Italian organised crime in Australia instituted to answer the question: 'Does the Mafia exist in Australia, and if so, indicate to what extent?' Bowen himself was quite certain of 'Ndrangheta's existence, having established that some Italian immigrants showed extraordinary allegiance to two seemingly insignificant Calabrian villages – Plati, which is often described as the 'heart of 'Ndrangheta' and San Luca, the 'soul' or the 'cradle of 'Ndrangheta'. These villages had come to international notice decades earlier when the area had earned the title of 'Kidnap Capital' due to local criminals who specialised in kidnapping members of wealthy, northern Italian families and holding them in caves in the surrounding mountains. Some of the proceeds of the ransoms, it was discovered, had been sent to Australia and 'invested' in the lucrative business of cultivating marijuana.

Detective-Sergeant Bowen took control of the investigation in August 1993 after the discovery of a huge marijuana crop in the Northern Territory. Police described the extent of criminality involved as probably Australia's 'most complex'. Eleven men, all of Calabrian descent, were subsequently charged, with Bowen concluding that Domenic Perre was the financier and organiser of the crop of 15,000 plants and associated drug workshops. His home was raided and subsequently a charge laid by Bowen against Perre for possession of an illegal listening advice. The court date for the charge was set for 3 March 1994.

The bomb went off the day before the hearing. Domenic Perre was arrested for the murder of Bowen and the attempted murder of Peter Wallis, an NCA lawyer who was seriously hurt in the blast. But the evidence was deemed insufficient and later that year, charges were dropped. Despite numerous police reviews of the case – and a 1999 coroner's inquest that found Perre had planted the bomb – the murder still remained officially 'unsolved'.

So what makes a 'Ndrina member? Who are these 'untouchables' who have grown from groupings of dispossessed, semi-literate village thugs into members of an international conglomerate that is estimated to have an annual income in Europe alone of €44 billion?

This brings us back to the gangster mentioned earlier in the infamous Getty kidnapping case. Saverio 'Saro' Mammoliti was a member of a 'Ndrina family from the Calabrian town of Castellace. When his father was killed in a feud with a rival clan, Saro and his three brothers took over the role of gang leaders. They expanded their territory and wealth by forcing neighbours to sell them their land at miniscule prices – or sometimes simply stealing it by fencing it off.

While his siblings remained in their rural fiefdom, Saro

became known as the 'Playboy of Castellace', dressing smartly and enjoying La Dolce Vita in Reggio Calabria and then Rome, driving around in his Jaguar sports car in the company of beautiful women. In 1972 he escaped from jail, where he had been sent because of his long-running feud with the rivals who killed his father, and lived openly without fear of recapture for the next 20 years. While officially on the 'most wanted' list, he wed a 15-year-old local girl at Castellace's parish church next to the local police station. Mammoliti was a fugitive when charged with kidnapping John Paul Getty III in 1973. He and fellow accused Girolamo Piromalli, an even more senior 'Ndrina member, were acquitted for lack of evidence, although Mammoliti picked up a secondary conviction for drug dealing.

The gangster, a long-time trafficker, had been caught in a sting operation by the US Federal Bureau of Narcotics whose agents approached him to supply heroin and cocaine. Mammoliti told them that, although he had supplies available in Tangiers and Amsterdam, he could only enter the American market with the permission of fellow 'Ndrine, including his accomplice Piromalli and others as far afield as Holland and Canada.

However, Mammoliti had enough influence to get away with soft sentences – or none at all. In one raid, telephone numbers for the Prime Minister's office and various Rome ministries were found in his possession. In a 1982 'maxi trial' against the 'Ndrangheta he was sentenced to 33 years but had it quashed by the Italian Supreme Court. In 1984, when charged with murder, he had his property seized and then handed back. He and his wife were arrested for corruption in 1992 but freed due to lack of proof. Within months he was back in court charged with a litany of crimes – the murder of a local landowner, six bomb attacks, 19 arson attacks, six major larcenies and the destruction of rival farmers' property.

At last, the charges began to stick. Mamolitti was jailed for 22 years for extortion and other Mob-related offences. In 1995 he received a life sentence for similar charges, with another 20 years subsequently added on as anti-corruption prosecutors assembled fresh evidence. In 2003, Saro Mammoliti finally decided to collaborate with the Antimafia Commision and became a pentito. It was only then that the former playboy revealed the full extent of corruption in his Calabrian homeland and told investigators how money was syphoned off from criminal enterprises into an array of business ventures. He also finally confessed that he had been one of the kidnappers of John Paul Getty Jr way back in 1972 – and would indeed have cut off a great deal more than the boy's ear had a ransom not been paid.